THE ONE AND THE MANY

THE SECOND
CORNING CONFERENCE

The One
and the Many

THE INDIVIDUAL IN THE MODERN WORLD

BY John Brooks

WITH ESSAYS BY CHARLES HABIB MALIK

RAYMOND ARON

ROGER M. BLOUGH

McGEORGE BUNDY

KENNETH O. DIKÉ

AUGUST HECKSCHER

JULIAN HOCHFELD

HARPER & ROW, PUBLISHERS
NEW YORK AND EVANSTON

MEMBERS OF THE ROUND TABLES

᪗ᓶ Note: *For brief biographies of participants, see Appendix*

PANEL I: Cornelis W. de Kiewiet, *Chairman*

Lawrence A. Appley
Raymond Aron
Harry S. Ashmore
Halbert L. Dunn
Sibylle K. Escalona
Franklin Ford
John A. Fuller
Victor Gruen
Philip M. Hauser
John Hersey
David G. Hill
J. Ward Keener
Jay Lovestone
Laurence J. McGinley
J. Stillman Rockefeller
Leo Schulgin
Muhammad Zafrulla Khan

v

18310

PANEL II: Douglas M. Knight, *Chairman*

Franz Alexander
M. A. Allam
Gilbert W. Chapman
John B. Coburn
Tengku Dzulkarnain
Herbert W. K. Fitzroy
Oliver Franks
Henry E. Guerlac
Melville J. Herskovits
Harold Howe, II
John A. Hrones
Eric Larrabee
Barry T. Leithead
Richard M. Paget
Muriel Rukeyser
Charles M. Scheff
Janez Stanovnik
Julius Stone
Frazar B. Wilde

PANEL III: Arthur E. Murphy, *Chairman*

Harold Boeschenstein
Ritchie Calder
Harold E. Clurman
William C. De Vane
William P. Fay
Oscar Handlin
August Heckscher
Dorothy Height
Kenneth Holland
John B. Kimberly
Salvador de Madariaga
Charles Habib Malik

David Rockefeller
James J. Rorimer
Mark Starr
Eberhard Strohal
Arnaud de Vogüé

PANEL IV: Paul J. Braisted, *Chairman*

Roger M. Blough
Mary I. Bunting
William L. Chapman
Merle Curti
Kenneth O. Diké
William K. Frankena
William Glasser
Pendleton Herring
James A. Houston
Patrick Hurley
Julian S. Huxley
Alfred Kazin
Bernard Kilgore
David E. Lilienthal
Walter H. Wheeler, Jr.
Charles E. Wyzanski, Jr.

PANEL V: James A. Perkins, *Chairman*

Amory Bradford
W. Randolph Burgess
John Dos Passos
Gilberto Freyre
Carl Gerstacker
Alexander Heard
Frank R. Moraes
Gabriele Morello
Whitney J. Oates

Charles E. Odegaard
Ralph Reiser
Samuel Sandmel
Graham Spry
Byron K. Trippet
John F. White
James C. Worthy

CONTENTS

꣠

PART II

INTRODUCTION

੭ई

THE SECOND CORNING CONFERENCE

੭ई

ON THURSDAY, FRIDAY, AND SATURDAY, May 18-19-20, 1961, ninety
men and women met at Corning, New York to devote themselves
for a brief but intensive period to the question of "The Individual
in the Modern World"—or, more specifically, in the words of the
invitation that had brought them together, the question of "the
extent to which the traditional ideal of the significance and dignity of the individual is vital and viable under the conditions of
the emerging world: an industrial civilization." The ninety came
from business, labor, learned societies, the arts, and public affairs
in the United States and abroad; the representation from abroad
amounted to about one-quarter of the total, or enough to ensure
that the chief topic under discussion would indeed be the world
and not the United States of America. Of the ninety, some were
international celebrities, front-page names; some were wielders of
great power, industrial or governmental, who ordinarily work in
a comparative anonymity that they are at pains to guard; and
many others, from both inside and outside the world academic
community, were persons whose lifelong study of some particular

aspect of the modern world made them, so to speak, expert witnesses. Between them, they represented both a cross-section of current world thought, and an agency whose combined deliberations might conceivably influence world thought in new directions. More briefly, they could describe the world as it is, and they might change it.

This was the Second Corning Conference. The first Corning Conference, held in May 1951, marked the centenary of Corning Glass Works, and, like the second, had as its co-sponsor the American Council of Learned Societies, a national federation of scholarly groups. Originally conceived by Arthur A. Houghton, Jr., president of Corning's division, Steuben Glass, the first conference had been planned to cut across the usual conference boundaries—conferences of scholars, conferences of writers, business conferences, labor conferences, and so on—and provide a meeting-place for brilliant and distinguished people of as many different sorts as possible, many of whom would be unlikely to meet or confer under any other auspices. Its roster of foreign participants had been comparatively short, and in line with this, its topic—"our industrial civilization from the standpoint of human values"—had focused attention on the developed Western nations. Its intellectual center had been unabashedly American, its premise that "there is more to living than making a living," and its goal to discover what, for an industrialized country like the United States, the "more" should be.

So an eventful decade later, Corning Glass Works Foundation had taken the lead in organizing a second conference, and had again called on the American Council of Learned Societies, now under the direction of Frederick H. Burkhardt, to be its co-sponsor. Based on the same general principles as its predecessor, the second conference was planned to be much more international in participation and subject-matter. This shift in intellectual center from a nation to a planet was surely in some sense a reflection of intervening events. Some of the obvious ones may be mentioned:

During the fifties the accomplishments of Soviet rocketry had challenged, if not ended, the United States' world military supremacy. Certain events, culminating in an alarming outflow of United States gold reserves, had raised questions about the United States' continued economic pre-eminence. The great part of a continent—Africa—had moved from colonial to free status, and had taken the first steps toward industrialization; indeed, as the one Great Fact of international relations, the so-called cold war had been challenged by something new—the rapid emergence of the underdeveloped countries, most of them in varying degrees politically uncommitted. And, of course, the invention and development of weapons systems capable of destroying civilization, if not humanity itself, had tended to make the very idea of nationality seem a little quaint. Like it or not, the world was becoming one. Ethnocentrism, one might say, had for people of all cultures become a considerably less tenable philosophy. When—as Arthur Houghton, speaking on behalf of Corning Glass Works, put it in opening the Second Corning Conference—"a small group of the finest minds of the world" came together in May 1961 to think things over in "this quiet, somewhat isolated little community," it was not only right but inevitable that they should think not about the United States alone but about the world.

The organization of the conference was as follows: For purposes of manageability, the general topic was arbitrarily broken up into the subtopics Work, Education, and Leisure. Six background papers, all of which are contained in this volume, were commissioned to be written by distinguished prospective conference participants. The six papers comprised two each on work, education, and leisure, one in each case written by an American and applying chiefly to the American scene, the other written by a participant from abroad and applying to a different, and in some cases contrasting, society. (Two of the paper-writers, Julian Hochfeld of Warsaw, Poland and McGeorge Bundy of Washington, D. C., were unexpectedly unable to attend the conference.) So that maximum use could be made of the conference time, the background papers were not read at the conference itself; they were sent to all participants in advance of the meeting to help form the basis of the discussions. The one prepared speech delivered at the conference itself was the keynote address, by Charles Habib Malik of Lebanon, and the one formal general session was a dinner meeting entitled "Views From Abroad," at which four foreign participants spoke briefly and then answered questions, some of them pointed, from other participants. For the rest, the conference consisted of five roundtables made up of from seventeen to twenty participants, each of which met for three two-and-a-half-hour sessions to take up, in free discussions, whatever matters they chose, in any order they chose, using an agenda of their own devising, or no agenda, as they chose.

In this sense, the organization was free-form, but in another sense it was directed—that is, the five roundtables were fixed, with no interchanging of members from one session to the next. The disadvantage of such an arrangement is obvious: that it permitted each participant to actually confer with no more than one-fifth of the others present. (That is, for the public record. A great deal of unofficial and unrecorded conferring went on between sessions, in hotel rooms and corridors and at the numerous social events.) But so is the advantage obvious. With the same groups remaining together through three sessions making up seven and one-half hours of talk, each participant had time to become familiar with the personalities and points of view of his fellow-panel members, and the time-wasting strains and formalities and *politesses* of getting acquainted were reduced to a minimum.

As to the absence of any agenda for the roundtables, its result was a remarkable diversity of procedure and tone of discussion. The panels developed characteristic moods and personalities. They handled the same subject matter in quite different ways; thus, considered together, their various slants of light give the conference a kind of prismatic wholeness. The participants had no hand in arranging the panel assignments, and no advance knowledge of who their fellow-panelists were to be. The planners had tried to arrange the panels so that each one would have a wide spread of points of view, productive of enlightening disharmony. It is a tribute to the planners—and perhaps even more to the participants—that not one of the latter complained about his panel assignment either before or after the conference.

Who were the participants? Their names are listed by panel in the front of this volume, their brief biographies are given in the appendix, and their parries and ripostes quoted in Part I; right here, some census figures may be helpful. Of the ninety participants, eight (Appley, Boeschenstein, De Vane, Huxley, Larrabee, Lilienthal, Starr, Worthy) were repeaters from the First Corning Conference. Twenty-one were from outside the United States; of these, three were from Asia, two from Africa, two from Latin America, three from Canada, one from Australia, one from the Middle East, and the rest from Europe. About one-third of the ninety were people primarily engaged in education and academic life; about one-fifth were people primarily engaged in industry. Four were labor leaders; three were clergymen; three were psychiatrists or psychoanalysts; five were primarily diplomats. A majority of the participants had published one or more books, and nearly all had published articles; nine were primarily writers. The rest were spread around in less classifiable occupations: government service of various sorts, foundation work, editors and publishers, a museum director, two youth leaders, a scientist, two judges. There were also—and, of course, this is a double listing, since they have already been counted by occupation—four women. Although many came much greater distances to be at the conference, surely none came under conditions of such hardship as James Houston, the Canadian government's civil administrator on West Baffin Island, who had been lucky enough to catch a Dominion Observatory ski-plane from his outpost to the nearest airline terminal at Frobisher Bay, and expected that his best way of getting home would be by dogteam. Evidently, he had not wanted to miss the conference.

In compiling this account, I have taken some small liberties with the order in which things were said, for the sake of clarity and coherence; I hope none of these liberties are licenses. Obviously, it could not have been compiled without the work of the stenotypists of the Buckley Reporting Service, whose unwearying efforts resulted in a transcript of amazing accuracy, and whose susceptibility to human error was hearteningly established by the presence in their record of such an occasional slip as the one that transformed a celebrated British novelist and scientist, as referred to in the possessive case by a fast-talking conference participant, as "Sir Sepe Snooze." (Surely Sir Sepe deserves a place beside Sir Toby Belch and Sir Andrew Aguecheek.)

A word about titles. The general aim has been to use them in such a way as to give the reader a chance to become familiar with the individual participants rather than to placate the latters' egos. With proper American reverence, all British Crown titles have been used. Academic titles such as "dean" and "professor" have been conferred or withheld, capriciously. The same holds true for the diplomatic tag "ambassador." As for "doctor," it has been ruthlessly omitted (other than in direct quotations) except in the case of members of the medical profession, on the ground that the use of it for holders of earned or honorary advanced degrees among such an accomplished and honored group would have tended to make the Second Corning Conference sound like a meeting of the American Medical Association.

J. B.

PART I

CHAPTER 1

∞§

AN OPENING PERSPECTIVE

∞§

THE SECOND CORNING CONFERENCE by common and tacit consent addressed itself to a single theme. It assumed man's survival, and aimed at a loftier goal: his fulfillment. It took the position that a man's reach should exceed his grasp even in a time when his grasp itself is shaky.

It had been decided in advance by the planners that the conference should not try to come to any conclusions. There was no plenary session, nor did the chairmen of the five panels make any formal attempt to summarize their various findings. Any document, any "manifesto" that could have been approved by ninety such different persons—such individualists—as attended the conference would have been a bland document indeed. There was no such manifesto. The decision reflected a prudent recognition of the limitations of conferences. On only a few matters was there anything like a consensus, and even on these matters there were usually vocal and persuasive dissenters.

Nevertheless, a perusal of the 350,000-word transcript of the roundtables leaves one with the feeling that certain things were said, repeatedly and forcefully. Patterns of thought emerged. I set down these patterns, as I see them, with the warning that they are not a consensus—they are a rather subjective impression of the way the conference's wind was blowing, arrived at not scientifically with a weather-vane, but intuitively with a wet finger held in the breeze.

Well, then, what was said at the Second Corning Conference? To begin with, its underlying value was individualism; almost the only questioner of that value's absoluteness was Frank Moraes of India, who introduced the idea that a scale has been thrown out of balance—that as things stand now the West leans too heavily to individualism as the East does to collectivism. And this was perhaps strange. Historically, individualism is anything but a worldwide value. In the Orient, it has always fought a rearguard action, as it continues to do today. It made little headway in Europe until the Renaissance. It achieved perhaps its highest estate in ancient Greece—but for a minority in a slave state. The rise of individualism for the many is a recent thing, coinciding with the rise of industrialism—which, paradoxically, is the force that now appears to threaten it. The whole mood of the conference was one of deep concern that so many of the most distressing problems of industrialized nations—conformity, mental illness, juvenile delinquency—seem to be related to a lost sense of personal identity and dignity. Indeed, the impact of these and similar problems on the world in recent years has been so great that a distinguished foreign participant, Sir Muhammad Zafrulla Khan of Pakistan, could in a between-sessions conversation express pleasure and surprise that an important conference held in America in 1961 should have concern for the human individual as its topic. This of the nation whose motto is *e pluribus unum!*

Accepting the value of individualism, the conference directed much of its attention to a question that was neatly formulated by Mary I. Bunting of Radcliffe College: Is there something innate in the organized production of goods that is inimical to the free expression of the individual; and if so, what can be done about it?

In the discussion of this and related questions, certain broad tendencies emerged:

1. There was a feeling—eloquently enunciated in the keynote address, and then repeated several times in the roundtable discussions—that the United States and Soviet Russia are remarkably similar in an increasingly important way; that is, in that (in different degrees) secular rather than religious or spiritual ideas dominate both systems. The contrast between a free and a directed economy was made, of course; but it was pointed out that Russia seems to be evolving in the direction of bourgeois competition, and repeatedly suggested that the great ideological struggles of the future may lie not in the present cold war but elsewhere.

2. The developing nations were recognized as being the biggest new factor in the world. Mr. Diké of Nigeria, by virtue not only of his personal charm and eloquence but of what he represented, was probably the conference's star. There was bitter disagreement as to whether, in dealing with these emerging nations, the developed industrialized countries should or should not think first in material terms and only later in spiritual or cultural ones. There was agreement that the large nations must avoid using economic aid as an instrument of foreign policy.

3. The pre-set categories for discussion—work, education, and leisure—often merged in the discussion to the point of disappearance as separate categories. This was surely proper. One man's work is another man's leisure; the same thing may be a third man's (or the same man's) education. Mr. Houston pointed out that for his Canadian Eskimos, hunting, which had always been work, abruptly became leisure as soon as handicraft work was introduced as a means of making money. On the supposedly entertainment medium of television, the few programs intended to be educational may be nearly the *only* source of entertainment to some serious-minded viewers. And so on. It was provocatively suggested once or twice during the conference that to the extent to which such categories of activity overlap in a society, it is a good society; in the ideal society, they would be indistinguishable.

On the subject of industrialization itself—to which the major part of the discussion was devoted, on the theory that it is the one great dynamic process acting on the modern world—there was some disagreement about how nearly universal it will eventually become, and even some blunt questioning as to whether, even at its best, it holds as much potential for the individual as do primitive societies. But there was general agreement that the process is irreversible and is destined to continue. A listing of the chief characteristics of industrial society was compiled, chiefly by Panel IV; they were (in no special order) complex organization, the use of science and machinery, specialization of work, constant change, urbanization of population, and the existence of far greater opportunities (or necessities) for individual choice of action than have existed in previous societies.

It was easy to agree on what industrialism is; the controversy came in what it does for people, and to people. Industrialism was accused of progressively causing unemployment as machines do more and more of the work of men; increasing the amount of leisure time to the point where the use of such time becomes a psychological and sociological problem; fostering materialistic attitudes to the exclusion of spiritual ones; having an adverse effect on physical and mental health due to increased tension; resulting, through its size and complexity, in individual lack of understanding and sense of powerlessness; destroying craftsmanship and pride in work through specialization; crowding people in inhuman, unbeautiful cities; causing bewilderment and neurosis by offering the individual too many choices; and, finally, threatening to destroy culture by subverting and denaturing the thought habits of the guardians of culture themselves, the creative artists, scholars and critics.

A grim picture. But, of course, each of these pennies had a "heads" as well as a "tails," and there were participants ready and willing to turn the pennies over. Industrialists, particularly Roger Blough of United States Steel, were ready with statistics to prove that in practice up to now, automation has actually created jobs rather than eliminated them. Increased leisure time was seen by many as presenting an unparalleled challenge and opportunity rather than a burden. On materialism, some insisted that spiritual values underlie industrialism as it is now, and others that they might in the future. On physical and mental health, some participants who have personally moved from agrarian to industrial culture offered themselves as examples of improved well-being caused by the change; others expressed the view that life under tension tends to promote individual self-fulfillment rather than oppose it. On feelings of confusion and powerlessness, many saw an answer in a re-dedication to old goals and ideals that have been largely lost. On the question of craftsmanship, some insisted that industrialism has created new and equally valid crafts and skills to replace the old ones. As to industrial cities, planners like Victor Gruen still saw the possibility remaining for our cities to serve the individual for both living and leisure. As to the adverse effect of industrialism on culture, here the concern and eloquence on the negative side tended to carry the day—but there was the countervailing argument that for a culture that possesses the power to know its weaknesses so well and criticize them so savagely and tellingly, all is not lost.

Indeed it is not. The problem, having accepted (with whatever reservations) industrialism and further industrialization, is to steer it in a favorable direction: not to make the best of a bad job, but to make a good job of the whole thing. Professor Herskovits of Northwestern, perhaps the conference's leading champion of primitivism, suggested that a beginning might be made by the attainment of "cultural modesty"—a general recognition by the people of developed societies that theirs are no better than undeveloped societies, but merely different. In a certain sense, cultural modesty was rampant at the conference. It was the industrialists—with exceptions, it is true, but by and large—who were fiercest in their criticism of industrialism as it is practiced. It was the writers and critics who were fiercest in their criticism of industrial culture, or lack of it; it was the educators who were the first to say that Western education has often failed. The only question Professor Herskovits might raise was the extent to which those self-criticisms were only family quarrels, not necessarily inconsistent with snobbery and smugness as soon as outsiders are involved. Still, the Finnish journalist Leo Schulgin, after listening to the Westerners in Panel I castigate themselves on both spiritual and practical grounds for most of a session, was moved to object by saying of the West, "You are not doing so badly." It is true that he meant specifically as regards the East-West military and political competition, but the comment might have applied in a wider context. Perhaps, as the psychiatrist Dr. Sibylle Escalona suggested later, self-criticism can be an easy way out—almost a form of boasting.

When the conference sought solutions, it turned, of course, to "education"—that talismanic word helpfully put at hand by the conference planners. The suggestion that individualism as the ideal of industrial society should be partially abrogated in the interest of winning the cold war was made—and generally rejected. A victory on such terms, it was thought, would be meaningless; indeed, our need in that competition is to strengthen our faith and aspiration. Whichever one of the failures of industrialism to serve individualism was a speaker's particular concern, he seemed for an answer to turn to education in one form or another. Specific reforms in American education were urged: a final end to racial segregation, wider and more appropriate education of women, wider and more urgent instruction in languages, maintenance of the liberal arts in the face of encroachments of technology, and so on. But—it was said, and several times seconded —formal education is no panacea; the academy is not a philosopher-king to take our worries from our shoulders and lead us to a better life; the sort of education that can help solve the problems of industrialism, beginning with self-education, is the task of all the leaders of society, and must go on as much outside school and university walls as inside them.

CHAPTER 2

✑

OVERTURE: THURSDAY EVENING

✑

Most of the conference participants arrived in Corning on the afternoon of Thursday, May 18, and set about getting settled at their rooms in the Baron Steuben Hotel and the Centerway Motel. The weather was not auspicious—a chilly breeze carried a spatter of rain—but even so, some of them took the occasion to look the town over, either by walking around its streets or by scanning it from the sheltered vantage point of a bedroom window at the Baron Steuben, which stands at the chief intersection. Famous and learned men from many parts of the world were suddenly in Corning's midst, and Corning seemed to be taking them in stride; when the novelist John Dos Passos mumbled his last name to the hotel's room clerk, the clerk assured him cheerily, "Nice to have you with us, Dr. Parsons."

What the famous and learned men saw was a small town that lies in a bowl of hills in the rugged and still quite wild country of south central New York State. Corning (population about seventeen thousand) became a company town in 1868, when the Glass Works (then called Brooklyn Flint Glass Company) was

9

floated up the Erie Canal from its previous home in Brooklyn. It is still a company town, its white frame houses sometimes standing cheek-by-jowl with the factory buildings. But the somber nineteenth-century implications of the term "company town" have been in large measure changed, even reversed, by the effects of twentieth-century ideas of corporate responsibility—of which, of course, the conference itself was evidence. (Another evidence of greater local importance was seen on the last day of the conference when, with most of the conferees present, ground was broken for a new Corning Community College, largely endowed by the Glass Works Foundation.) The Chemung, the little river that runs through Corning, was swollen by spring freshets to quite respectable proportions. The Glass Center, barely finished when the First Corning Conference had been held ten years earlier, was by now an old hand at welcoming distinguished visitors and initiating them into the wonders and mysteries of Corning's favorite material.

The setting seemed a good place for serious talk about important problems because it was off the beaten path without being out of touch, quiet without being solitary. In addition, whatever else this setting may or may not have been, it was American. It gave the cosmopolitan gathering a firm and self-assured parochial backdrop. The names of the towns and villages that surround Corning make a kind of American litany: Odessa, Dundee, Beaver Dams, Big Flats, Athens, Van Etten, Horseheads, Painted Post, Candor.

The formal opening of the conference—a brief meeting at five-thirty in a small auditorium in the Glass Center, consisting of welcomes to the participants and explanations of the ground rules—served the additional purpose of getting the participants into one room where they could make each other's acquaintance, or renew it. This purpose was even better served at the two events that followed: a party outside the Glass Center, and dinner in its club. Since the earlier spatter had now become a resolute downpour, the outdoor party was held under a hastily-erected canopy of canvas (or, more probably, of some sort of glass). Inevitably, a little rain got through the canopy's eyelets and seams, and dripped onto the heads, dignifiedly sparse-haired or formidably gray-maned, of the distinguished guests. They could not have taken this in better part than they did. Indeed, the small hardship of foul weather, cutting across the awesomely efficient management and Lucullan fare provided by the conference's hosts, seemed to add a cheerful human dimension. Those who had come primed to denounce industry in the conference sessions found themselves momentarily softened and disarmed: even industry in all its awesome power evidently could not fix the weather.

Delivered in the Glass Center's large auditorium, which holds more than one thousand persons, the keynote address was the only event of the conference open to the general public, and the citizens of Corning—augmented, of course, by the participants—responded by filling the room nearly to capacity. The evening's speaker, who appeared after brief introductory remarks by Corning's executive committee chairman Amory Houghton and the American Council's president Frederick Burkhardt, was, of course, Charles Habib Malik, professor of philosophy at the American University of Beirut, Lebanon, and former president of the United Nations Security Council.

Mr. Malik's keynote address appears in full elsewhere in this book (see page 135), and so an extended account of it is not needed here; but since its impact on the whole conference was so great, some comments on the manner of its delivery and the nature of its reception may be in order, together with a brief outline of its main points. Ambassador Malik is an impressive man, whose face seems to suggest moral earnestness and practical political sense in almost equilibrium; trained in mathematics and physics before he turned to philosophy, and having remained an academic while becoming his country's leading international political figure, he represents a combination of qualities that the West has often lacked in its leaders. His Corning address, controversial as it proved to be, was eloquent in language and almost fierce in delivery.

It began with the rounded assertion, "The derivation of man from and the reduction of man to material, economic, and social conditions is the great heresy of this age." The Marxist materialist conception of man has become increasingly dominant in recent years, said Mr. Malik, not only in the Communist realm but in the West as well. His argument was that more and more as time goes on, we tend to think of economic and material betterment as *the* form of human betterment, to the exclusion of any other values; to conceive of man, philosophically, as an economic animal; and finally, to identify the individual only in terms of his current stage of economic development—as nothing but a certain point on a known graph curve. Such criteria, which Mr. Malik said he found to be current among the most responsible leaders of Western thought as well as among those of the Communist world, he pronounced "nauseatingly superficial and false." Malik distinguished seven major and distinct types of modern society—African, Chinese, Russian, Indian, Moslem, Latin, and Western (that is, Western European and English-speaking), each containing its characteristic type of individual. Insisting on such pluralism as providing the only view of the modern world that can avoid the disastrous pitfalls of a single world view, Mr. Malik argued that the "myth" of the existence of a univocal modern society resulted from precisely the materialist fallacy he had previously been attacking—the view that everything can be leveled down to the plane of matter, of the body and its desires, of the economic process.

Because of such thinking, said Mr. Malik, "Western civilization is in real trouble today." Where, in his view, does its salvation lie? Only in "the old paths, where is the good way"; that is, in its traditional faith in God. Modern man has the possibility, and the obligation, to be free—the possibility of "a personal self-consciousness infinitely rich and infinitely true," which can be

achieved only if he will take "the offensive of love and helpfulness . . . which affirms that the greatest things in life can only
come through sorrow and suffering; the offensive of the spirit
which is contrite and the heart which is broken."

And how did the participants, many of whom came close
to being the very Western leaders that Malik had been chiding
for their materialism, react to these passionate remarks, which
were intended to set the tone for their deliberations? Some chose
to ignore them, or at least to avoid discussing them—perhaps
out of tactful disagreement; perhaps out of the feeling that Mr.
Malik had merely revived an old debate on which there was
nothing left to be said; or perhaps out of a certain American
embarrassment toward the discussion of questions of faith that
was to become a topic of considerable discussion before the conference was over. Some participants heartily agreed with Mr.
Malik's diagnosis, but wondered how a return to traditional
Western faiths could be accomplished, and how it could be translated into more fruitful national policies.

At least one—Janez Stanovnik, director of the Institute for
International Policy and Economics in Belgrade—was to express
flat disagreement with Mr. Malik. Speaking in his roundtable
the following morning, Mr. Stanovnik said, "We cannot hope for
human beings becoming more human without making it possible
for technological change to achieve its final goal, that goal being
to make the economic background of human societies more firm
and strong." In another roundtable, David E. Lilienthal, former
chairman of the Tennessee Valley Authority and now chairman
of the Development & Resources Corporation, expressed another
sort of reservation, which also contained an element of agreement.
Listening to Mr. Malik, said Mr. Lilienthal, "I was rather uncomfortable. I was associated with a rowdy Peck's Bad Boy next to
me—and I was even rowdier—but I gathered that this contempt
for materialism [of Malik's] loses sight of the fact that this is
just our way of covering up the fact that we [in the United

States] are somewhat embarrassed when we're altruistic. I personally am not embarrassed; I don't think anyone should be. There are moral concepts back of industrialization."

Thus, with the stage already set for debate, the first day of the conference ended.

CHAPTER 3

⋅⋅§

FRIDAY MORNING

⋅⋅§

Friday morning: leaden skies over Corning, but no rain. After breakfast at their quarters, the participants boarded buses to Houghton Park, the spic-and-span preserve of glass and grass where the conference was to be held, its opening panel sessions at nine-fifteen. The heartland of the conference had been reached.

Much of the character of the discussions was to derive from the makeup of the five roundtables and from the diversified surroundings in which the five panels met. As a figure in a painting gains meaning from its relationship to other figures and to the texture of landscape, so the things said at Corning, set down in the pages that follow, can best be understood in relation to where they were said, and among whom.

As to the panel assignments in general, the planners had grouped the participants with care to achieve a balance of points of view, and possibly now and then with a sly sense of humor. For instance, Lawrence A. Appley, president of the American Management Association, discovered that in Panel I he was going

15

to choose his phrases in such a way that they would be proof against any objections from Jay Lovestone, director of international publications of the AFL-CIO. In Panel IV, Mr. Diké of Nigeria (population around forty million) was to have a chance to compare conditions in relatively underdeveloped areas with Mr. Houston of West Baffin Island (population about two hundred and forty people). In Panel V, Mr. Moraes, former editor of the *Times of India,* would sit near Amory Bradford, general manager of the *New York Times.*

Four of the five panels had American labor leaders, and all of them had American industrial leaders. (But Mr. Blough and Walter H. Wheeler, Jr. of Pitney-Bowes, in labor-leaderless Panel IV, had a raft of professional intellectuals to contend with instead.) The less developed countries were represented in all but one of the panels, and each of them had a foreign representation of at least three. Three had spokesmen for the psychiatric or psychoanalytical point of view, and each had a creative writer: two of them novelists, one a poet, one a literary critic, one a literary jack-of-all-trades, one a theatrical critic and director. Three groups had a clergyman or theologian on hand.

As to the five roundtables in particular: Panel I's meeting-place was the Corning Glass Works board of directors room on the ninth floor of the Administration Building: a rectangular room, with a fine north light, dominated by a bearded portrait of Amory Houghton Jr. (1837-1909), onetime president of Corning, son of the company's founder, grandfather of the current Corning executive committee chairman, and great-grandfather of the current Corning president. The panel chairman, President Cornelis W. de Kiewiet of the University of Rochester, is an authority on modern European history with a special interest in British Colonial and post-colonial Africa; the panel itself was a characteristic cross-section of the conference as a whole. (See p. v.) One participant in Panel I commented later that its emphatically executive setting may have subtly influenced it to take more the point of view of the industrialist than it might have done otherwise. But this must also be said: The dominant role in Panel I over the three sessions, if there was such a dominant role, was that of sharp criticism of industrial life coming from industrialists themselves. As to the manner in which the Panel I discussions were conducted, it is only necessary to say that Mr. de Kiewiet is an enthusiastic amateur bee-keeper; he knows that bees are soothed by a calm mien and are excited to disorder and violence by the smell of fear.

Panel II, chaired by Douglas M. Knight, president of Lawrence College, met in the cafeteria on the ground floor of the Administration Building. The cafeteria had been deactivated as an eating place for the term of the conference, so the participants were undisturbed by the clatter of dishes (although they were occasionally bemused by the hum of a large refrigerator) ; indeed, being capacious, and having glass walls that opened out on grass, trees, a parking lot, and the sight of Glass Works employees coming and going, it provided an interesting sort of conference room; it seemed to open out on the world rather than be enclosed from it. Panel II turned out to be what might be called a mood group. It had its ups and downs; its participants seemed to influence each other, at different times, toward hope and toward deep pessimism. It produced, late Friday morning and early Friday afternoon, some of the liveliest colloquy of the conference, which its chairman guided with tact. He also brought to each session no less than three pipes, which he arranged on the table in front of him and smoked in rotation, occasionally slipping in a cigar for diversity. In the experience of one seasoned observer of conferences who was on hand, Mr. Knight is perhaps the only three-pipe panel chairman now operating.

Panel III's venue was the first-floor conference room of the research and development laboratory—a plain enough room with nothing particular to distinguish it or influence the course of its deliberations. Its participants were another matter, having much to distinguish them. (See page vi.) Their chairman, Professor Arthur E. Murphy of the department of philosophy at the University of Texas, conducted the discussion with smiling geniality; as one panel member, Mark Starr, put the matter, Murphy was a "permissive" chairman, tending to hold the reins loosely and let the talk go where it would. One of the fortunate results was that in no other panel was the interrelatedness of work, education, and leisure brought out so clearly. Perhaps the particular mark of Panel III was its Western character; it was the only group containing nobody from east of Mr. Malik (Lebanon) or south of Mr. de Madariaga (originally from Spain). This regional quality made for a welcome frankness of Western self-appraisal.

Panel IV, meeting in the research and development laboratory's third-floor library—an airy and book-lined place with fine natural lighting—was led, or rather intelligently left on its own, by Paul J. Braisted, president of the Edward W. Hazen Foundation. In a way, Panel IV was a glamor panel, featuring several newsy names as well as having among its number the conference's attractive cynosure, Mr. Diké. Perhaps as a result of this, a motion-picture film crew that was covering the conference showed a particular liking for Panel IV. One might have thought that the frequent presence of this crew and its rather awe-inspiring equipment would have stiffened or constricted the discussion, but, if anything, the effect seemed to be the opposite. Reading the record of Panel IV, one has the feeling that in the confrontations that took place, and in the manner in which some of the participants reacted to each other, a kind of history was made.

The setting of Panel V was strikingly different from all the others. It was the basement auditorium of the research and development laboratory: a windowless cave in the best modern conference-room tradition, fully isolated from any distracting visual contact with the outside world, and even isolated from the outside weather by an air-conditioning system that created an ambience something like that on a mild day in Antarctica. Here sat three of the conference's visitors from overseas—Gilberto Freyre of Brazil, Frank Moraes of India, and Gabriele Morello of Sicily. Under the comparatively firm direction of its chairman, James

A. Perkins, vice-president of the Carnegie Corporation of New York, Panel V hewed to the line, avoided quibbles over definition, and methodically pulverized the conference's three subtopics in systematic succession. The discussion focused strongly on the situation in industrialized countries, the United States in particular, but the foreigners provided a refreshing check against any tendency toward acceptance of old shibboleths or toward self-congratulation.

It was immediately evident on Friday morning that the panels were going to differ widely in their procedure. Panels I and V resolved to take up work, education, and leisure in sequence, one to a session; Panel II began with each participant giving a brief statement of what, in his opinion, is the basic problem of the individual in modern society; and in Panel IV it was quickly agreed that all three sessions should be devoted to a single question. Panel III, influenced by the presence there of Ambassador Malik, began with a discussion of the previous evening's keynote address, and is therefore the logical point at which to begin this account of the roundtable proceedings.

Mark Starr, the longtime educational director of the International Ladies' Garment Workers' Union, questioned the keynote speaker's attack on materialism as being too broad. "Let's not tip the baby out of the crib," said Mr. Starr. "No civilization can be developed unless its material basis is assured. . . . Unless we have a sufficient amount of food, clothing, and shelter, then all our playing around with philosophy, or the arts, or culture, are misopportune." Dean William C. De Vane of Yale University replied to this by saying that he thought Mr. Malik had spoken as he had by way of redressing a balance that has swung too far in the direction of materialism; he agreed with Malik, he said, that the West must recover its tradition coming out of Greece and the Near East, "which, fundamentally, is in praise, in honor, in the service of the individual"; if we continue to rest as we tend to do at present on material things, said Dean De Vane, then our society will not be worth preserving. Professor Ritchie Calder of the University of Edinburgh echoed Mr. Starr, raising the warning that the word "democracy" has a hollow sound to a man with a hollow belly; in competing with the Russians for the favor of underdeveloped countries we had *better* be materialistic, or we will lose; and furthermore, the people in such countries may be and often are quite content with their own spiritual values, and look to the West only for material help.

Salvador de Madariaga, the Spanish author and diplomat in exile, came in largely on Mr. Malik's side, and with an interesting objection to Mr. Starr's remarks:

> It is simply not true, absolutely not true, that the human being who is below a certain standard of material comforts or material necessities is incapable of understanding the higher truths and higher values. On the contrary, I think that prosperity is more likely to deaden the sense of freedom than poverty. . . .
>
> Diogenes lived in exile, and he was capable of doing some independent thinking, and all he wanted was for anybody to get out of the sun. Now, this seems to me a very important point, because we are, in the West, powerfully contributing to the success of the Communist heresy in this very dangerous stage of the history of the world—the heresy that what's the good of talking freedom to people who haven't got enough food to fill up their stomachs? This is the wrong doctrine. . . . I should be sorry in a discussion in this free city of a free world, if we were to accept as gospel truth ideas which, in my opinion, are senselessly put forth by your spiritual enemies of the other side.

The subsequent contribution of Harold Clurman, theatre critic and director, moved the debate ahead by introducing the suggestion that the West's primary mission is to itself: not to reform the values of the rest of the world, but to reform its own—which, he agreed with Mr. Malik, are now too materialistic. This led Miss Dorothy Height of the national board of the YWCA to point to one obvious and crucial area for self-reform. Too many Western individuals have a sense of powerlessness to influence the huge and bewildering society that surrounds them, Miss

Height said; for example, as a Negro educator she is powerfully aware of a powerlessness to teach that, even in the United States, all men are equal and have equal opportunity. Far beyond such specific problems, she said, she feels that our most important mission is to restore to individuals the sense of real worth and of being able to make some difference to the situation.

So some of the most important cards were already on the table; some basic problems had been stated, and could now be tackled. Arnaud de Vogüé, president of the Compagnie de Saint-Gobain, and Eberhard Strohal, deputy editor of the *Kurier* in Vienna, both agreed with Mr. de Madariaga that people who have known privation as to both freedom and food rate freedom the more important human need. Mr. Malik concurred with Miss Height that the West—or in this case, specifically the United States—has serious problems not directly related to materialism, in particular the racial problem, which "incapacitates" the United States in international affairs; but at least such problems can be freely discussed here, and the guarding of such right to free discussion is of first importance. August Heckscher, director of the Twentieth Century Fund (and the author of a background paper which is to be found on page 250), stated the view that a key United States weakness in dealing with the world is parochialism —that is, we who once thought of democracy as a universal idea have come to think of it as a local one, without applicability to other civilizations in other stages of development.

Now came a sort of marshaling of forces. Dean De Vane picked up Miss Height's remarks on the sense of powerlessness, and compared it, ominously, to the situation of "the little men in Germany under Hitler who thought they would not have any effect"; now, he said, we must take freedom in an active sense rather than a passive one. Mr. Clurman in his turn picked that up:

> I don't think anybody here need defend freedom. . . . I am very critical of my own country, the United States, but I always said I'd rather be unhappy here than happy any place else. I would rather fight and quarrel here than have freedom anywhere else.

I think all of us feel the same way. . . . Let's get on with our business [of trying to solve our problems], because I think we are more
or less in agreement as to certain basic premises.

The rest of the session was largely devoted to specific Western
problems and their solutions, in this conspicuously all-Western
panel. Mr. de Madariaga led the group off on its new tack, aiming toward some definitions. Roger Blough's "extremely able"
paper (see page 173), he said, had led him into trying to find a
definition for "work." What he came up with was "the endeavor
to act on physical life so that it becomes less like physical life
and more like the life we [as human beings] represent." This
was undoubtedly the most metaphysical of the many definitions
of work that were heard during the conference, yet it led Mr.
de Madariaga to a practical conclusion: that there is a substantial
connection between work and freedom. The labor done in an
unfree society is not, by his definition, true work. As for leisure,
it is only "an elegant word"; Mr. de Madariaga put far more
value on "idleness," which he said is generally forgotten or under-
valued in Western civilizations:

I am very fond of the fellow who does nothing at all, because I
think that fellow is preparing creativeness for his children or his
children's children or what may come later.

Among the industrious and seldom-idle men sitting around
the table, none seemed to take exception to that. Instead, Mr.
Starr went on to deplore another Western tendency, the tendency
to "put the dollar sign where it shouldn't be." It makes him
mad, Mr. Starr said, when he sees youngsters persuaded to go
to college because a degree will get them a bigger salary; educational values are not, or should not be, dollar values. Mr. Starr
proposed that what modern Western society needs is "social planning by consent. . . . The helplessness of the individual is somewhat compensated when he finds a group of people who agree
with him, and out of group activity he can find the power to
influence development which he could not do as an isolated
individual."

That idea stirred up a lively controversy. "How do you get social planning by consent?" demanded Harold Boeschenstein, president of Owens-Corning Fiberglas Corporation. Most social planning, said Mr. Boeschenstein, grows out of inertia rather than consent: The strong and confident merely impose their will on the lazy and unsure. He pointed to the first Henry Ford's experiment of giving plots of land to his employees, and recalled how a good many of the employees had soon hired other employees to work their plots—simply because they preferred being entrepreneurs to being farmers. Professor Calder emphasized and broadened the objection with another example—the Western attempts to get all the nations of the world to agree on a declaration of human rights, which were opposed in India and China on the ground that the duties of man come before the rights of man. Basic philosophies differ so widely that not everyone will consent to being planned for—even when to the planner his own wisdom seems self-evident.

Mr. Heckscher came out strongly for the possibility of social planning with consent—"I think it is the very hope of our social order and of our political order, too." He emphasized the importance of minority rights to dissent, and added that he did not think voluntary organizations and volunteer civic activities were playing as great a role in American life at present as they should. David Rockefeller of the Chase Manhattan Bank said he thought the base of the problem, for planners and planned-for alike, was our sheep-likeness, our inability to find direction from within—not that we lack the right to dissent, but that we lack the will.

Oscar Handlin, professor of history at Harvard, declared roundly that he disagreed with almost everything that had been said so far. To him, he said, the right to dissent is not in itself a terribly important right, or the main distinguishing feature of our society as opposed to others. He found the distinguishing feature in the realm of voluntary action—non-governmental, non-coercive planning through voluntary contributions and work. As to American materialism and putting the dollar sign in the wrong places, Professor Handlin said he felt this is partly an illusion. Our production is not for its own sake, as is often supposed: "It remains characteristic of our society, as of few others, that people give away these rewards, that they do not think of them as ends in themselves but often as means toward ends." Professor Handlin even had a good word for production lines: The routine of the Old-World peasant, tied down as he is by tradition, custom, weather, and the nature of the soil, may well be more deadening than that of working on an assembly line, and certainly the latter allows more leisure.

This expression of approval of the industrialized West brought a degree of agreement from William Patrick Fay, ambassador of Ireland to Canada; but Mr. Fay nevertheless wondered whether the American tendency to de-emphasize the state and emphasize the voluntary organization in social planning always works for the broadest possible common good. Mr. Clurman asked Mr. Handlin, "Since you seem to feel we are, more or less, in fine shape," what further development in our culture would Mr. Handlin recommend? Mr. Handlin replied that he saw many shortcomings; he mentioned the commercialism of mass communications as one. (So did almost all of industrialism's stanchest defenders, all through the conference.) But even here he saw voluntary, free-enterprise activity as the best road to solution, and mentioned New York City's radio station WQXR as a private venture that has brought good music to a larger audience than some of its government-controlled counterparts in Europe. James J. Rorimer, director of the Metropolitan Museum of Art, entered the reservation that public taste will not improve through exposure alone; specific education is called for.

That brought the panel to its last topic of the morning, cultural education to meet the mass leisure of industrial society. Mr. Starr raised a worrisome practical problem. When the rubber workers in Columbus and Akron achieve a thirty-hour week, do they use their increased leisure for creative or cultural activities? By and large, they do not; they "moonlight," or get a second job, and so the shorter work week ends up meaning not greater leisure but simply a rise in the material standard of living. "It shows the paucity of imagination," said Mr. Starr. Miss Height ended the session with a comment that seemed to go under what Mr. Starr had pointed out—and, incidentally, to introduce the morning's first mention of women:

> One of the tasks of education may well be the redirecting of our thinking and understanding of the meaning of work. . . . The thing that often stands up for me is the kind of thing that happens when you ask a woman what does she do. She will say, "I'm only a housewife," or you ask a voluntary organization worker what she does and she says, "I'm only a volunteer." . . . Whatever one does, if it really expresses the capacity which he has, and if it contributes to the good of the society, and if it meets a need—or if it is a response to a need—it is significant. . . .
>
> We have downgraded the importance of good workmanship in a voluntary group, the importance of doing well, whatever it is we are doing, as a means of discovering the real meaning in life. I tend to think maybe this is one of the places where we can see coming together . . . a greater task of education.

If Panel III's morning was devoted in the main to two great questions (Can industrialism have a spiritual component? and How much and what kind of social planning in the West?), Panel I's was forthrightly devoted to the single topic of work in modern society. First there was an interesting series of attempts at definition, excerpts from which will bear quoting.

Harry S. Ashmore, editor-in-chief of Encyclopaedia Britannica, Inc.: "Work is the amount of energy that you have to put into obtaining the means of subsistence. Could you begin there?"

Father Laurence J. McGinley, president of Fordham University: "I think one concept is important here, and that is when you have two men doing the same thing, to one it is work and to the other it is recreation. The man to whom it is recreation can stop when he wants."

Halbert L. Dunn, special assistant on the aging to the United

States Public Health Service: "Work is the expenditure of energy in a force field directed toward purpose."

Lawrence A. Appley, president of the American Management Association: "I want to question the possibility that there is work without fulfillment. If there is work without fulfillment, this is work without purpose. . . . The man who is standing all day putting nuts on bolts in a very routine job, or the man who is swinging a pick and shovel, is performing some important work that is part of the overall purpose of the organization."

Victor Gruen, president of the planning, architecture, and engineering firm bearing his name: "I am working as an architect when I sit in my office, and I have to deal with clients, some of whom I don't even like; but when, on a Saturday or Sunday, I go to my own study and design something and my wife says to me, 'Why do you work again?' and I say, 'I don't work, I enjoy myself,' this is recreation."

Sir Muhammad Zafrulla Khan, vice-president of the International Court of Justice: "I will pose one question by using an illustration. Are we here this morning at work or not?"

John A. Fuller, chairman of the board of Shawinigan Chemicals, Ltd. of Canada: "Mr. Chairman, I am just a practical businessman. . . . I would think labor is doing something you don't particularly like to do, but you have to do because you need shelter and you need food."

Jay Lovestone, director of international publications, AFL-CIO: "I don't think we should set ourselves absolute definitions of or distinctions between labor and work. . . . To me, the concept of labor and work is not something static or fixed. It changes. It is social. . . . Let us rather approach the problem of how labor or work will . . . produce more in a material sense so that we can enjoy more in a spiritual and cultural sense."

Raymond Aron, French journalist and professor: "The definition of work or labor varies from society to society. . . . The main characteristic of modern society is, I should say, differentiation. . . . We are in a society where we don't know if work is positive or negative, if it is a pleasure and a fulfillment or just a necessity; because in the past, there was almost always either a negative or a positive content to the notion of work or labor, but now, work has become purely neutral." (For an amplification of this idea, see Professor Aron's background paper on p. 157.)

John Hersey, novelist: After drawing examples of two workmen—one a declaimer of the *Iliad* in ancient Greece, the other a West African farmer tying the thatch of someone else's roof to fulfill a community responsibility—Mr. Hersey spoke of work as communication: "The reward both of those workmen have is a social reaction of some kind, a sense of the work producing something new in his relationship with other human beings."

Dr. Sibylle K. Escalona, professor of psychology at the Albert Einstein College of Medicine: "It seems to me that we are all agreed that a general definition is useless. . . . It is terrible to be hungry, and everybody knows it, and that does not need any discussion. But beyond that, the kinds of things that have been found in all the studies of the psychology of unemployment with which I am familiar have been a sense of worthlessness, a sense of not feeling oneself." No work, one might say, no sense of identity: a definition in reverse.

Dr. Escalona's remarks put an end to the search for a definition, but they did not prove that the attempts had been fruitless. Far from it; as well as introducing the participants to each other's points of view, the attempts had introduced most of the prevailing attitudes toward work in modern society. The discussion could move on—and move on it did, to the topic of Professor Hochfeld's background paper on work considered from a Marxist standpoint (see p. 276). This paper, as informal conversation the previous evening had abundantly shown, had proved a stumper to a good many of the American participants. Their trouble seemed to be not so much disagreement with Hochfeld's Marxist ideology and conclusions as inability to comprehend his style or relate his insights to anything in their own experience. In commenting on this difficulty in communication, Professor Aron said

some things that may perhaps serve as a touchstone to some of
the problems of the Corning Conference—and, indeed, of the
modern world:

> This morning, I had breakfast with Mr. [David] Lilienthal, who
> explained to me that he couldn't find any clear meaning in the
> paper of Hochfeld. In answer, I told him I thought it was a per-
> fectly clear paper, and I tried to explain it to him. . . . This paper
> is absolutely unintelligible to the majority, not only of the practical
> men in the United States, but to many intellectual men of the
> United States. Yet, this paper is perfectly clear to any European
> intellectual.
>
> The fact that the communication is so difficult between the
> intellectual community of the United States and the intellectual
> community of Europe and Latin America has a lot to do with
> political difficulties.

"Do not understand me too quickly," André Gide once wrote,
and Aron's comment, by pointing to the problem, reminded the
Panel I participants, coming as they did all the way from Pakistan
to California, not to understand—or misunderstand—each other
too quickly across cultures. Thus warned, they went on to take
up some work problems which at present apply to Europe as
well as the United States, and will certainly have wider scope
in the future: the problems of worker dissatisfaction under industrialism, and of potential ills associated with automation.
Taking the hopeful view on the former question, Mr. Appley
cited the conference's host as example of an industrial company
preserving craftsmanship rather than destroying it: the Steuben
glass blowers, their faces showing their absorption as they work,
fully conscious that they are part of an art. Mr. Ashmore replied,
"The only thing I have to say in rebuttal is that this is unique."
"It shouldn't be," said Mr. Appley. "But it is," insisted Mr. Ashmore. Mr. Gruen agreed that it was exceptional, if not unique.
This led Mr. Lovestone into a discussion of a labor unionist's
attitude toward management paternalism. "We are very suspicious," he said, adding that some union suspicions are well
founded, others less so and should have been got rid of long

since. You couldn't do in Corning what they do unless you had unionization, he declared: "If you did it otherwise, it would be paternalism, and there would be resentment." Furthermore, it would not work in many other industries: "You couldn't possibly do that kind of work in the garment industry, because the 'big capitalist' in the garment industry is the union." But here the future looks brighter: "We get a little suspicious [of management paternalism], but that can be overcome as the union becomes stronger and as the union develops a sense of social responsibility, and as the union loses the notion that the way it can do business best for its members is by driving the company out of business."

Mr. Ashmore now brought up the question of automation. Mr. Blough's paper (see p. 173) makes the point that on the record up to date, as he interprets it, automation has actually created jobs rather than causing unemployment by eliminating them; but Mr. Ashmore's concern was not unemployment but the use of increased leisure. As the average work week grows shorter and time off increases, won't we, Mr. Ashmore inquired, have to begin to build our lives in a different way? Yes, indeed, Mr. Gruen agreed; and one way to rebuild them is to rebuild the places where so much of that increased leisure time will be spent—the places Mr. Gruen spoke of as the public environment. "The greatest sin of our mechanized technological society has probably been that in developing it we have destroyed the public environment," he said, modestly omitting to add that Victor Gruen Associates has already done something, in particular places, about rebuilding it.

Dr. Escalona, pursuing the topic of increased leisure, said she thought it necessary to talk about boredom. She didn't agree, she said, that the few remaining skilled crafts are the only tasks that are proof against boredom: "I think I know very few tool-and-die makers who are bored on the job. Garage mechanics very rarely are. Peculiarly enough, cleaning ladies very rarely are. They may hate the job and have totally unsatisfactory conditions to battle, but they are not bored. I think postal employees are among the most bored bunch of people I know. It had gotten to be a joke in our hospital that certain families with difficulties severe enough to bring them to the psychiatric unit come really disproportionately often from postal employees." To generalize this fascinating analysis, Dr. Escalona said she thought the component of work that prevents boredom is somewhat the kind of thing Mr. Hersey had been speaking of—"a direct involvement where you use your muscles or your brains in a very immediate way to build a roof or to make some kind of alteration and to achieve a visible, tangible goal." The study of boredom, its causes and cures, will be an increasingly important one from now on in technological society.

Mr. Dunn cited a couple of rules for employers that, he said, have proved helpful in keeping employees interested in their work: Keep them informed and knowledgeable, so far as possible, about what they are doing, and find ways to consult and listen to employee views.

Chairman de Kiewiet wound up the session with the comment that the Western problems under discussion must finally be considered in the context of the great fact, perhaps deplorable but nonetheless inescapable, of our competition with Russia:

> There is a mobilization of work which gives the Russian state a tremendous accession of power. Now, we are under the challenge from the Russian state. . . . At the present moment it substantially leads in a great section of the world's population. . . . I think one of the great questions that needs to be faced by American society is the degree in which it can safely continue the humanization of labor and, at the same time, meet these incredible challenges that lie upon us. If, for example, we were to be challenged and accepted the challenge . . . could we mobilize the resources to do it? Are we perhaps being driven inexorably in a direction where we have to simply remobilize our power, our labor—have to withdraw from some of the gains and advantages that we have painfully won for ourselves?

And that, in fact, was to be Panel I's principal topic in its next session that afternoon.

Different as had been their starting points, Panels III and I had come at the end of the morning to the same question: How to humanize work and deal intelligently and creatively with increased leisure. Panel V, like Panel I, began by getting resolutely down to Work. Its strong representation from less developed countries brought about a welcome check on Western shoptalk; indeed, after some introductory remarks by Chairman Perkins, it was the foreigners, led by Gabriele Morello, director of the Istituto Superiore of Palermo, Sicily, who started the discussion by giving views of work in their own countries. According to Mr. Morello, the industrial optimism embodied in Mr. Blough's paper simply does not apply to southern Italy at present. As industrialization comes there, he said, "there doesn't seem to be a clear correlation of industrial growth and income, and of growth and satisfaction among the people who do work." Culturally, said Mr. Morello, Sicily has remained an agricultural, tradition-directed society: "The desire for change, the desire for innovation, the desire for leisure, which are the really modern concepts of work, have not yet been absorbed by a population which is still much more bound to the fear of losing the job that they have, with all the consequence that this implies."

Frank Moraes, the Indian author and journalist, said that he thought his country's situation more or less corresponded with Mr. Morello's, and went on to affirm one of the ideas that was among the whole conference's bones of contention: that the material must come first, and the spiritual afterward. (As we have seen, Mr. de Madariaga was attacking it that morning in Panel III.) Hungry men don't think through their minds, said Mr. Moraes; they think through their stomachs, and it is no use talking to a man about freedom of individual expression when he has no freedom from want. Furthermore, he went on, the idea that the West is materialistic and the East spiritualistic is to him nonsense: "It is only the accident of history that the industrial revolution in the West occurred one hundred years before it struck Asia." Mr. Moraes saw the West as having undergone "a sort of mental spring fever"—the Renaissance in the fifteenth century, the Reformation in the sixteenth, the great scientific discoveries in the seventeenth, and the Industrial Revolution in the eighteenth—and the East as having missed all this. Only in the light of this vast difference, said Mr. Moraes, can the Indian approach to industrialization be understood. He saw the contrast as being a clearcut one between a West that puts too much stress on the individual and an East that puts too much stress on society, and the solution for both lying in a balance of the two concepts.

Gilberto Freyre, Brazilian sociologist, next offered a striking Latin American view. He comes from a country, he pointed out, that had slavery until 1888, and has begun to industrialize only quite recently. Mr. Freyre then pointed out some characteristics of Brazilian society. In pre-industrial Brazil, he said, work was associated with slavery and was not accorded dignity. Nor was prestige based on economic wealth; indeed, there were no banks, and if a man had many gold coins he had to conceal the fact assiduously, or the coins would be stolen. A far more important measure of prestige was the number of children a man had; unlike gold coins, they could safely be shown off! Then, gradually, came industrialization, and with it various new values. On the one hand, work became more dignified because it was no longer associated with slavery; but in another sense, it became degraded because the worker "began to be mass and ceased to be individual." Meanwhile the prestige of wealth began to rise, and as money became more important, so did time: "With that expression, 'time is money,' another phrase came into Brazil, and that was the 'English hour,' meaning that one should be more careful about appointments. If you say two o'clock, you don't mean a half an hour after two." Out of such changes Mr. Freyre drew the conclusion that from the experience of his country, "You cannot say that the process of industrialization is good or bad. It may be good or it may be bad. It depends upon the psycho-social orientation that you give it."

The panel's fourth foreign visitor, Graham Spry, agent general of the government of Saskatchewan in the United Kingdom and Europe, rounded out the opening non-United States views on industrialization and industrial work by speaking of the alliance between African-Asian and Anglo-Saxon elements in the British Commonwealth to force South Africa out on the grounds of its racial policies. Mr. Spry saw this as a hopeful sign in the development of worldwide trade relations, and in part as a promising consequence of general industrialization.

Then John Dos Passos, the novelist, gave the first United States viewpoint:

> I would like to get away from politics and back to the individual, to an individual man. I feel that the word "individual" is always used apologetically today. . . . I feel that the individual, one man by himself, is the whole story.

But alas, Mr. Dos Passos went on to say, the individual does not seem to be the whole story of industrialization. Speaking particularly of the baneful influence of television, he went on to chronicle individualism's recent setbacks in the area where he lives—Tidewater Virginia—and to conclude that "all of the modern forms of industrial production are working against a basic biological fact . . . which is for individuality." True or false? The panel debated the point, with variations, for the rest of the morning.

James C. Worthy, business consultant, said it seemed to him that along with the forces Mr. Dos Passos had been speaking of was an opposing one: a substantial contribution of technological progress to diversity—a multiplication of different occupations that actually contributes to individuality. Charles E. Odegaard, president of the University of Washington, likewise took a rather optimistic view of industrialization, pointing out its democratic tendencies (a man's occupation no longer stigmatizes him as to social status), mentioning its characteristic of increasing a man's flexibility of choice, and maintaining that even the watcher of television is, like the reader of a book, reaching out to communicate with other human beings.

This led Samuel Sandmel, provost of Hebrew Union College-

Jewish Institute of Religion in Cincinnati, to put the question, Does not increased opportunity for personal choice lead not to increased personal freedom, but rather, by causing bewilderment, in precisely the opposite direction—toward automatic conformity? Leaving that question temporarily in the air, Carl A. Gerstacker, chairman of the board of Dow Chemical Co., raised the matter of industrialism's tendency to specialize work. "Our people no longer become salesmen, they become salesmen of acetylsalicylic acid," said Mr. Gerstacker, and with this change goes a diminution of the amount of satisfaction a man can take in his work. But if an industrialist was worried about job specialization, such were the paradoxes of the conference that two college presidents rose to defend it. President Odegaard of the University of Washington replied:

> I am a little troubled by some of this disenchantment, because I have the feeling that a man is a little healthier animal than may be implied, even under industrial conditions. I was thinking, Mr. Gerstacker, as you were talking about [specialization], of a good friend of mine who is a very good eye specialist. . . . I remember one time at a dinner party he turned to my wife and began talking about something he saw that day, some eye condition on some human being, and suddenly he realized that he had been awfully enthusiastic, and he said, "You know, I guess there is really nothing that I love like a sore eye." The capacity to find value, even if it seems preposterous to the critic next door, in human activity, is pretty enduring, I think.

And then President Byron K. Trippet of Wabash College:

> There are an awful lot of people in my part of the world who still work hard, and get an awful lot of satisfaction out of it, even though they may be highly specialized. . . . I come from a line of people who made work almost a supreme value of men. My grandfather worked from sunup to sundown, doing all the multitudinous things on a farm, and now I am rather highly specialized, and still working pretty hard. I really don't see much difference.

Chairman Perkins paused to sum up: On the one hand, the

panel seemed to be saying, industrialization brings increased freedom and increased possibilities, not to mention freedom from social oppression and physical want; on the other hand, it brings mass standards and uniformity, the things lumped together in such phrases as "Coca-Cola civilization." The concern of Mr. Morello and Mr. Dos Passos was "the heavy hand of groupness"; of Mr. Odegaard, Mr. Worthy, and Mr. Trippet, the development of a capacity to deal with the new multiplicity of opportunities. Mr. Moraes modified this summary by adding the warning that it would be a mistake to assume that the whole panel considered individualism an absolute positive value; in his own view, he re-emphasized, "the mistake the free world makes is to put too much expression on the individual," just as the totalitarian world puts too much expression on society.

Thus the subject of work under industrialism came back, as it had to in all panels, to its inescapable context—the world power struggle among industrialized nations. Mr. Morello said that his difficulty, in listening to the succession of American panelists who had spoken, was that of finding himself in agreement with all of them, even when they disagreed with each other—and yet feeling that an essential question was being evaded or begged. "What kind of end are we now looking for?" Mr. Morello asked, and "Where is this whole thing going to go?" The Communist nations have a goal in sight; that is, the raising of their standard of living to one comparable to that of the United States; while "this slogan of individualism in [Western] society doesn't show very clearly where all this is going, and it doesn't have really a driving force which makes it an appealing goal for a number of other societies."

Mr. Sandmel agreed, and added an interesting thought in the form of a paradox: When individualism and it alone becomes the end and goal of a society, then by implication the individualism of the society is reduced. Mr. Dos Passos agreed; without retreating a yard from his position that "one man by himself is the whole story," he suggested that the most desirable goal in modern industrial life is successful teamwork—not deadening bureaucracy (which Mr. Dos Passos saw as a large and depressing mark of similarity between Western and Russian Society), but teamwork of free men cooperating freely. The idea was further formulated by John F. White, president of the National Educational Television and Radio Center:

> I wonder if perhaps the term that we are struggling for is not . . . responsibility. In an industrial society when the accent is on the individual we must, if we are to achieve integration, insist that the individual assume responsibility beyond the product of his compensated time.

Whitney J. Oates, professor of classics at Princeton, amplified further:

> If I were counseling an undergraduate with respect to his choice of career, I would say that it was perfectly obvious that he should choose a career compatible with his capabilities, his natural endowments. However, I would say that once you have selected several, maybe one or two, which do answer this, there is an obligation on his part as a human being to contribute by his work—to call it for short—to the public good.

Randolph Burgess, former United States permanent representative on NATO, was more specific:

> The real question, I think, is the one . . . that I asked when I read Roger Blough's paper, excellent as it was: whether all of this adds up to the requisite amount of drive to equal the Communist menace; whether all that we do to teach people who are working, and to minister to their satisfactions, adds up to making opportunity as attractive as security.

The matter of whether industrialization serves the cause of the individual—or how it can be made to serve that cause better than it does now—also engaged the attention of Panel IV, up in the Research and Development Building's airy library. As has been related, Panel IV lost no time at the outset in asserting its collective individualism by adopting an entirely novel discussion procedure: leaving the three topics of work, education, and leisure to come into the talk naturally and incidentally, the members of Panel IV resolved to devote all three of their sessions to the single question, *How can the process of industrialization be influenced so that it will favor the fullest development of the individual in society?* Through this procedure, adopted at the suggestion of the British biologist Sir Julian Huxley, Panel IV's Friday-morning subject became *de jure* what Panel IV's, and to a lesser extent Panels I's and III's, had been *de facto*.

There were two particular colorations that the Panel IV discussion of this topic had from the first. One was an emphasis on the role of the intellectual and the creative artist, and this was probably due to the presence of such an articulate and provocative spokesman for literature as Alfred Kazin, the literary critic. The other was the leitmotiv, sometimes muted but never entirely absent, of the hopes and problems of now underdeveloped but rapidly developing nations, and this was certainly due to the presence of such a candid and engaging spokesman as Mr. Diké of Nigeria.

The first man to speak to the question propounded by Sir Julian and accepted by the panel was Walter H. Wheeler, Jr., chairman of the board of Pitney-Bowes, Inc. The basic answer to the question, he said, is "communication—a tremendous amount of it." If industry can let the worker know the importance of his work, he will feel his worth as an individual. But does that answer go far enough? In the opinion of the panel, as evidenced by the subsequent discussion, it does not. Chairman Braisted commented that Mr. Wheeler's answer seemed to apply chiefly to highly industrialized areas—the only areas where a critical "communication problem" is generally recognized to exist—and asked Mr. Diké for his possibly different viewpoint. But Mr. Diké demurred: "I think you are really asking me to discuss something which has yet to be in my society," he said, "and my first reaction would be to ask, What has been your experience? What has happened to your area, and how can we learn from it?" In effect, Mr. Diké was sitting in on his own future; and with what he heard, he might be able to modify it for the better. Who can blame him for wanting to listen and learn?

Mr. Kazin was ready to tell Mr. Diké one thing that has happened—and also to raise a question that broadened (as well as complicated) the basic one adopted by the panel. Why, Mr. Kazin wanted to know, has hostility between the life of industry and the life of the mind been taken for granted, both in England and America, since the very beginnings of the Industrial Revolution; whereas in Russia today the intellectual feels that thanks to industrialization he has a new life? Sir Julian suggested that one factor in creating the hostility might be something that has now largely been corrected; that is, the bad industrial working conditions of the nineteenth century which outraged such a writer as Dickens. Merle Curti, professor of history at the University of Wisconsin, added that as industrialization advanced, writers and intellectuals came to feel that the value placed on their role by society tended to become smaller or more uncertain. While agreeing with those two answers, Mr. Kazin went further—in a deeper psychological sense, he felt, the material goals of industrialization, the ranch house or the second car, are too easily arrived at, and the individual is disappointed and frustrated; he comes to feel a kind of generalized discontent at a life that is not challenging enough; "and this is surely part of the reason for the extraordinary vogue of irrationality in modern Western philosophy."

David E. Lilienthal, chairman of the Development & Resources Corporation, now spoke in a way that must have been more encouraging to Mr. Diké. Industrialism is not so bad on the individual, said Mr. Lilienthal, and to the extent that it is bad, it is less so than what precedes it—the poverty and boredom of much agricultural life. As to increased tension and conflict, are they not good, considered as goads to individual self-awareness?

Next, Mr. Diké could hear the views of such a pillar of industry as Chairman Roger Blough of the United States' fifth-largest corporation. And what did Mr. Blough have to say? That he agreed whole-heartedly (and, perhaps bewilderingly?) with Mr.

Kazin, the intellectual; he hoped that such a conference as this one might do something to lessen the deplorable gap between industry and culture. Mr. Blough went on to make some remarks about industrialization rather less optimistic in tone than his background paper. First of all, he said, there is no longer a choice, anywhere, between industrialization and non-industrialization, because the former is inevitable; the process is irreversible. Second, it is not an easy or comfortable process. "Our basic problem is how to work and live in an industrial society as comfortably as you can, realizing that life is not going to be comfortable for anybody at any time under any circumstances. . . . But somehow or other we have to make the best of it and do the best we can with what we have to work with."

This striking and almost Puritan view of industrial life, coming from the very horse's mouth, provoked Charles E. Wyzanski, Jr., United States district judge for Massachusetts, to raise a fundamental question: "We have assumed the virtue of individualism and its value, but why do we think that the values of individualism are a desirable set of values?"

Dr. William Glasser of Los Angeles, California, Panel IV's resident psychiatrist, replied that the need for individual sense of identity and worth is basic to human psychology. Mr. Wheeler, on the other hand, replied in moral terms, saying that he had no trouble accepting the assumption that individualism is right and collectivism wrong. "I don't see how we can escape it," he said.

JUDGE WYZANSKI: Well, half the world is escaping it. Maybe we don't belong in that half, but let us not assume it's inevitable.

MR. WHEELER: Because half the world has not yet been industrialized sufficiently to make a concept like this possible.

The chairman asked Mr. Diké if he cared to comment on *his* view of individualism. But Mr. Diké said that he had one great matter on his mind, and that was the industrialization of Nigeria; let the philosophical chips fall where they may, "We are actually hankering for industrialization in the hope that it makes for the development of the individual man more than our agricultural economy will ever do . . . and we also feel that we can never catch up with the rest of the world until we industrialize."

Mr. Houston, the Canadian civil administrator on West Baffin Island, offered for comparison his experiences of the effect of small-scale industrialization on his test-tube sample community— one might say frozen sample—in the Arctic. As the Eskimos there have passed from a hunting society to an early-industrial society (bypassing the stage of agriculture, because, of course, agriculture is climatologically impossible), Mr. Houston has seen first a new sense of excitement and satisfaction in work, and now the beginnings of the restrictiveness and boredom that are so worrisomely evident in more highly industrialized groups.

How, then, to emphasize the good things and minimize the bad? Pendleton Herring, president of the Social Science Research Council, commented that the panel seemed to be looking back, putting under a microscope the experience of industrialization up to now; he suggested a more fruitful approach would be to look ahead—to try to suggest ways, for example, that man can use the increased choices open to him under industrialism in a creative way rather than reacting to them with bewilderment and uniformity. Patrick Hurley, professor of geology and chairman of the faculty at Massachusetts Institute of Technology, was willing to accept the challenge to look ahead; and looking ahead, he saw hopeful things as well as knotty problems: the elimination of drudgery through automation, leading to the question of how to use increased leisure, leading to the need for new concepts in education.

Mr. Blough, who had evidently been saving up comments on the remarks of several previous speakers, now released them. To Judge Wyzanski's question, Do we really want individualism?: Yes!, said Mr. Blough, declaring that to him it seemed to be a matter of biological need. To Mr. Diké's almost wistful hope that the inevitable industrialization in his country may end in a releasing and flowering of the individual: It can be done, said Mr. Blough, in effect. On Mr. Hurley's point about new concepts in education: In Mr. Blough's view, "industrialization itself is, in a very real sense, more or less an educational process"; you learn by doing, and the mental exercise of meeting new situations produces the very mental capacity needed to meet them.

These strong affirmations prompted Dr. Glasser to say that the industrialization of, say, Nigeria must in itself be individualistic; the Nigerians, that is, "must achieve their own individualism there—whatever it is, for them. If they try to take an identity other than their own identity they won't achieve what they are working for. We can't tell them this. This is something they have to develop for themselves." Mr. Diké nodded vigorous agreement, and Judge Wyzanski went on to add the warning that planning for individual creativity, if carried too far, may become self-defeating. Some individuals do not fulfill themselves best under the most ideal conditions (art flourishes under limitations). And, said Judge Wyzanski,

> Maybe we ought not to seek for them solely security, peace, comfort, and on the whole that kind of adjusted life which will make it unnecessary for them to consult Dr. Glasser. It might be very desirable that they should live under a certain degree of tension. . . . This means challenge and response—a possibility of failure as well as the possibility of success.

In other words, said Bernard Kilgore, publisher of the *Wall Street Journal*, "Let's don't force everybody to eat strawberries and cream."

Mr. Wheeler now returned to the theme that he had introduced earlier; that is, the existence of a basic immutable morality and the need to implement it. Harking back to Mr. Malik's keynote address, he said that he found the whole world, agrarians, industrialists, and intellectuals alike, suffering from "a lack of the development of sufficient practical moral concepts." Messrs. Kazin and Lilienthal and Sir Julian wanted the speaker to be more specific. Mr. Wheeler replied that so far as the United States is concerned, we all know in a general way what is right and try to live by it, but are hampered by a certain embarrassment at the very idea of moral concepts which makes us shy away from formulating our morality more precisely. Mr. Lilienthal agreed that such embarrassment exists, and thought it unfortunate. To which Mr. Kazin replied:

> I must confess that both Mr. Wheeler and Mr. Lilienthal slightly astonish me. I hadn't realized, living as an American, in what I consider the most self-congratulatory culture of the world, that we were afraid of using the word "moral." Why we use no other word about ourselves—from the dropping of the atom bomb on the Japanese to our attack on Cuba. Good heavens, the rest of the world considers us exactly the kind of hypocrites that they considered the British in the nineteenth century. Perfidious America— that's what we are, because we are so moral.
>
> Just look [for example] at the advertising pages of any big American magazine. Every product that's put out so as to become useless in two weeks is always put out with the cry that we are moral and good. And this spirit of self-congratulation, I think very frankly, does not come from hypocrisy; I think it comes from innocence about our own provincialism.

This dash of cold water had, at any rate, the effect of ending any tone of self-congratulation among United States panel members. As if to mediate their intramural differences, William L. Chapman, vice-rector of the University of Buenos Aires, said that in his opinion while general statements about morals and ethics can be made about individuals, they cannot be made about whole societies. There was some shaking of heads at this statement, so Mr. Chapman amplified: Speaking of an Argentine president who had broken most of his campaign promises within six months, he said that many people had concluded that the government was immoral; he, Dr. Chapman, insisted that it was rather the president who was immoral.

The discussion now went through a period of increasing abstraction. Judge Wyzanski, Mr. Wheeler, Sir Julian, and Dr. Glasser propounded their respective notions of morality, a polarity developing between Sir Julian who held that new forms of society need new frameworks of moral ideas, and Mr. Wheeler who held out for absolute moral law. Finally it came down to the question of individual freedom of moral choice, and Sir Julian commented, a bit glumly, "We're back at Socrates." Mr. Blough came in to suggest that whatever conclusions were being reached, whatever moral guidelines were being laid down, they should be thought of as guidelines for ourselves to follow rather than as instruction for others.

Mr. Diké had been long silent. The time for the session was running out. Whether the morning's discussion among the learned representatives of the advanced societies had given him a picture of what industrialization in Nigeria is going to be like, and how its pitfalls may be avoided, is a question of moment; at any rate, now Mr. Diké said:

> I have been listening to this for some time now, and I naturally think back to my own very highly communal society, where the moral principles which guide conduct are clearly known to everybody, sanctions are accepted, and the moral questions you speak of here are really obligations. You *have* to conform to them. . . .
>
> It's quite clear to me that one of the views that has come up in this discussion is that somehow your own type of industrial society tends to fragment and departmentalize individual actions in a way ours does not. In other words, I'm saying that we [in Nigeria] do not separate morality from our everyday conduct as a whole. In fact, I'm beginning to wonder, when we are talking about the role of the individual in society, whether we may not have to modify it for each area according to its state of development.

Is there a relationship between moral confusion and difficulty in communication, both of which seem to come with industrialization? Is successful communication more a matter of moral clarity than we generally realize? Subsequent discussion, in Panel I and elsewhere, seemed to suggest an affirmative answer.

Down in the cafeteria, Panel II was going its own way, adopting what one of the participants—Franz Alexander, director of the psychiatric department of Mount Sinai Hospital in Los Angeles, California—called the "meistersinger method": each participant in turn giving a brief opening statement of what he considered the basic problem. Dr. Alexander expressed the fear that too many of the meistersingers would sing the same aria, but as it turned out, he need hardly have worried; the arias were astonishingly, even bewilderingly various and tuneful.

John A. Hrones, vice-president of the Case Institute of Technology, sang first; he felt that the writers of the background papers had tended to be too idealistic in aiming toward maximum self-expression for *all* individuals in modern society, and that a more reasonable goal might be to bring about relative increase in the number who are able to achieve it. Julius Stone, professor of jurisprudence and international law at the University of Sydney, Australia, expressed the view that to be meaningful the discussion would have to take account of how various peoples come to hold the values that they do, and how these values are maintained. To Herbert W. K. Fitzroy, administrator of the University Center in Richmond, Virginia, the basic problem was simply stated: "We've drifted into a pattern of work. We seem to be drifting out of a pattern of work. I think it's important that we do not drift into a pattern of leisure." Harold Howe II, superintendent of schools of Scarsdale, New York, was concerned that the panel examine the constantly-changing pressures in industrial life that tend to deny individuality.

Dean John B. Coburn of Episcopal Theological School in Cambridge, Massachusetts put his emphasis on the questions, How shall the individual proceed to become truly free? and how shall the spiritual values spoken of in the keynote address be translated into practical life? Dr. Alexander's own aria asked a related question: What shall a man do, now that his basic physical needs are well taken care of in industrial society, to realize himself fully? Gilbert W. Chapman, president of the New York Public Library, saw the first problem, if not perhaps the last one, in the need to define modern society—to examine exactly what has been achieved rather than take it for granted.

Melville J. Herskovits, professor of anthropology at Northwestern University, raised a problem that the panel was to return to often in its later discussions—how to avoid the trap of ethnocentrism, of assuming without question the superiority of developed societies and of our form of individualism over the forms of it found in more primitive cultures.

Henry E. Guerlac, professor of the history of science at Cornell University, said he thought the panel must take up the question, "Is individualism a relative concept—a concept that is dependent upon the place of the individual in the group, however small, however large?" Whereas the concern of Charles M. Scheff, president of the American Flint Glass Workers' Union of North America, was more empirical; he saw the basic problem as being that of getting education to be more specifically directed toward meeting current conditions than it is now. Sir Oliver Franks, chairman of Lloyds Bank and former British ambassador to the United States, emphasized the belief, often stated at the conference, that we must take general industrialization as the given of the situation—it is inevitable whether we like it or not; therefore the basic problem seemed to him to be that of fitting people coming from traditional societies into the new framework. M. A. Allam, secretary-general of the Afro-Asian Youth Bureau in Cairo, Egypt, basically agreed with Sir Oliver, feeling that the conference should concentrate on how to combat the recognized disadvantages of industrial society.

As Professor Herskovits had put his statement in the form of a warning against ethnocentrism, Muriel Rukeyser, poet and biographer, put hers in the form of a warning against the acceptance of certain assumptions that the participants seemed to be making—particularly the assumption of a polarity between work and leisure in an industrial society. The assumption was that work is what you do to earn a living, and leisure what you do in the time left over. But, said Miss Rukeyser, speaking as a poet, she finds that she has to devote her "leisure" time to taking outside jobs that will provide her with a living, because her life work does not and cannot. (It has been said that only two poets now living in the United States are able to earn their keep by poetry.) Thus her leisure time is her work time, her work time—since it is what she enjoys, and what does not pay material rewards— is her leisure time; and the false opposite was blown sky high. Speaking next, Richard M. Paget, management consultant, said in an almost stunned way that it was now obvious leisure was going to have to be redefined, and asked the panel to examine "the impact of influences of a spiritual nature on the individual in seeking to orient himself to this maelstrom which we have painted."

Eric Larrabee, the journalist and author, carried on what Miss Rukeyser had started by attacking another false opposite, that between the individual and the group; he wanted the panel to think of them as in interplay rather than in opposition. Barry T. Leithead, president of Cluett, Peabody & Co., reaffirmed that the basic problem was, indeed, the obvious one: how to preserve individual freedom against the threats posed to it by industrialism.

The last of the opening round of statements was that of the panel's only participant from a Marxist nation—Janez Stanovnik, director of the Institute for International Policy and Economics in Belgrade, Yugoslavia. Mr. Stanovnik, as might have been expected, disagreed with Mr. Malik's keynote address: "We cannot hope for human beings being more human," he said, "without making it possible for technological change to achieve its final goal, to make the economic background of human societies more firm and strong." Beyond this, he saw the problem as being how to steer industrialization so that, instead of creating organization men, lonely crowds, waste makers, and so on, it may result in "putting man more on his own."

What a multiplicity of basic problems! Mr. Paget would seem to have spoken well of "this maelstrom which we have painted"! But diverse and often conflicting as they were, the opening statements had served to get the participants acquainted with each other's points of view, and had seeded the soil for the free discussion that now followed. Chairman Knight, gallantly striving to sum up what had been said, discerned four themes: (1) the centrality of technologically oriented societies in the modern world; (2) the necessity to consider "men in their completeness and complexity," rather than fragmented by false opposites; (3) the impossibility of clearly pigeon-holing work, education, and leisure; and (4) the necessity of transcending one's own culture and avoiding a parochial view.

But Professor Stone and Mr. Larrabee, going on from there, discerned another complication; to them there seemed to be really two sets of problems, differing both in character and potential solution—the problems of highly developed societies and those of less developed ones. Mr. Stanovnik didn't think the problems were essentially all that different. He affirmed his basic agreement with the American economist Walt Whitman Rostow (whose book on the subject, interestingly enough, is subtitled "A Non-Communist Manifesto") that all society develops through comparable economic stages, irrespective of cultural background and the ideology of government. Mr. Stanovnik suggested that the desire for economic security, leading to individual freedom, was the factor that makes the whole world kin. Certain societies, and Mr. Stanovnik mentioned the Russian one as being among them, have been diverted from this basic goal; but the whole world was heading in the Marxist direction of economic security through industrial development. (And here, while differing diametrically in value judgment, he agreed in fact with his antagonist Mr. Malik.)

Now followed an arresting exchange of American points of view, in which individuals seemed to speak almost as allegorical representations of their training and interest—a psychiatrist, a teacher of science, a cultural anthropologist, a clergyman, a poet.

Dr. Alexander, echoing what that same morning Mr. Starr was saying in the first floor conference room and Mr. Moraes in the basement auditorium, quoted a Latin proverb that he translated, "First one must live, then one can philosophize." Going on from there, he posed the question, "Do we live to eat or do we eat to live?" When material things are no problem, what does one do next? Turning for analogy to the animal kingdom, he spoke of the young doe that, having a great deal of energy that is not needed for survival, instinctively cavorts and runs. This frivolous exercise of native faculties, of which Dr. Alexander spoke in psychological language as "functional pleasure," serves the long-term practical purpose of preparing the animal to escape from beasts of prey in case of need. This "functional pleasure" seemed to Dr. Alexander to be the essence of ideal leisure in a well-fed industrial society; but, alas, we have lost the knack of cavorting, of using our excess creative energies for the sheer joy of using them. "As yet I haven't heard the expression 'creativeness' in this room," he said. "Leisure and creativeness are extremely close and related."

Professor Guerlac, allowing that he was speaking "a little bit from my own point of view as a historian of science," objected to the notion, propounded by Mr. Stanovnik, that society is moving toward some final and immutable goal. Instead, he said, the essence of the technological situation is change—"a built-in element of constant and often radical change. The notion that we will somehow work out a permanent adjustment to a stable type of industrial society is something of which I am not at all sure." Change, then, to Professor Guerlac, is our tradition, paradoxical as that may sound; "I think we should be aware of this constant necessity of adjusting ourselves."

Professor Herskovits, who was to emerge as the panel's gadfly to technologists and all their works, rose with objections to all of the three speakers who immediately preceded him. To Mr. Stanovnik, and to Dr. Alexander to the extent that he agreed with Mr. Stanovnik, Herskovits said that he thought that extreme caution was in order when emphasizing the universal desire for more material goods: "There isn't any society that doesn't feed itself. If it doesn't, it disappears." To Professor Guerlac, he said that he questioned the inevitability of industrial change, or, indeed, of industrialization itself. He could conceive of societies that might develop from here on without industrialization, and pointed to India as one that is "very quizzical about the value inherent in the industrial process." The problem of modern leisure—the reason we have forgotten how to cavort like Dr. Alexander's doe—he saw as the problem of industrial specialization:

> You've got to learn to play. We have specialists in teaching people how to play. We have specialists in the supernatural. I think this is one of the reasons why the industrial civilizations are among the most secular civilizations mankind has ever known. . . . You leave the manipulation of those forces which are outside the technological aspect of life to specialists in manipulating the supernatural.

Dean Coburn, rising to this challenge, started from Dr. Alexander's doe and functional exercise:

> What is it to be a doe? The functional exercise of that jumping up and down enables the doe to become a deer, to run away when there is danger. We are faced fundamentally with this problem, it seems to me, of the ultimate meaning . . . of deerhood, or manhood. What is it to be a man? We concentrate as man upon the underdeveloped country to develop this technical society so that these basic human needs of men in terms of goods, production, can be met. Therefore there is a tremendous optimism about this because it simply means that we need to apply our minds to the technical process. We have evidence that it can be done. . . . I'm not sure this optimism is completely justified. If we look to the West where the technical society has been developed most, we find underneath the optimism an underlying pessimism. This pessimism comes up through the arts very largely, the theatre, creative visual arts, novels, poetry, existentialism, philosophy, and in certain areas of religion there is a sense of coming up against nothingness.

It may be worth noting the remarkable congruence between what Dean Coburn was saying, from the standpoint of a theologian, to the men of science and technology in his panel, and what Mr. Kazin, at almost the same time, was saying, from the standpoint of the creative arts, to the industrialists up in the library.

But Mr. Stanovnik was not willing to accept the characterization of his view as being that the ultimate man is simply an animal with an adequate roof and a full stomach. The process of industrialization to him is more than a striving for that, he said. It is, in fact, the change from *sordidae artes* to *artes liberales*: "If technology means that man gets free from just exercising brute force, he then becomes free for what I would consider a higher capacity of human labor." In speaking of the need and desire for technological change and growth as being a unifying factor of all humanity, he had not meant that the end product would be the same in all societies. Indeed, "What we are moving toward is a kind of diversity of identity"; freed of material need, men in different sorts of societies may differ from each other, in the sense of being individuals, more than ever.

It was near noon; outside the great glass windows of the cafeteria, Corning employees were passing on their way to lunch; and the debate was at something of an impasse. Perhaps not logic but a poet's insight was needed, and perhaps the conference planners, conjuring up the names of people to shed light on the problems of industrialization, had done well to invite a poet—and such a poet as Miss Rukeyser, who now musingly spoke a kind of prose poem:

> This discussion that is so moving reminds me very much of the passage in Sir Charles Sherrington's book [*Man on His Nature*] of which Dr. Guerlac and I talked last evening. The description of the forming of the embryo eye, the eye of the embryo forming in the dark, without light, for life and not for infant's sight—for the mature sight, in all its clarity of focus. It seems to me that the talk that has just been going on is with that conviction. Sherrington speaks of the embryo eye as moving toward a future requirement. I think that we have been talking in terms of a future requirement of which we are now aware, so that it becomes a present requirement. So that we wonder, What is the human requirement that is on us in this society and in exchange with other societies? What is the human requirement?

CHAPTER 4

وهم

FRIDAY AFTERNOON

وهم

Noon hour at the Glass Center Club was devoted to a Trimal-
chian luncheon such as might have stunned the bodies and dead-
ened the minds of ordinary mortals. But the participants were
no ordinary mortals. They were all back at their places in the
five panel meeting rooms at two o'clock; and furthermore, the
Friday-afternoon panel sessions, taken all together, were as striking in their ideas and as far-reaching in their implications as any
in the conference. Friday morning's feeling out, the introduction
of individuals and of ideas, was over; Saturday morning's attempts
to round out, to put on the record, to conclude if not actually
to decide, were still ahead. Friday afternoon was the central period
of free give-and-take, of full and unhurried self-expression, when
the kaleidoscopic procession of ideas was perhaps at its brightest.

Panel IV—the group in the library under the chairmanship
of Mr. Braisted—spent part of Friday afternoon making a helpful
contribution which may serve as a starting point for this summary. At the suggestion of Mary I. Bunting of Radcliffe College,
it decided to pause midway to attempt to arrive at a pure descrip-

tion, devoid of moral judgments, of what it was talking about—
that is, of industrial society. What characteristics does it always
have, whether in the United States, Nigeria, or somewhere else?

Appropriately enough, the first speaker to this topic was Mr.
Blough of United States Steel. Mr. Blough started by stating
what, in his view, it is not: Industrial management is not a
wielding of power for its own sake, and anyone who thinks of
it in those terms has "a very infantile point of view." It is rather
a sense of obligation that preoccupies the industrial-management
man, said Mr. Blough—obligation to the organization, to its employees, to its customers, and to society—and that sense should
be put forward as the system's first characteristic.

Mr. Herring of the Social Science Research Council, who
spoke next, had a definition ready: Industrialism is "an organized and rationalized effort to produce material goods . . . characterized by a differentiation of function and a division of labor."
Sir Julian Huxley insisted on the addition of the fact that industrialism involves the use of machines, and Mr. Blough came back
to reintroduce Mr. Wheeler's characteristic—"communicated information." There were subsequent additions by other members
of the panel, many of them closely paralleling the things that
had been brought up that morning in Panels II and V, and finally
Chairman Braisted, with help from Mrs. Bunting, arrived at a
summary of what had been said: that industrialism, in essence,
is marked by complex organization, the application of science, a
greater sense of awareness on the part of the individual and more
opportunities for him, specialization of work, and constant change.

Industrialism, the panel agreed, is on the way to becoming
more or less universal—because there appear to be no countervailing forces opposing its world advance. Its chief products—
although there was some disagreement about the latter—are material goods and human leisure. And its goal, in the broadest sense,
is the fullest possible development of the individual. As much as
any generalization produced by one panel seemed to speak for
the whole conference, this description of industrialism did; it
may serve as a reference point for what follows.

Granted that it exists and is thus and so, is industrialism boon or bane? It was Panel II that, on Friday afternoon, tackled this question in a full-scale debate carried out on both practical and philosophical levels. The debate was a suggestive one precisely because it rejected the assumption that universal industrialization, being inevitable, is therefore beyond value judgments; it challenged, and defended, the system at its very roots. Speaking broadly, the sides lined up thus: for industrialism, with reservations, Guerlac the science historian, Larrabee the journalist, and Stanovnik the Yugoslavian economist; against it, Herskovits the anthropologist and Alexander the psychiatrist; at various points between, supplying information and comment, Miss Rukeyser the poet, Scheff the union leader, Allam the Cairo youth leader, Stone the Australian law professor, and some others.

Professor Guerlac led off for the defense of industrialism by attacking the notion that it has destroyed craftsmanship. Rather, he suggested, it has brought into being a new set of craftlike specialties to supplant the old ones. Corning itself, he pointed out, has its specialists in the respected old craft of glass blowing, but are they necessarily more skilled, or more profitably absorbed in their work, than the key machinists of Bell Telephone, for example? Mr. Larrabee said he saw sentimentalities on both sides: The sentimentality of industry in putting the brightest possible face on industrial work, and the opposite sentimentality of intellectuals in assuming that all repetitive work is obnoxious to the worker. For his own part, on balance, he found himself more on the side of the industrialist and "in considerable opposition to the cultivation of what seems to me to be an old-fashioned image of what industrial work is like." (The famous Charlie Chaplin movie *Modern Times,* for example.)

Professor Stone brought in the subject of automation, speaking of it as a "self-correcting mechanism" to take the excess of repetitive work out of human hands; yet the machines cannot truly think, and their failure to perform that vital function makes man more rather than less important. Agreeing, Mr. Larrabee illustrated with an anecdote about a petrochemical plant on the

Gulf Coast: The men who twiddled the dials of this largely-automated plant were told their jobs were about to be declassified from skilled to unskilled; they reacted by suspending all personal judgment, and operating the dials as if they were themselves automatons; within forty-eight hours the plant nearly exploded, and the old job classification of the dial twiddlers was hastily restored.

Now came Dr. Alexander for the prosecution. "As a psychiatrist, I deal with people and I see how they react," he began, a bit ominously; one of the things he sees is that a man does not want to be part of a process—he wants to make something that is his work and no one else's.

> Take the canoe builder . . . the Polynesian craftsman who produces a canoe. Maybe two or three help, but that is still one team, and the distance between his work and the product is very short. He produces a functional canoe, which is good. [But he adds] a prow with a beautiful carving of a woman or some kind of a monster. While he's producing the canoe, which is economically a very rational product, he can also put in poetry or his fantasies to satisfy his needs which are specifically human.

Industrialism, said Dr. Alexander, has radically separated the poet from the rational producer; the attempt to speak of new kinds of craftsmanship, of the industrial worker's self-fulfillment in his work, is merely "rationalization" designed to "preserve the status quo."

Miss Rukeyser—a poet not, for the moment at least, separated from rational producers—was in the middle. It is a question, she said, of whether one can avoid the trap of letting the routine gesture of industrial work *become the whole response to life*: "Do we let the marvelous things in industrialism limit our response to the world; and if not, then how do we extend that response?"

Professor Herskovits was pessimistic. "I do think," he said, "there is something in the relationship of work to creativeness that causes the industrial establishment to produce a psychological vacuum in the lives of many industrial workers, if not the major-

ity. . . . It would be very difficult, I should think, for a worker
in a Chevrolet plant to identify himself with any particular Chevrolet and to say, 'You see that automobile? It's a good automobile.' " Referring to his old favorite teacher, Thorstein Veblen,
Professor Herskovits spoke of the concept of instinctive workmanship; the existence of a widespread do-it-yourself movement
seemed to indicate the existence of incomplete satisfaction in
compensated work.

Gilbert Chapman, the industrialist turned librarian, disagreed:

I think the assumption we make that man does not like a repetitive job, that he is an artist and he is creative and he wants to
point to a Chevrolet—I don't think man's mental development
has come to that point. . . . I don't think the average man of
limited education is as interested in creating as he is in security.

And Mr. Scheff the labor leader was even more down-to-earth:

I know what automation is going to do to the industrial worker.
It's going to displace a lot of these workers. . . . The thing that
bothers me . . . is how we are going to take care of the displaced
or unemployed individual.

But Dr. Alexander was not to be put off by such immediate
considerations. "I don't think it is right to consider creativity
as a privilege of the few," he said. "The Polynesian canoe maker
is not a college graduate. He is an average man who carved a
boat. . . . Everybody is creative." Mr. Larrabee gave the discussion a new turn by suggesting that the sentimentalities he had
spoken of previously were operating in the present discussion.
Is the Polynesian canoe maker really free? Isn't he a prisoner of
a society of scarcity, ridden with fears and taboos?

That raised the hackles of Professor Herskovits, the panel's
co-champion of primitivism. Fears and taboos? The Zulus who
have come to live in Durban have higher blood pressure now,
on the average, than they had when they lived in the bush. This
has been systematically measured. "If one lives in primitive societies, as I have done," he went on, "one finds there is about the
same degree of freedom of choice, the same freedom from fear,

that there is in our society. . . . Magic is, certainly, no more dangerous than electricity." Or take the matter of polygamy, so much deplored in industrialized countries: In primitive societies, Professor Herskovits pointed out, it serves a practical purpose as a method of hygiene because it tends to prevent a young woman from becoming the child-a-year drudge that she so often becomes in our own society. His conclusion followed logically. Industrialism is not progress but change; our society should be looked at as neither better nor worse than the Polynesian, but different.

Professor Guerlac detailed the case for science and technology as a humanizing factor:

> We often forget that a number of very important social accomplishments did result from [the Industrial Revolution], that the intelligent care of the insane, and attitudes toward the criminal law, crime and punishment—a great many of these things, I think, are demonstrably influenced by the scientific occurrences of the eighteenth century. I think there is a positive social ideology in science.

It was Mr. Allam who now, so to speak, pulled up the reins on Pegasus, as Mr. Scheff had done earlier. The debate was interesting, he said; but meanwhile, what do we do about industrialism's twin problems of unemployment and excess leisure? The tug at the reins was timely; it led Dean Coburn to suggest that what the panel members, whether espousing industrialism or its opposite, were looking for was a common denominator to apply to the human situation. Professor Stone put the impulse in the form of a parable. He has, he said, invented a new technological wonder that could make the 1963 Cadillac a great success: a button that doesn't open windows, doesn't defrost the windshield, doesn't do anything to any mechanism, but simply "presses back and makes the driver feel wanted." But the question is, Is technology and the technological attitude of mind capable of producing such a humanly useful appointment?

How far can science alone take us? That was the last phase of Panel II's scene-setting debate, and Professor Guerlac, as the apostle of science, was quick to emphasize the difficulties. Science and scientists are just emerging from adolescence, and Professor Guerlac took the fact that some scientists assumed the lead in advocating the first military use of the atomic bomb as all too eloquent evidence that the adolescence is not over. Mr. Hrones of Case Institute was inclined to qualify this by saying that it is the bad scientist who gives science a bad name—the scientist, that is, who "not realizing the limitations, undertakes the solution of the unsolvable, and claims that he has a generalized solution." Seizing on such a concession, Professor Herskovits agreed that scientists are naïve about human problems. So did Dr. Alexander, who broadened the base of the criticism by stating that the very culture produced by science and technology—our own—tended to do nothing less than leave out man: "Science not only didn't answer questions, but led us away from the big questions because we forgot to ask them any more. For what? We raised living standards. The question, again, after we reach the [present] level, is, For what? I don't think this 'for what' has been or can be answered by science."

Dean Coburn said, "I think Dr. Alexander has presented perfectly the religious question, with which I would be in complete agreement. As far as the answer is concerned, I'm not sure we would agree."

This broad-based questioning of industrialism at its roots, which went on almost exclusively in Panel II, gives shape to the tackling of specific problems, and the search for specific solutions, that was being conducted simultaneously in the other panels. Panel I in the board of directors room and Panel III in the first floor conference room were going after the great question that had been either stated or implied in almost all of the morning sessions. That is, Is individualism enough? As a cultural goal, does it contain the dynamism necessary for competition with a formidable military and economic rival—Russia—or must some individualism be sacrificed by the West in the interest of holding its own in that competition?

In Panel I, Philip M. Hauser, professor of sociology at the

University of Chicago, stated his negative answer to the first question in forthright terms. "I would say," he said, "that the American worker does not begin to have an imagery to which he is dedicated that provides motivation and incentive of the kind the Communist worker has." Point number two: "Christianity has failed the Western world"—in that it no longer provides men with the dedication, zealousness, or fanaticism if you like, that the Russians and Chinese have found in their secular political faith. And the same can be said of Judaism and Islam. The increased leisure brought by industry appeared to Professor Hauser to be a vice, to the extent that in becoming a nation of consumers we have declined in productivity—in the very competitiveness necessary to our survival.

Raymond Aron entered disagreement on one point of Houser's. It was his belief, he said, that production in Soviet Russia had nothing to do with individual dedication; rather, "It is perfectly clear that the main inspiration on which the Soviet system relies is self-interest . . . the ordinary tricks of so-called capitalism. . . . Certainly, the Soviet leaders and the Communist Party men may be very dedicated people, but the economic system of Soviet Russia does not function or intend to function on the basis of individual dedication to communism." Nevertheless, interposed Harry S. Ashmore, in his opinion there was no question that by the nature of its organization Russian society can move more directly toward a goal than can ours. He wanted to hear from Leo Schulgin, the Finnish journalist and Russian expert, on the subject. Mr. Schulgin agreed with Mr. Aron that Western disadvantage is not due to Russian dedication, but he also agreed with Mr. Ashmore that Russia's totalitarian methods give it the advantage in getting practical things done quickly; "Nevertheless," said Mr. Schulgin to the Westerners on the panel, "you are doing very well. I don't see any reason for being afraid of competition—afraid that in ten, fifteen, twenty years you will be politically outnumbered by this other bloc." The key, he thought, was Western mobilization of effort: "Even if a cold war, there should be a kind of mobilization." And this mobilization, he allowed, would involve a certain setting aside of the goal of individualism.

To J. Ward Keener, president of the B.F. Goodrich Company, it appeared that a mistake in emphasis was being made by the panel. "We have been talking in terms of our failure to meet Russian competition as though it were economics," he said. "In my opinion, it is politics. And the politics in it is that we have not had people at the top of our government who have understood what communism was."

Jay Lovestone of the AFL-CIO, speaking as a student of Marxism in Russia and elsewhere, set about putting the question in still another perspective. Russia, he said, must not be thought of entirely in terms of politics; we tend to forget that Russians were great scientists and artists long before the coming of communism. Nor is it true that Russia was a backward country; it was, said Mr. Lovestone, the sixth-ranking economy in the world before the Bolsheviks took over. He went on to speak of our drawbacks in dealing with uncommitted nations—the confusions of our free and undirected society and the ever-present millstone of our racial problem—but also of our advantages: "We have social justice to export," said Mr. Lovestone. "With all the criticism we can make of our social system, there is more social justice and the worker gets a bigger share of the social profit in this country than anywhere else in the world. A lot of it is due to the trade unions. . . . We lack a spirit of dedication. We have to convince the American people that they are fighting for survival. . . . The academic world must be conscious of this. You professors don't realize the profound influence you have."

The hortatory mood persisted; Mr. Dunn, the government expert on the aging, urged that the United States ask itself not what it is against but what it is for; and Professor Hauser returned to the point that we must "find something positive in a society like ours almost surfeited with the 'vice of production.'" Then the mood of gloom about this "vice," if such it be, appeared to deepen—particularly among the Americans present, who seemed to see the Western plight as worse than it looked to M. Aron of France, Mr. Schulgin of Finland, or Sir Muhammad Zafrulla Khan of Pakistan. "Does anybody see any prospect for reform in commercial television? I don't," declared Mr. Ashmore, referring to an area of American life that, almost every time it was mentioned at the conference, was mentioned with the deepest concern, as a surface symptom of an inner sickness. No one answered Mr. Ashmore; and Mr. Appley of the American Management Association broadened the attack by accusing the United States of having fallen into a national climate of immorality. He brought in Mr. Diké of Nigeria, who, while physically confined to Panel IV, seemed to some extent to be symbolically present in all the groups:

> I wish Dr. Diké were here right now. Last evening he said to me, in essence, "Please don't bother our religion. You don't understand it. It means something to us; it cannot mean the same to others. Leave it alone. Please don't bother our tribal setup. You don't understand it. It is a family structure, not a political one. We know in Nigeria that we have to be industrialized to survive. You are industrialized. You have made every mistake in the book. Would you please tell us how to avoid making these mistakes. . . ."
>
> I feel that the trouble with our industrialization now is that there isn't enough soul in it.

And Mr. Appley brought forth some exhibits as evidence:

> I believe you were probably all as shocked as I was over the article in *Life* magazine a week or two ago about the happiness of a family being nearly destroyed because the father had returned some money that he saw fall off an armored truck, and the community ridiculed him for being honest and returning the money. . . . Where an Ingrid Bergman, after her public disdain for morality, could receive an Oscar; . . . how a Hoffa can still walk the streets a free man; how a Sewell Avery, director of a million-dollar industry, could be removed only by senility.

The concern was general, but not in all cases so grave. Father McGinley of Fordham, echoing Mr. Wheeler and Mr. Lilienthal earlier in Panel IV, felt that Americans are more moral than they seem, and are hampered in the expression of moral and spiritual sentiments by embarrassment. Sir Zafrulla saw the West's spiritual position as serious but far from hopeless. He differed with Mr. Malik that man has become an "economic machine," and declared that in his view there is nothing wrong, from a spiritual point of view, with economic development; the whole man can advance, "body, mind and soul must march forward in coordination." As for the "failure" of Christianity, Judaism, and Islam, he saw it rather as the failure of those religions' adherents:

> The problem is to rediscover the soul and bring about a marriage of spiritual values and the values in the technological and scientific side that we have discovered. All knowledge, all accession of knowledge is a bounty of good for the service of man. It is, indeed, a manifestation of the truth revealed in the very first chapter of Genesis. . . .
>
> There is nothing wrong with the rapid advance of technology and science in this age. The only question is whether we shall apply the new knowledge . . . to benefit the service of man, or use it for its destruction.

That we are losing battles in the cold war because of a certain apathy, because of a lack of clear goals, because of immorality; but that the cause is far from hopeless, and that we must avoid the mistake of blaming it all on science and technology *per se*: so seemed to be the consensus in Panel I on Friday afternoon. Panel III, the all-Western group in the first floor conference room, was going at the same questions in a spirit of self-criticism that finally, painfully, won through to a note of faith.

If the West suffers from a lack of goals, what should its goals be and how should it implement them? Mr. de Madariaga suggested the use of Western youth in a broader way than is possible within the framework of the present United States Peace Corps; that is, "An unarmed international corps which would, in certain cases, be sent to see to it that things happen according to what the international authorities have decided, and which would not

be the object of suspicion, precisely because they are not armed."
For example, he thought the presence of such a corps in Budapest in 1956 might, by exerting moral pressure alone, have pre-
vented the use of Russian tanks. "I am only giving this as a
possibility," he admitted. "It might be Utopian and impossible
to realize."

Irish Ambassador Fay pointed to one difficulty of Western
goal-setting: "We are afflicted with a profound skepticism. We
just do not know what we believe. . . . Large numbers of the
most highly educated people in the West are skeptical whether
there are any values at all." Kenneth Holland, president of the
Institute of International Education, and a participant who had
been mostly silent up to now, objected to this. The West has its
ideals, all right, he said; they are embodied in such documents
as the United States Constitution, the charter of UNESCO, and
the United Nations Declaration of Human Rights; our trouble
is that we don't live up to them. We belie our principles by
(for two examples) making alliances with Trujillo and with
Franco Spain. Mr. Malik picked up Mr. Holland on the Declaration of Human Rights, of which the former United Nations
Security Council president said, with far too much modesty, "I
had something to do with that." Here, he said, was the embodi-
ment of the West's faith in the individual—and in more than
just the West's faith, because when it was voted on in the United
Nations in 1948, there was not a single dissenting vote, and
even the Russians had stood up and agreed with it:

> One can say it was adopted by the whole world. I can talk to you
> for at least three hours about its history during the thirteen years
> it has been in existence and about the tremendous effect it has
> had to the human nations. At least eighteen have taken it as part
> of their constitutions. It has had more effect upon legislation all
> over the world than any other international document in recent
> years.

But Mr. de Madariaga, to his great regret, flatly dissented:
"How can people believe in a Declaration of Human Rights

which is vouched for by Mr. Vishinsky?" He saw the Declaration as being honored chiefly in the breach, and by the United States among others: "You go to Paris, you go to Madrid, you go to Rome and London and talk to the young about freedom, about respect for human rights, and they laugh, because they have seen the governments of the world just merely making paper birds with the conventions of the Rights of Man. . . . The West has no moral authority, because the West has been talking grand and acting bad for many years." Now Mr. Malik assumed his old United Nations role of practical politician. If anyone could produce a better document that the nations of the world might agree upon, such a man would find Mr. Malik enlisted under his banner: "It seems to me existence has about it an advantage that ideas cannot possibly have."

> MR. DE MADARIAGA: The text is wonderful. I do not think we could better that text. What I meant was not that the text was bad, but that it was approved by Vishinsky.

> MR. MALIK: Not approved. . . . He never voted for it.

> MR. DE MADARIAGA: He never voted against it.

> MR. MALIK: Because he couldn't, and because world public opinion would have been against him. It was a great victory. It was one of the few victories in the United Nations of that order.

> MR. DE MADARIAGA: The point is that associating with people of that kind who are violating that text all the time is vitiating that text, and worse than that is vitiating the moral authority of the West.

David Rockefeller of the Chase Manhattan Bank sought to resolve this honest—and in its implications, tragic—difference by enlarging the context. Whether one quests for the ultimate or practices the art of the possible, the West has lost some of the motivation, which may be called faith, that went into the Crusades and the Puritan Reformation. Here Malik, de Madariaga, and Rockefeller were together: It is up to us to recover the faith. And Mr. de Madariaga made a concession to practical politics by adding, "I will say that I was tremendously impressed by the inaugural speech of President Kennedy, because I thought that was going to do the trick."

With these concessions achieved, the talk moved toward hope. Miss Height of the YWCA said that one of our troubles is that we tend to take for granted things established long ago, and so to lose sight of them in day-to-day affairs; but, with effort, they can be recaptured. Professor Handlin of Harvard was almost the only participant willing to mitigate the lashing that the West had been applying to itself:

> I do not think we have done terribly well, but we have not done badly, either. There are parts of the world in which the principles that we believe in, that we only half-expressed or half-formulated, have taken hold, and there are very few parts of the world in which we have been defeated in a genuine contest of ideology. Where we have been defeated, it was by force.

In other words, to the extent that the Cold War is an ideological struggle for the minds of men, especially in underdeveloped and uncommitted nations, the West has not lost it yet—ample cause for concern though there may be. To end this account of the afternoon's discussions on this topic, it may be well to swing the camera of our attention back to the directors' room, and cite something that the novelist John Hersey said there—not simply because it evoked general agreement among his fellow-panelists, but for its own value. Aid to underdeveloped countries, said Mr. Hersey, is, after all, an act of human brotherhood, not an instrument of national defense; and to the extent that it is allowed to become an instrument of national defense, it will be "bad defense, if any, and inconsistent with American ideals."

> I think the only sound offense is one which thinks of people in these countries as fellow human beings, fellow citizens of the world, and that it would be an unsound kind of development that did not have the capacity to identify with those human beings as human beings—to study very carefully the kinds of development we propose to offer them in order to have it accommodate to their

needs, not just on an economic level as we see it, but on a cultural level as they see it.

Whenever the conference sought solutions, it turned toward education. Asked the direct question, "How can we make the most of the strong points of industrial life and minimize its bad points?," it seems safe to say that nine-tenths of the participants would have included the word "education" in their answers. But "education" is an easy word to say; to be in favor of it is no solution to anything. In the Friday-afternoon sessions, three separate panels—III, IV, and V—devoted themselves more or less specifically and technically to the subject of Western education. What is its present state? What are its problems? What are its hopes? (For a background discussion of these questions with particular reference to higher education, see McGeorge Bundy's paper on page 209.)

In Panel III—which divided its time between the debate on Western goals and ideals that has already been described, and what follows—it was appropriate enough that Mr. Malik should fill the role of brief and informal keynote speaker on education. Mr. Malik simply presented a list of topics that he thought worth pursuing, as follows:

1. The problem of science education—"how to liberalize and universalize it so that everybody lives intellectually in this scientific age and is literate about it."

2. Adult education: how, in particular, to counteract or supplement the effects of television and the press.

3. How to educate these media themselves, to introduce greater responsibility and quality into them.

4. The problem of improving public taste and the appreciation of beauty and art.

5. The teaching of the classics—"in that regard, I think the United States had led, during the last thirty or forty years."

6. The need for greater emphasis on general fundamental ideas and philosophy; closely related to which is

7. The problem of improving debate and discussion, recapturing the almost-lost art of conversation—"especially how to argue from first principles."

8. The question of liberal education: "I feel very strongly that one of the greatest contributions of American education to contemporary civilization is [in this field]. Europe does not quite have it in the sense in which you have it."

9. The importance of the English language, which seems to be in the way of becoming a world lingua franca.

10. The challenge to the West (and the United States in particular) to support educational systems abroad.

Presented with such a comprehensive agenda, the panel proceeded to treat it as cavalierly as all good agendas should be treated. Point Ten quickly became the focus. Referring to it, David Rockefeller asked whether, with reference to such underdeveloped areas as Africa, Mr. Malik felt that American support should focus on higher liberal education, technical instruction in agriculture and technology, or the grammar- and high-school level. If one must be chosen, said Mr. Malik, he would choose higher education on the theory that in the long run improvement on that level would seep down to the others.

Mr. Holland, speaking from personal experience, pointed out that liberal education is, at this stage of the game, just what the underdeveloped and developing countries do not want; a census of foreign students in this country in 1960 showed that most were studying engineering, the medical sciences, and the physical sciences, and less than one-fifth the humanities. (On this point, see Mr. Diké's background paper on page 224.) He objected in part to Mr. Malik's emphasis on higher education, saying that in some places, Latin America in particular, "secondary education is probably the place where emphasis should be placed."

Professor Calder of Edinburgh underlined the importance of the problem by speaking of the Belgian Congo, where Lovanium University, opened to Africans seven years ago, had produced only seventeen African graduates at the time of the Congo's liberation. The country became self-governing without having any qualified people in very many fields.

MR. ROCKEFELLER: Would you go so far as to say that the recent history of the Belgian Congo would have been very different if Lovanium had been founded thirty or forty years ago?

MR. HOLLAND: Very different. You would not have this situation, or have had it, either.

Drawing on recent experience in Africa and Latin America, Miss Height said that the developing nations' hunger for technical and compartmentalized education was resulting in a costly loss to themselves; their education "is not dealing with the whole person. It is dealing more with the parts." And why not? Well, suggested Mr. de Madariaga, perhaps because the teachers from the developed countries had nothing more to offer. If so, then who will teach the teachers themselves? Chairman Murphy said, "It does seem to be true that we are deluding ourselves if we simply say, 'We'll educate people to solve the problems we cannot solve.' If we are going to teach on large matters, I wholly agree with Mr. de Madariaga that we have to have something to teach, and you do not get that in the schools of education ordinarily as they are now organized." "That is the dilemma of education itself," suggested August Heckscher.

Quis custodiet ipsos custodes? The realization that education stands, so to speak, on its own shoulders, turned the spotlight on Western education at home rather than abroad. John R. Kimberly, chairman of the board of the Kimberly-Clark Corporation, interestingly presented an industrialist's point of view. The world is too much with us, he said, in effect: The arbitrary requirement of a college degree for many jobs causes many students to go to college when they lack the intellectual capacity to benefit from it; industrial society's demand for technical skills results in a slighting of humanistic studies; too often we fail "to give these young people an intellectual curiosity beyond the

area of training that they get in their formal education." Dean
De Vane of Yale documented from his own experience the notion
that many college students think of their courses, and even their
extracurricular activities in college, as specific vocational preparation.

Harold Clurman eloquently synthesized the panel's views of
our educational failures, and added some of his own:

> This morning Mr. Starr said . . . that when people got increased
> leisure, they took other jobs and did not do anything, as he put
> it, to improve or widen the scope of their personality. My response
> is that most people do not know they have a personality. . . .
> Should we not seek to develop a picture of the whole person?
> What is it to be a human being? What is it to be a feeling person?
> Why do we live? In other words, fundamental moral, ethical, reli-
> gious questions, if you will, so that all our techniques are not to
> make a human animal function well in the way of inhuman ani-
> mals, but a human animal who is a whole person. . . . That sense
> we lack in this country. . . .
>
> We seem to be a little impudent in all our propaganda, because
> we take for granted that just voting, just having free speech, is
> enough. Free speech to say what? Freedom to do what? Education
> to do or be what? Culture to affect what? We have no sense of
> ourselves, except that we can eat better, drink better, sleep better,
> talk with a finer vocabulary, and vote for some equally confused
> person.

But at this gloomy point, the tide turned, and Panel III's
discussion of education ended with three speakers whose attitude
was that of promise and resolve. The union-education man Mark
Starr insisted that "we are not quite as fouled up as Mr. Clurman
says." He asked the participants to consider how sharp was the
cleavage between the gentleman's liberal education and the workman's practical education under the old British system. Progress
has been made: With all its shortcomings, Western education
today *does,* to a certain extent, train the generalist as well as the
specialist; *does,* to a certain extent, train the whole man as well
as the economic man. True, there are problems (and one of
these that Mr. Starr mentioned was an important one to get

into the record—that is, the hesitancy or outright fear of many teachers to express their own political views freely in a conformist climate of community thought) . But there is hope, and Mr. Starr saw the hope as lying in a greater emphasis in our schools on individual responsibility, especially in relation to international affairs.

Mr. Heckscher, speaking about American higher education, associated himself in general with the optimism of McGeorge Bundy's background paper; he saw taking place a gradual breakdown of the old idea that with the awarding of a degree education ends and life begins, and an increasing extension, through community adult education and programs for adult return to universities, of education into adult life. And Miss Height, speaking again of education in Africa, managed to put the thing in a way that was both hopeful and admirably simple. The West has something to tell, which is precisely to explain how it has been able to achieve what it has, not just materially but in other ways, such as the task of preparing young people to meet responsibility. One of our immediate tasks is to put aside our self-consciousness and give the developing nations a straightforward account of our successes as well as our defeats.

Panel V, isolated in its basement, attacked education like a wasp dismantling a caterpillar. Its was a useful discussion, circumscribed by the fact that the six foreigners present were to some extent excluded by the specific reference of most speakers to the American situation. This was hardly the fault of Chairman Perkins, who, in leading off, asked that the participants take the subject in its widest possible framework, and not feel bound by formal systems or university walls. Responding to that, Dean Alexander Heard of the University of North Carolina's Graduate School took about as wide a framework as one possibly could— and at the same time spoke for a limited sort of education. Western education, he suggested, is nothing less than a matter of survival. In serving that aim, over the near future it is going

to have to concentrate on such things as scientific development
and research activities, with a probable concomitant sacrifice in
such fields as, say, medieval studies, and even in the culturally
important work of adult education to meet the demands of increased leisure.

Mr. Odegaard of the University of Washington did not take
the other side explicitly, but seemed to by implication. He stated
that in his view much of the "psychic energy" that has built
the United States—and that is needed now more than ever—has
come in part out of its educational system. To continue producing this energy, he urged that our education now become broader
and less specialized than ever, so as to prepare people to take
intelligent advantage of the increased options offered by industrialism.

Mr. Gerstacker of Dow Chemical raised two practical needs
in American education: the re-education for new jobs of workers
who are displaced by technological advances, and the training of
housewives in how to use their free time more usefully.

Echoing much that had been said in Panel III, Mr. Trippet
of Wabash College pointed out that the chief goals of education
mentioned so far had been (1) to make a specialist, and (2) to
make a citizen; he wanted to add (3) to make an individual.
He felt that there might be a danger in relating education too
much to national purposes or the reconstruction of society, and
in thinking of it as a national panacea:

> It often occurs to me, as I listen to the numerous proposals for
> reconstructing American educational levels, that I am listening to
> competing gospels of human salvation, and that in turn reminds
> me of the kind of error that was made in the nineteenth century
> by economic reformers: if you solve the economic problems, you
> solve all human problems. If there is anything empty in the world,
> that idea has been demonstrated to be empty by the history of the
> last few years. I wonder if there isn't somewhat the same danger
> in education in this country today. We are expecting formal edu-
> cation to perform all manner of tasks for society.

Mr. Sandmel enthusiastically seconded that. Avoid panaceas in education! Avoid thinking of education itself as a social panacea!

Mr. Oates of Princeton made the case for liberal education with a story that he credited to one of his colleagues on the plains of New Jersey. There was the dinosaur—a big, tough, mean, strong beast, but a specialist. Certain climatic changes took place, and the race of dinosaurs became extinct. A student, asked for comment on this sequence of events, replied, "Sir, the dinosaur evidently did not have a liberal education." Having entered that plug for the liberal arts as a road to survival, Mr. Oates went on to say that he was not pleading for liberal education *only*. In his view, the key to our society is pluralism, and that pluralism is—as it should be—reflected in many educational institutions of many different kinds, ranging from the trade school to the liberal arts college. And the trade school as well as the liberal arts college, he suggested, can contribute to the fulfillment of the individual, so long as it is the right individual. People differ; should not schools differ to accommodate them?

Chairman Perkins now listed what he considered to be some grave deficiencies in our higher education, whether its first goal be considered the making of specialists, citizens, or individuals. In the first category, he said that until recently our scientific and mathematical training at the grammar- and high-school levels was so inadequate as to choke off many promising talents. In the second category, "linguistically we are ignoramuses in this country—I think it is a continual disgrace," and, furthermore, a clear-cut political liability for an industrially mature nation that must of necessity have constant contacts all over the world. In the third category—or, perhaps, spread-eagling the three of them— Mr. Perkins, enlarging on a point of Mr. Gerstacker's, spoke of our education of women in terms as stern as those he had used for our language training:

> How long can this country's educational system continue on the assumption that we do not need the talent, the enormously varied high-powered talent represented by the women of this country? It is a national disgrace that we are continuing to educate our women as if they were going to lead nineteenth-century lives.

Mr. Perkins' conclusion was that, in many ways, our educational systems are not meeting the requirements of our society. Just as Panel III had faulted our educational achievements in broad philosophical terms—that is, in terms of the kind of people our schools and colleges turn out—so now Panel V, led by its efficient chairman, had diagnosed some of the particular symptoms of failure and thus suggested some first steps toward cure. But, as in Panel III, the harsh statement of our failures and limitations now led to a reactive thrust of optimism.

Mr. White saw hope for the future, and even a certain amount of accomplishment in the present so far as adult education is concerned, in his specialty, educational television. Mr. Trippet now returned, even more forcefully and comprehensively, to the point he had made earlier that we must avoid debasing and denaturing our education by forcing it to be merely the solver of transient problems, the social panacea—the replacement for the disintegrating American family; the adjuster of maladjusted youngsters; the trainer of military manpower; the occupational therapist for people with too much leisure; and so on. We must, he insisted, allow and urge our schools to emphasize "what is timeless, what ignores national lines, what is worldwide in its effect"; and to achieve this end, we must guard and protect above all the many small liberal-arts colleges across the country, of which, according to certain gloomy projections of present trends, eighty per cent will be gone in another decade.

That was seconded by Mr. Dos Passos, the novelist.

At the chairman's insistence, the previously-silent foreigners present spoke their pieces about American education.

Mr. Morello of Sicily said that he professed no competence on the subject, although he had taken a master's degree in economics at Stanford and "considered it his alma mater." With that prologue, the aspect of American education that Mr. Morello pointed to was its ethnocentrism. "Where the Americans really fail is abroad": the kind of approach, reflecting American education, that gives rise to such travel advertisements as "See Rome in three days, Pope included." What Americans tend to miss when they go abroad, said the speaker, is "a thorough understanding of the internal problems of the people they are facing"; and, obviously, the failure is closely related to the deficiencies of language-training mentioned by Mr. Perkins.

Mr. Moraes of India began with even more disclaimers than Mr. Morello, not even embracing an American alma mater. His view of the subject, he said, was specifically that from India—which, one may comment, gave it a special value. Said Mr. Moraes: Every year a large number of Indian students come to the United States, largely for scientific and technological training. The vast majority of them go home disappointed and frustrated—not by their experiences here, but rather by their return to India. In the United States, they are trained against the background of a nation that has all the technological tools readily at hand, but back in India they often find themselves unable to apply what they have learned merely because of the absence of equipment. And the difficulty extends into the intangible area of culture, too: "It is impossible for them to adjust themselves from the American environment back to the Indian environment."

The search for a solution obviously led back in the direction of what Mr. Morello had been saying. If the Indian students' American teachers had been more aware of the physical and spiritual climate in India, the problem might have been avoided. Beyond that, Mr. Moraes said he suspected Americans, in thinking of education, put far too much stress on formal institutions and "book learning." In India, a man who is uneducated in the formal sense is not therefore considered either uninformed—or unwise.

Just as the last two speakers had tended to emphasize differences between United States and other views of education, so Mr. Freyre of Brazil now emphasized similarities—and, by so doing, was able to close the discussion on a note of fellowship:

> In the face of Professor Oates' definition of education, and I agree with it, that education should be for the development of the human being in all his dimensions, we are all undeveloped. Not only

those in the underdeveloped countries, but those in the developed countries. That is a basic human unity. I think that with all our differences, differences between the developed countries and the underdeveloped countries, we have something in common in the face of certain problems—educational problems included.

And he went on to suggest a way that Brazil in particular might serve as educator to other peoples, developed and under-developed—a way that, while not put forward as a criticism of American education, may have been taken to heart by the American educators present:

> I think, though I am afraid of not being modest enough in this, that Brazil has the mission of being a sort of mediator between European peoples and non-European peoples, between whites and blacks, since we do not have race prejudice in Brazil—it is insig-nificant—and since we are as a nation an expression of the contri-bution of different races and cultures.

While Panel III was taking up United States education largely in its effects on our relations with the rest of the world, and Panel V was concentrating on its internal problems, Panel IV, up in the third-floor library, was gradually broadening its dis-cussion of the topic into a consideration of education's effects at home—that is, on the current state of American culture.

Professor Hurley of Massachusetts Institute of Technology set forth a sort of Platonic ideal for American education. He visual-ized an enormous broadening of formal education at its highest levels, technical and otherwise, leading to an American society in which thirty per cent of the population would attain the degree of Ph.D. The increasing complexity of life would be met by the creation—by some means, it is true, that are not at present foresee-able—of a mass educational elite. As for the other seventy per cent, he visualized improved non-formal mass education not leading to advanced degrees: such education to be provided not only by schools and colleges but by the mass-communications media and all other means at hand, and recorded on a "record of educa-tional experience" that each individual would have, and could present to a prospective employer. Most of these unblessed by the doctorate in this educational Erewhon would, at least at first, be women. And here at least a start has been made. Nodding in tribute to Mrs. Bunting across the table, Mr. Hurley spoke of Radcliffe's new and much-discussed program for the education and re-education of women in mid-career. Such adult education for women—considered either as a means toward self-fulfillment for the intellectually-frustrated housewife, or as the mobilizing of a wasted national resource—seemed to Hurley one of the pressing immediate needs of our educational system.

Judge Wyzanski concurred, with both gallantry and conviction:

> I do not think we have ever sufficiently concentrated from a male point of view on what our society loses from not utilizing women after they have reached the point where child-bearing or child-rearing is no longer their primary or partial function. . . . It is rather striking that there has never been a commission of males who have cared to concern themselves with this problem. It would have been more appropriate if the President of Harvard, rather than the President of Radcliffe, had chosen to speak up about this problem.

Mr. Lilienthal mentioned another reservoir of human resource that is, at least at present, being inadequately tapped by our educational system, "particularly in the South, but also elsewhere in the United States"—that is, the Negro population.

Mr. Chapman of Buenos Aires had doubts about Mr. Hurley's ideal. Why so many Ph.D.'s? Why must everybody be a university man? The same goals are in everyone's mind in Argentina, he said, but he nevertheless questioned them: Must the university and its official stamp be the measure of all higher education? "I think this is a very good question," replied Professor Curti of Wisconsin, and went on to say that he thought American universities were tending to overvalue the degree, to make it an "institutionalized stereotype." Mrs. Bunting, concurring, pointed out that at present it is sometimes almost impossible to study at our major universities unless you sign documents stating that you are interested in getting a degree. Mr. Hurley himself hastened to agree about degree-mania; he said that he had been using the Ph.D. only "as a level, as a measure of depth" in projecting the future.

Judge Wyzanski, mitigating the case, pointed out that besides the universities there now exist such first-rate, and far less degree-oriented, institutions as the New School for Social Research in New York City and the Aspen Institute in Colorado. In other words, opportunities for adult education at high levels do exist; it is a question of extending them.

Mr. Wheeler of Pitney-Bowes turned to the relation of education to industry. In this century, he said, there has been a "literal revolution" in the attitudes of business management toward its responsibilities toward stockholders, employees, customers, community, and nation. But "we have a long, long way to go," and Mr. Wheeler thought that one of the primary goals in future education planning should be to aim toward a furthering of this salutary revolution in management thinking. Advancing this thought, Judge Wyzanski seemed to call for a return to the old idea of putting character ahead of intellect. What was the basis of the attained distinction, for example, of the participants at the Corning conference, or the people at this very table? "They have grown in character and intellectual distinction by assuming the responsibility of making choices—often erroneous choices." (See the remarks, already quoted, of Mr. Starr in Panel III.)

All seemed to be agreed that one of the great problems of education in an industrialized society is keeping up with the rapid rate of social change. Mr. Chapman pointed out that in Argentina this flexibility is encouraged by allowing representative students to help run the universities—a method that severely shocks many United States university presidents. Mr. Kazin, as one who had taught both in the United States and abroad, spoke of American students' lust for knowledge, but utter lack of tradition: "More and more, American students give me the impression of not knowing that the wheel or fire has been invented, and that they are trying to do it themselves." How can we get our students to have not quite such a complete lack of a sense of the past? The very nature of our system appears to emphasize the present and the future almost to the exclusion of the past, and that, said Mr. Kazin, is one of the things that bothers him.

There followed an interlude devoted to the question—indirectly related to education—of the form industrialization will take in the underdeveloped countries, the panel's specimen country being, of course, Nigeria, because of the presence in the room of Mr. Diké. He himself, speaking of education in the United States, echoed the theme of the foreign members of Panel III: "One of the things which make your education rather one-sided is that your youths are not brought sufficiently into touch with the differing cultures of the world." Specifically, that we tend to think of industrialization everywhere as being bound to follow the pattern that it has followed here, while Mr. Diké saw the industrialization of Nigeria as being entirely Nigerian.

> The stage which you have reached, that has enabled you to think about leisure in your own industrial society, we have yet to attain. In fact, we are so eager to industrialize that we tend to forget all the evil that goes with it. That evil is not yet with us, and our primary concern, at this stage, is to push forward as much as we can in order to catch up with the rest of the world. . . .
>
> We are likely, if we are well guided, to avoid the kind of mistakes which you have under study, in connection with your own development.

Why, several participants wanted to know, does Mr. Diké think that Nigeria can accomplish that? Because, he replied, Nigeria starts with an industrial *tabula rasa*—its economy at present is still ninety-eight per cent agricultural—and it is free to plan each step, with the experience of the developed countries both as a guide and a warning. Professor William K. Frankena of the University of Michigan was a bit doubtful. "I think Dr. Diké underestimates the changes that will accrue to his country and his culture if they industrialize," said Professor Frankena. "You can't just take industrialization and not take the things that come with it. . . . Your mores will change; your moral concepts will change a great deal. You will automatically put a great deal of store on material goods." Mr. Diké insisted that he knew all that: "What I am trying to say is that we hope that that change, when it comes [in Africa], will produce something basically Nigerian or Ghanian or whatever."

Sir Julian Huxley took this opportunity to introduce a theme that he has made something of a personal crusade—the population problem. (The week before, during a television interview in New York, he had said that uncontrolled population growth is such that unless something is done, man himself is in danger of becoming "the cancer of the earth.") The experience of India, he said, was that no matter how much equipment, technical know-how, and capital are available, such a country cannot be industrialized unless and until the birth-rate is brought down. The same, he assumed, would apply in Africa.

The sense of the panel seemed to be good will toward Mr. Diké's ideal, combined with skepticism that it can be realized. This was human. Mr. Diké, after all, was saying, "What you have done, we can do better with your help," and the Westerners were replying, "We'll try to help, but results are not guaranteed. Our record is one of partial failure."

But had not Panel IV, in its zeal to find the new directions by which United States education can best help industrialism serve the cause of individualism, tended to fall into the trap of making education a panacea? To a certain extent, it had; and now it was reminded of this by Dr. Glasser, who said, "I am concerned with the fact that as our industrial society becomes more mechanized and dehumanized to a certain extent, our education seems to be following along the same lines." That expression of concern headed the discussion away from the tendency to think of society collectively, and toward a consideration of the role in industrial society of those natural-born arch-individualists, the creative artist and the intellectual critic. Now Mr. Kazin, instead of Mr. Diké, became the cynosure. He said, first of all, that he did not want the context of the discussion to disintegrate into "the two situations"—overdeveloped *vs.* underdeveloped, technological *vs.* agricultural, haves *vs.* have-nots. There is much in common between the people involved in the two situations, he pointed out, and it is limiting to think of them in terms of polarities. Specifically, Mr. Kazin didn't feel that he should have a guilty conscience, culturally speaking, because he is, so to speak, industrialized:

> I've had in my own life the experience of moving from a fairly primitive culture, too. My parents were illiterate. They were immigrants. I had the experience of knowing what it's like to move up from this relatively primitive background to this high eminence in which we are seated right now, and I must say that I am not as impressed as I used to be when I was young and trying to make my way by the sheer process of getting an education. . . . I'm more impressed by all sorts of distortions and anti-human, narrow attitudes which are involved in that thing itself. . . .
>
> I think it's still one culture. We are all one species.

The main "anti-human, narrow attitude" that Mr. Kazin spoke of in connection with United States cultural life was a certain homogeneity of thought in the most educated circles. That is, everybody tends to be a liberal; everybody tends to orient his thinking according to the discoveries of psychology and psychiatry; everybody neglects religion or uses it for propaganda; everybody tends to be "depthless, lacking in that sense which Aristotle said was the very mark of philosophy, which is to regard with wonder the fact that things are as they are." This dull, gray, shallow uniformity of intellectual thought seemed to Mr. Kazin to be the melancholy product, up to now, of mass education in the United States.

Dr. Glasser, the panel's psychiatrist, whose specialty had been under attack by Mr. Kazin, came in with a disarming intervention:

As to Mr. Kazin's comment on psychiatry and psychology, I am in the midst of this thing and I couldn't agree with him more. . . . We're in an age of psychology and psychiatry, and whenever there's a cooperative nursery-school meeting they get a psychiatrist to speak and give the little women around there the wisdom on how to raise their little children. The women accept this like it is dripping right from the Lord's mouth. . . . I'm fighting the same battle Mr. Kazi is as hard as I can, and it's pretty hard.

Why this unholy grip of psychiatry on the American mind? "Partly, I think, it's magic," said Dr. Glasser. "We have developed a rather systematic magical cult which people want to believe. . . . I had a patient come to me and say, 'I'm here. Do psychiatry.' She was there, and I did psychiatry as best I could."

But presently Mr. Kazin himself was under attack. Judge Wyzanski objected to the idea that unity of thought among the educated classes is our problem. Indeed, he said, "There has never been a society so clearly believing that a variety of tongues makes the best tune," and as an index of diversity he cited the great differences in regional cooking throughout the United States. Mr. Kazin protested that he had not been speaking of social diversity, of which he agreed that the United States has a wealth; he had been speaking of "the cult of the common man as opposed to the common man's cult of the hero"—that is, the general leveling and shallowing of thought, the tendency to denigrate thought itself by identifying mind with behavior, power with administration, administration with psychology.

Sir Julian discerned for the writer, the thinker, the critic, the artist—"for short, the intellectual"—two social functions: to introduce variety, and to curb and correct variety when it goes too far. Judge Wyzanski spoke highly of several American writers, and expressed the view that according to Sir Julian's criteria for their function, they have done well. Mr. Lilienthal was less enthusiastic; what bothered him was the number of intellectuals who, feeling somehow alienated and frustrated, become critics of industrialization, "but, if I may be blunt about it, will not take the trouble to see what the facts are." Sir Julian agreed in general:

I think what we want to do is not merely to have the outside critic, the Utopianist, the satirist, but we also want the intellectual to give some of his time and intellectual energy to positive studies of concrete problems, such as, for instance, the industrialization of a new society like Nigeria's.

Mr. Kazin replied to his critics by accepting many of their objections, and reformulating his own critique of industrial culture as it now exists. He granted that industrialism satisfies wants and creates rising expectations. The problem, he said, arises out of those very accomplishments: "Industrialism creates a kind of dissatisfaction precisely because it satisfies so many wants. The more people live in this kind of society, the more they expect of themselves. . . . That is why we feel a sense of frustration at a time when our industrial society is much more humane, much more social-minded than it ever was before. . . . Having their goals statable, fillable, people adopt a kind of attitude toward life that is one almost of contempt for themselves, which is not in the least the fault of industrialism or capitalism or even of socialism, where it exists—but simply a fault in the very nature of the process itself."

Sir Julian said: "Yet surely it's fairly simple in a way. We ought to begin by saying that [the accomplishment of industrialism] isn't merely the satisfaction of wants. It is the creation of opportunity, which is a very different thing." The challenge of the future is to resolve the paradox whereby greater opportunity leads to not more freedom but less.

CHAPTER 5

◈

INTERLUDE: FRIDAY EVENING

◈

ON FRIDAY EVENING, the Second Corning Conference had its moment of drama—and in a certain sense, its moment of truth.

Scene: The Corning Country Club, where the conferees, after being transported there by buses and limousines, had warded off the chill of a cloudy and penetrating spring evening with refreshments on the lawn, and had then been treated to another of their hosts' overwhelming dinners. Occasion: A general session of the conference, entitled "Views from Abroad," and consisting of brief remarks by four of the foreign participants, followed by general discussion. The discussion period would provide the only time when any participant who chose to could address the whole conference.

On the platform, as the evening's opening speakers, were four participants with whom readers of the foregoing pages will be amply familiar: Mr. Freyre of Brazil, Mr. Stanovnik of Yugoslavia, Mr. Diké of Nigeria, and Mr. Moraes of India. Serving as moderator was Robert D. Murphy, for many years a top United States diplomat serving in posts all the way from Munich to

Algiers to Tokyo, and now president of Corning Glass International.

The tone of the session, or of the greater part of it, was one of almost excessive decorum, moderation, and constructiveness. Mr. Freyre, speaking first, began by saying that his remarks on Brazil would be largely favorable—"but please do not think from this that I am an absolute patriot, who never criticizes his own country. On the contrary, I have been accused of being too critical of Brazil, and, some years ago, there was a group of patriots who wanted to burn my books in a public square in the traditional style. One of them went so far as to say that the author of the books should be included."

Mr. Freyre maintained that on the question of individualism, Brazil can, and always could, give itself the highest marks. Because of the nature of its society, which was originally based not on national conquest or on the Catholic Church, but on the patriarchal family, it has been able to avoid the problems of radicalism and militarism that have plagued most of the other Latin-American countries. It had the first woman governor in the American continent—in the sixteenth century. It had the first Negro president of any republic south of Panama in 1910. And, said Mr. Freyre, it continues to keep up its impartial regard for the worth and independence of the individual, regardless of sex or race; indeed, in the speaker's view, individualism in Brazil runs so rampant that it becomes almost a national sin, by holding back social progress that might be made if the Brazilians were more socially-minded: "and that sin is not peculiar to Brazil. It is an Iberian sin."

Mr. Stanovnik presented a warm statement of Yugoslav ideals cast in humanitarian terms. He started from the assumption that economic development is, for the present civilization, the basis of humanism. He saw the major powers in the world as divided into two camps, one dedicated to a society of high mass consumption, the other setting itself the economic target of catching up with, or if possible overtaking, the first. He himself, Mr. Stan-ovnik said, spoke for a third force, for whom economic development means not merely more consumer goods (here the speaker invoked the familiar symbols of automobiles and television sets), but rather a restoration of human values. "I am deeply devoted to socialist thinking," said Mr. Stanovnik, "but I have never thought that the ideal of socialism is just producing steel or producing economic power to compete with the other fellow. . . . I don't think that is or should be the socialist aim or target. I think if socialism remains faithful to its historical tradition, it should restore human values. . . . The final aim should be man."

Mr. Moraes summarized the view of the world situation that he had put forward in his panel that morning: that the East tends to be overly society-centered, while the West tends to be overly individualistic; that the contrast is based on the historical fact that the Industrial Revolution hit Europe a century or more before it hit Asia, and should in no case be attributed to the much-touted spirituality of the Oriental mind, a concept that Mr. Moraes dismissed as nonsense; and that the goal for everyone should be "an integrated individual in an integrated society." To the extent that the conference could mark a path toward that goal, he thought, it would have succeeded in its purpose.

Mr. Diké, speaking for his own country, was not to be out-done by Mr. Freyre in the matter of women's status. So Brazil had a woman governor in the sixteenth century? Well, said Mr. Diké with a smile, at the end of the *fourteenth* century Queen Amena of Zaria was the greatest tribal ruler in Nigeria, holding sway over eight million people. But "our problem now is not with the past"; it is, rather, the developing of a none too homogenous concatenation of some forty million people into a modern nation. Most specifically and pressingly, the problem for Nigeria is education, and the strides that are being made in that direction are nothing less than headlong. In the days of British rule, Mr. Diké pointed out, not more than two per cent of national income was spent on education, whereas since the granting of independence—which took place a scant seven months before the conference—the figure in some regions of Nigeria had risen to over forty per cent. "We realize that we are miles behind many countries in the world," said Mr. Diké; "we realize that until our manpower is trained, the task of developing our country cannot be carried out." And the speaker made no bones about the fact that one of the reasons he had come to the United States was to express thanks for American assistance already granted toward the carrying out of this mammoth task, and "to make contacts that would enable me to explain to Americans and to other scholars who have been invited here what the needs of Africa are, and how much we value your assistance."

Mr. Murphy now threw the meeting open for comments and questions. The first to rise was Mr. Holland of the Institute of International Education, who directed to Mr. Diké the practical question, "How can we in the United States work more effectively with Nigeria in improving education there?" In replying, Mr. Diké cited the Ashby Report, the result of a study directed to this very point. The prime need, he said, is for teachers and teacher training at all levels, since at the present time some eighty per cent of the teachers in Nigerian schools are untrained; and the financing of a program to correct this situation—"I must speak selfishly," apologized Mr. Diké—should above all be an international undertaking.

Sir Julian Huxley gave a biologist's explanation of the relatively late survival of indigenous—and in the anthropological and cultural sense, barbaric—civilizations along the West Coast of Africa. His explanation was disease; every time the Western traders or the North African Moslems left the immediate coast they died of malaria, blackwater, and yellow fever, and their horses of nagana disease from the bite of the tsetse fly. (At the same time, he warned, with examples, against the colonialist notion that all progress in Africa has been correlated with the penetration of Western civilization.) Sir Julian was high in his praise of Mr. Diké's ideal of preserving these indigenous and valuable cultures during and after the process of industrialization: "I think it is wonderful to find somebody in Dr. Diké's position who is aiming at this important goal."

Mr. Stanovnik, in answer to a question from Raymond Aron, enlarged on the idea that he had expressed earlier that the important watershed in the world today is not between East and West but between developed nations and underdeveloped nations—or, as he quoted a recent published statement of Sir Oliver Franks, between North and South. And in pressing this point, Mr. Stanovnik detailed some of his own nation's differences with the Soviet Union:

> We don't think that there is anybody who should write a recipe for us as to what is a socialist society and what is not a socialist society. In Sweden, for instance, a Social Democrat party is now in power and has been for about thirty years, and we feel that there is nobody who can say that the Social Democrat party in Sweden knows less about socialism than they in China know.

He himself thought, said Mr. Stanovnik, that if the gap between the have and the have-not nations is not solved, and becomes progressively more profound, then civilization will be more seriously threatened by that difference than it has ever been by the difference between East and West.

On the theory that a quotation from a man can be a challenge to him, Chairman Murphy suggested that Sir Oliver Franks had been challenged. Would Sir Oliver rise to meet the challenge? For a moment, it appeared that he wouldn't, as participants murmured to each other and looked around the room for the British ex-diplomat. But finally, the moving of a portable microphone to his table having been established as the cause of delay, Sir Oliver's classic profile was seen, and his voice heard:

> Here I am, a cheerful, unrepentant, ex-colonial power. When I look around me tonight and I see Americans, Indians, Nigerians, all very happy in their independence, I feel that, one way or another—perhaps not very willingly—we have done a lot of good in the world. (*laughter*)

What Sir Oliver had to say further was that on the main points he agreed with Mr. Stanovnik. It does little good to think of the world in terms of East-West tension: "We are all, developed or less developed, of equal importance in terms of human interest and human history. What is important is that we should move forward together, not in fear but in confidence, trying to create a higher standard of living in the whole world so that our unity increases rather than our disunity."

Mr. Stanovnik, in answer to a question from Mr. de Madariaga, pressed his point further with an example that was close to home for both himself and the conference's host nation. In Yugoslavia, he said, Americans are well regarded, despite the two countries' political differences: Indeed, "You will find countries where you have been pouring in much greater assistance, and where you are not so well regarded, if you are not even hated." Why is this so? Mr. Stanovnik stated flatly that it is because American aid to Yugoslavia has always been given without any political, economic, or military strings attached. Such non-interference, he said, is the very key to successful diplomacy through economic aid. As to the question of freedom, Mr. Stanovnik insisted that the West is wrong to assume that one of the field-marks of freedom is inevitably the presence of many different political parties: "Individuals should be free, but the precise institutional framework of this freedom in each society will be decided on its own tradition."

Now the thunderbolt struck. Mr. Lovestone of the AFL-CIO arose, Mr. Lovestone—who was of course one of the earliest and most vocal highly-placed defectors from the ranks of Stalinism—wished to question some of Mr. Stanovnik's assumptions, and to do it in language more pointed than any that had been heard previously in the conference. Here the transcript, abridged, may take over:

> What I can't understand, particularly in the face of all the emphasis our Yugoslav friend placed on helping the underdeveloped countries, is how it comes about that on most of the basic issues in the United Nations, the Yugoslavs vote with the Russians, even

when the Russians spit in their faces. Very often, when the Russians spit in their faces, they think it is the morning dew. . . .

We have never attached any conditions [to our aid to Yugoslavia], and I am indebted to our Yugoslav friend for pointing it out. The United States is financing the building of communism in many ways in Yugoslavia. Without our help, I maintain the Yugoslavs could never have resisted and resisted well—and we are glad that they resisted. . . .

The Russians say they want to wage ideological war against us. I will make a deal with them. Let's work out an agreement. We should conduct ideological propaganda in every totalitarian country, and we should let the Communist Party conduct ideological propaganda, as they do, in our countries.

I say to our Yugoslav friend, the important issue is what you say, but the explosive issue, the vital issue, is not the question of helping. We are even prepared to work with the Russians to help the underdeveloped countries, but they won't work with us, because they don't want what we want in the underdeveloped countries. They want to use their economic assistance for subversion, and we want to use it for creation. . . . The difference is that the Russians want to sovietize the world on the basis of the Kremlin pattern, and that we, in the West, won't accept that. (*applause*)

Mr. Stanovnik replied:

Mr. Chairman, this time I am going to be very short, because I am sure you will agree with me if I say that that is the way which will bring you the shortcut to isolation and to defeat. (*applause*)

So in the midst of general agreement that East-West tensions are not the paramount issue in the world today, East-West tensions asserted themselves. Instead of coolly and detachedly analyzing world problems, the conference was suddenly enacting them.

The session almost pointedly did not pursue further the subject. But its tone was changed, and it moved in a gloomy direction. Professor Hauser of Chicago brought up what is often called the population nightmare, citing figures to prove that if Asia by the year 2000 is to match the living standard of Europe in 1950, it must increase its continental income by the fantastic factor of twenty-three. Mr. Moraes objected that he had no faith in paper projections, which have so often in the past been proved wrong. Sir Julian Huxley declared that they weren't paper projections but "calculations in the flesh":

> What is happening is that [India] and many Asian countries and underdeveloped countries are multiplying, reproducing their human flesh so fast that there won't be enough capital and skill to industrialize them, unless they get the birth rate down.

> MR. MORAES: Theoretically, you are right, but what if an atomic war happens, meanwhile? That might decimate people and solve the problem.

Two minutes later, Mr. Wheeler of Pitney-Bowes said:

> I think we have imposed upon our illustrious panel sufficiently, and I would say you should call a halt, and give them a rising vote of thanks for this very interesting evening. (*standing applause, whereupon the panel discussion was adjourned at 10:30 P.M.*)

What was to be made of this sudden and disconcerting turn in the conference—this startling change in the pitch of its engines? At least one participant, John Dos Passos, found it a high rather than a low point. To him, said Mr. Dos Passos, speaking at his roundtable the following morning, the Stanovnik-Lovestone exchange and what had followed it was "a marvelous scene" which "gave visual and dramatic form to what we have to face": on the one side, the Balkan Communist who had "phrased his side of the story so perfectly"; on the other side, the American "reformed Marxist using the old Marxist vituperation"; as audience, "the overfed people at dinner"; and, caught helplessly between the two adversaries, Mr. Diké, standing for the people of an undeveloped country who only "want to be left alone and to be helped to pull themselves up by their bootstraps." It might have been a scene from one of Mr. Dos Passos' novels, and perhaps some day it will be. "It has been haunting me ever since," he said the next morning. "I still see the whole thing, and I still hear every word, particularly the last words of the gentleman from the Balkans, and Mr. Moraes' neat capping of the whole little drama by his remark about how a few million deaths from radiation might solve the population problem. . . . If a dozen people out of this whole gathering managed properly to evaluate that scene, it will have made worth while all the man-hours and all the money that has been put into getting this conference together."

What was Mr. Dos Passos' own evaluation of the scene? "It seems to me," he said, "that the adrenalin has not started to flow in this country, and the things that need to be done are extremely urgent." The things that he recommended most urgently were "a crash program in languages"; a program to teach people how to deal best with situations caused by radiation accidents ("apart from wartime, atomic reactors like gas plants occasionally blow up") ; and vastly increased emphasis on civilian defense in general. To Mr. Dos Passos, the scene had been a particularly vivid allegorical representation of a world on the brink of madness, calmly and even smugly watched in the very process of explosion by its sagest and most powerful citizens.

It is doubtful that most of the other participants agreed fully with Mr. Dos Passos' interpretation. Some probably saw the scene as a mere ripple in an otherwise largely constructive discussion, an expression of special points of view that could be largely discounted; others may have thought of it as not allegorical at all but merely a projection of personalities rather than issues, or an indication that the hour was late and the time for adjournment at hand. One thing, though, did seem certain—that the conference was no longer talking, as parts of it had seemed to be more than once during the day, in terms of easy generalities, diplomatic politeness, and tactful agreements. The Friday-evening session had given the conference a fresh teeth-hold on reality.

CHAPTER 6

SATURDAY MORNING

From the editor's notes:

Eight A.M.: The glint of bright sunlight on Corning, after two days of rain, leaden clouds, and damp chill. A sign; a portent; an emergence from a tunnel into daylight.

Headlines in the Corning Leader: *"Big Two Talks May Be First of Series" (East-West tensions). "France, Algerian Rebels Open Peace Negotiations" (last days of colonialism). "Restaurateur Deplores Expense-Account Threat; Pictures Midtown Manhattan a Distressed Area" (internal problems of developed societies). "Apalachin Crime Meeting Cost Government Over $1 Million" (problem of national moral climate). "Winemakers in California Doubt Soviet Claim of Producing Sparkling Wine in Three Weeks" (Cold-War competition). "World Hopeful, Wary." (Hopeful, wary indeed.)*

Seen from a window in the Baron Steuben: Elsie's Hair Styling; Brown's Cigar Store; Bacalles Grill; The Casual Shop; Harold's Army & Navy Store; Sullivan's Liquors. Beyond, one of the hills that make up the bowl that holds Corning; on its slope, a church spire, a civic building, a Romanesque clock tower. Chiefs and wise men of the world called together here through the concern of a wealthy merchant in a time of crisis. A dramatic conception: Can it not perhaps bear some small but nourishing fruit?

Several preoccupations colored the final panel sessions on Saturday morning. The time was short; it was now or never to say what one wished to say, or perhaps had come to say. There was a tendency to pick up the loose threads, to introduce into the record ideas and subjects that had been glaringly omitted so far. There was a tendency to express second thoughts, marshalled overnight, on certain things that had been said and allowed to stand the previous day. And finally, of course, there was a tendency to summarize.

The most notable subject to be "picked up" was leisure, which had been one of the trinity of topics prescribed by the planners for discussion in the roundtables—and which, to a striking degree, had so far been either touched on lightly or ignored entirely. It may be interesting here to gather together some of the general statements on leisure that had been made on Friday, or were made now. Professor Aron in Panel I: "We cannot require the content of leisure to be better than the content of the life of the people concerned." Mr. Hersey in the same panel: "I think leisure should be life." Dr. Alexander in Panel II: "Leisure, I'm afraid, was an unfortunate expression that came in." Mr. de Madariaga in Panel III: "Leisure is only an elegant word." Mr. Rorimer in Panel III: "We will begin with the Middle Ages, when Saint Benedict said, 'Idleness is the enemy of the soul.' Then, perhaps, we might take Benjamin Franklin: 'I look upon indolence as a sort of suicide.' Even Carlyle says, 'In idleness there is perpetual despair.'" The general queasiness on the subject reached its height in Panel IV, where Chairman Braisted repeatedly tried to introduce it with such comments as "And now I feel it is time we took up leisure," only to have the panel obstinately ignore him over and over again. Indeed, when the conscientious chairman finally got a sort of response to his urgings, it was not a very encouraging one. Mr. Lilienthal: "It's quite evident that just as this panel is against sin, we are against leisure." Mr. Blough, a moment later: "Now, to go on to leisure . . . I suggest that we abolish it, as we apparently have."

Why this general tendency toward evasion of what almost all the participants seemed to agree is an important problem of industrial societies? Partly, no doubt, it was caused by the character of the participants themselves, all of whom are busy people with a minimum of what is commonly thought of as leisure in their own lives. Another reason was the difficulty of definition—dramatically pointed up by Miss Rukeyser, the poet, on Friday morning, when by referring to her own case she had so devastatingly proved that leisure is *not* "what you do when you are not working for a living." But surely a third and more comprehensive reason was the general realization that the more interesting and fulfilling to the individual a society is, the less easy it is to draw the lines between work and leisure or even between work, education, and leisure—that, in effect, treating leisure as a separate and compartmentalized thing is tantamount to recognizing and systematizing a weakness in the present industrial society rather than reaching toward something better.

Still, the existing problem—dramatized by Mr. Starr when he had pointed out that many industrial workers simply used their increased "leisure" to take on second jobs—has to be dealt with. Precisely because it begged the question of definition (it cheerfully accepted leisure as "non-work"), Panel V was able to have a rather fruitful discussion of the topic.

Mr. Bradford of the *New York Times* introduced two key choices that the individual faces in determining how to spend his leisure in an industrial society. One is the choice between spending it in the company of others, or spending it alone; the other is the choice between spending it in the area where one works, or spending it somewhere else. He further suggested a contrast between the situation of people working in or near large cities, who for the most part go somewhere else for their leisure, and people working in small communities like Corning itself, who are more apt to find their leisure close to home. Mr. Freyre implemented this by mentioning an extreme case of city-dwellers who find a strong need to go somewhere else for leisure—the residents of Brazilia, the jungle-bound, single-industry capital of Mr. Freyre's country, where the monotony of the physical landscape (augmented, no doubt, by the monotony of the inevitable political conversation) is such that people there "are even developing a sort of mental disease" unless they have frequent opportunities to escape for a time.

Mr. Sandmel introduced the idea that since industrialization creates more leisure hours, the management of corporations, in their capacity as the leaders of industry, must assume a responsibility to provide counsel and guidance as to the use of that leisure. The business consultant, Mr. Worthy, rose to protest against the premise—or at least to change it. Industrialization, he contended, does not necessarily produce increased leisure time. For example, the industrial management groups in our society have less leisure than any other groups, and may well have less leisure than any one segment of any society of the past; "Quite likely the leisure class of America is the working class." Mr. Bradford came back to the prevalence of "moonlighting" among industrial workers. They work six days a week by choice; thus Mr. Worthy's "leisure class" voluntarily liquidates itself. The only possible conclusion seemed to be that Americans, at least, whether involved in industry on the management side or on the labor side, resemble the participants at the conference: they simply do not seem to like leisure. (And this, as Mr. de Madariaga had suggested, may be their greatest weakness.)

Now came a fascinating and perspective-giving comment on industrial work hours from a man who knew his subject—Ralph Reiser, president of the United Glass and Ceramic Workers of North America. Mr. Reiser first said that he disagreed with those who had suggested that management's responsibility for workers' leisure extends to guiding or directing it. "People don't go for directed activity," said Mr. Reiser. "An individual wants to call his own shots." Then, on the matter of work hours:

> You have got occupations in glass that we call "scoring out." The fellow gets to the high tempo, and he would like to stay at that tempo and get his work out and maybe score out in four hours. You take the Corning plant: when they had the blow shops in there, those men wouldn't work any more than a six-hour shift. They get into a tempo, and if they break for eating or anything like that, it would take them a half-hour to get into shape again.
>
> During the war the Army and Navy put a lot of pressure on— they were blowing radar tubes—and they wouldn't go over a six-hour shift. In eight hours they produced less than they did in a six-hour one. This was pretty hard for the procurement officer to believe.

It is also, no doubt, enough to drive a management time-study man to distraction. What is he to do with a situation where men can turn out more work in less time than they can in more time? Shoot himself, perhaps; at any rate, Mr. Reiser's down-to-earth remarks led Panel V to a far more flexible view of the industrial worker's relative hours of work and leisure.

Mr. Dos Passos commented that in his observation, just as leisure in the United States is the prerogative of no particular class, so there is a classlessness in the use of leisure. Whether it be fishing, camping, boating, hunting, or whatever else, "the banker and the steelworker have exactly the same recreation gambit right along"—the survival of that Veblenian symbol, the yacht, to the contrary notwithstanding. Mr. White of the National Education Television and Radio Center felt that the idea of classlessness extended to the continuing sense of social responsibility in leisure time; just as others had said that the employer should be concerned with the quality and content of the employee's leisure, Mr. White said that the employee on vacation has the responsibility not to put the community and its needs out of his mind during his free time.

Mr. Gerstacker of Dow Chemical introduced an aspect of

industrial leisure that he thought had been inappropriately neglected so far in the discussion—that is, the greatly increased leisure of the housewife, brought about by improved household appliances, and resulting too often in a more or less purposeless life. Mr. Gerstacker's comments, along with one he had made on Friday morning, clearly established him as the conference's chief pleader for housewives; still on family affairs, but in a different vein, he now showed his mettle by offering a valiantly candid explanation of executive preference of "work" to "leisure":

> Travel has been mentioned. . . . When I travel in my work, it is usually more pleasant than when I travel in my leisure time for pleasure. I know where I am going to go and what I am going to do, and often other people help me in accomplishing this. I have less decision-making in work travel than when I travel in leisure.
>
> In leisure travel, I take my wife and daughters, and we have problems. I have decisions to make . . . so I prefer my work travel to my leisure travel. . . . Mr. Reiser, I imagine when you go to a Miami Beach meeting, this is work; but I imagine that in a sense, when you are all through you enjoy this more than when you take your family to the beach or take them to some other place—at least in many cases.

Another brave man, Mr. Reiser did not demur, except to say that the only reason his union convenes in Miami Beach is because accommodations there are relatively cheap, and in any case the delegates really do spend all their time there working.

The question of the role mass communications, especially television, play in American leisure could hardly be postponed longer. Here Mr. Sandmel introduced the premise: "I am not talking about moral corruption, I am talking about the sheer waste of time that goes beyond all measure. Some waste of time is good, but we, I think, live in a society in which we have become attached to wasting time beyond all reason, and wasting it on the most unyielding, superficial banality." Mr. Morello of Sicily codified the indictment. Leisure, he suggested, may be divided into consumption and investment; the tendency in industrialized countries seems to be to emphasize the former at the expense of the latter.

No one had specifically brought up the television industry yet (except Mr. Odegaard, who said that he missed the presence of David Sarnoff of RCA, the doughty defender of television at the First Corning Conference), but surely no one in Panel V failed to grasp the allusions that had been made. Television was the butler with blood all over his shirt; nobody needed to accuse him of the murder by name. Yet now Dean Heard of North Carolina rose to offer the butler a modest defense. There are, he said, many television programs that are constructive. And a generation ago, didn't everybody talk about how terrible and corrupting the movies were? Did the movies actually corrupt that generation, on the basis of later evidence?

Mr. Dos Passos expressed the belief that the chief drawback of television is that it keeps children from playing, the activity in which their knowledge and creativity is most naturally developed. Mr. Freyre added another thought—that any form of leisure-time activity in which the participant is an entirely passive spectator may tend to develop a cast of mind recipient to totalitarianism. But Mr. Freyre was glad to admit that the passivity of television-watching in the United States is balanced by its exact obverse in the use of leisure time—that is, the flourishing do-it-yourself movement.

The panel's final consensus on television, insofar as there was such a consensus, was, in relation to the conference at large, rather mild. What corrupting effects on the young are, up to now, observable? Not many: "I must say that the young people that I see beginning to come to college now, that have been brought up on television, seem to compare very favorably with their predecessors," said Mr. Trippet of Wabash College. "We are selling more musical instruments to kids, for example than we ever did before." Mr. Dos Passos said that he could accept the cartoons, but not the Westerns. No one seemed prepared to level such a broadside against commercial programming as that of FCC Chairman Newton Minow—or, for that matter, as that of Professor Aron in his Corning background paper. (See page 157.) The absence of Mr. Sarnoff from the discussion table may have had something to do with this. Bull-baiting is no sport without a bull to bait, and critics agreeing with each other tend to bore even themselves. A much more stimulating intellectual test is trying to find something good in commercial television. Panel V tended to play this Socratic game; it was the only panel that did, and even here, the defenders of the television status quo seemed a bit tentative and half-hearted.

On the broader context of American leisure in general, Chairman Perkins discerned that the panel seemed to have divided our use of non-work time into three categories: time used for recreation, time used for self-improvement, and time used in meeting civic and public responsibilities. Professor Oates of Princeton wanted to add a fourth category. He quoted Mr. de Madariaga as having once said, "The trouble with you Americans is that you do not know how to lie in the sun." Whether or not the accusation was just—and the presence of suntans on so many American skins, at all seasons of the year, might argue the contrary—Mr. Oates wanted "lying in the sun" to be admitted to fully-accredited status as an approved use of leisure time. The motion having been accepted without objection, Mr. Odegaard wanted to add one more distinction. The life of the United States' West Coast, he declared, is far more conducive to constructive use of leisure than that of many other regions—and, in particular, than that of the industrial cities of the East and Midwest. "One of our problems is to figure out how to deal with the metropolis so that it provides not only the environment for the manufacturer of products and a place for people to live, but also a place for people to play." Here again, an opposing tendency must be noted and set against Mr. Odegaard's commendable regional pride. As was brought out in another panel discussion soon to be described, many people find their most sympathetic playground in and around a great industrial city.

Chairman Perkins, feeling that the center of most of the discussion had been too much the United States, called on the foreigners present; and three of them, by commenting specifically and factually on leisure in their own countries, did just that.

Mr. Morello returned to television, in terms of its place in present-day Sicily:

> If I may go into a personal experience, there is some research that we are engaged in at the present moment. It is to see the effect of television on a great illiterate society. The conclusion which seems to emerge at this point . . . that they jump from the pre-alphabet society to the screen-image society, is a rather positive one. It brings people into contact with a world that was entirely unknown, and although it may give rise to aspirations that are probably out of reach in the short run in the structure of these people, it certainly broadens their cultural horizon in a way that could hardly be reached at the same tempo through the written word. . . .
>
> I think it may not be necessarily the same thing in another context of society. . . .
>
> CHAIRMAN PERKINS: Mr. Moraes, do you want to say anything?
>
> MR. MORAES: We don't have television in India.

Mr. Perkins assured Mr. Moraes that he hadn't intended to restrict him to television. But Mr. Moraes still remained one-up: In India, he said, leisure—and even, indeed, recreation—"also means study, in a sense. That is, reading. Because we take our pleasure rather solemnly."

Not so in Brazil, said Mr. Freyre, who wound up the session by salting it with the day's first mention of one of mankind's oldest and most honored forms of recreation, dancing:

> I think that Brazil is one of those countries that in the near future, with the probable development of automation and the probable beginning of a fast-growing industrial society, will have something to teach to separate industrial societies in the matter of what to do with free time; because there are a number of folk traditions in dance and song and recreation that have been preserved there, as in other Catholic Iberian countries, that have disappeared from

the super-industrialized, literate and progressive countries of northern Europe and in the United States.

Upstairs in the first floor conference room, Panel III was taking up leisure in direct relation to work, with particular reference to one of the important consequences of the organization of industrial work—this is, urbanization.

It was appropriate enough that Mr. Heckscher, who had contributed a background paper on leisure, should introduce the discussion. "The problem of leisure, really, is largely a problem of substituting urban leisure time for rural leisure," he said. It was, indeed, no great problem on the farm; but the man transferred from the farm to the city, bewildered by its multiple distractions, and endowed with increased free time by shorter work hours, has a profound psychological adjustment to make. How does he make it, or how should he? "I raise the question without really being able to answer it," said Mr. Heckscher, but on another point he was more definite. Automation, which is so greatly changing the character of work from predominantly blue-collar to predominantly white-collar ("they make roads with great machines and dig ditches with ditch-diggers"), is also eventually going to create an unemployment problem. Here, he took direct issue with Mr. Blough's conclusion that automation creates more jobs than it displaces. "Certainly, that has been true on the record and up to this point," Mr. Heckscher conceded. "However, I myself cannot believe that that is going to continue indefinitely— at least, not if we somewhat stabilize our desires, and curtail our frantic search for innovation. If you are going to scrap your products and require completely new tooling every five years or so, I suppose one could go on indefinitely recreating the tools which make automation possible. If we are going to stabilize our tastes and our desires . . . automation is going to have effects far beyond those that Mr. Blough, for example, sees."

Mr. Calder of Edinburgh called attention to some statistics that he thought might give perspective to the discussion. Man's physical work, he said, is the most expensive energy in the world; in the present situation of the United States, according to some calculations, the energy expended by one man flicking one switch does the equivalent work of one hundred and forty slaves toiling for a day without any machinery. And from there he went to the population problem: In an underdeveloped country with a large and uncontrollably growing population, people must be kept at work, and thus the transition to the vastly cheaper energy supplied by industrialization simply cannot be accomplished. For such countries, it is a question of finding a way to solve the economic problems attendant on automation; whereas for already-developed countries, the problem is largely that of leisure.

Mr. de Madariaga returned to the question of urbanization—the magnetic attraction of the cities, the siren song of the movie marquee and the juke box, "particularly in the south of Europe, in Italy, Spain, and Greece, where the flight from the land is quite apart from any allurement of industry to the cities; it is probably out of boredom." The same thing, he said, is happening elsewhere—in Latin America, for example, where huge slums are being created and perpetuated in Rio de Janeiro and Buenos Aires by such migration. Should we not begin to work on an international basis to find ways of arresting this depopulation of the land, perhaps by making the rural life more bearable?

David Rockefeller, agreeing that the shift has to be dealt with, questioned the view that it is caused primarily by the boredom and discomforts of rural life and suggested that the cause may be the mechanization and industrialization of agriculture that makes the demand for manual work on the land so much less. At any rate, the process is going on, and in a massive way. Mr. Rockefeller quoted estimates that the United States population will increase before the end of this century by between sixty and eighty million—and that *all* of these additional people will live in urban centers.

Mr. Kimberly of Kimberly-Clark controverted a common notion by asserting that one of the reasons for automation's rapid spread is that it simply permits higher standards of quality control in manufacturing than are possible when quality control is done entirely by human efforts. That automation had permitted industrial growth such as would have been impossible without it, Mr. Kimberly considered self-evident; a top executive of Bell Telephone had told him that if that company were not automated, in five years from now it would be necessary for every girl in the United States to be a switchboard operator—and still there would not be enough!

But as things are going, Mr. Heckscher objected, there soon will not be any human telephone operators at all.

And yet, Mr. Kimberly countered, automation has not caused a drop in the Telephone Company's employment rolls.

This paradoxical ability of mechanized industry, up to now, to have its cake and eat it, seemed to be either a source of encouragement or of annoyance, depending on the individual participant's point of view. Mr. Kimberly went on to say that in his view the first task in the industrialization of underdeveloped countries is to educate them to the advantages of a developed economy, of which many of them are largely unaware. As to our domestic situation, he was optimistic:

> I think in our trial-and-error method we usually come through at the last minute with something that seems to work. What we are planning to do in the next ten years is subject to change every year as far as we are concerned, but I am very hopeful that, if we are cognizant of the problems in the areas in which we are concerned, those problems of education, work—and leisure is the smallest problem of the three in my book—will be reduced.

Mr. Rorimer, saying that he devotes "most of my time to thinking of what others should do with their leisure," wished to differ with Mr. Kimberly's downgrading of leisure as a national problem. He felt that our leisure is to a great extent being wasted, and the problem neglected, and as evidence he cited that at a recent museums conference it was stated that every one of the museums in the country is virtually bankrupt. "I think it is industry's job to take its surplus and help the institutions that can provide education, music, and the arts," said Mr. Rorimer. Mr. Kimberly's reply was that he had simply meant the problems of leisure can be solved through education, rather than by being dealt with separately.

Referring to Mr. Rorimer's suggestion about industrial aid to the arts, Ambassador Fay said he wanted to emphasize "something of fundamental importance—namely, that private industry, on its own, cannot be expected to do anything anti-economic." But, protested Mr. Heckscher, industry does uneconomic things all the time, "sometimes out of the generosity of its heart and sometimes out of the tactics of the union." (Mr. Heckscher had, of course, a strong card in hand that he disdained to play: the very conference at which the participants were sitting was hardly an economic activity.)

Mr. de Madariaga reduced the point to a parable: A friend of his, a Spanish writer, was criticized for being lazy, and advised that if he wrote more articles, he would be a rich man. The writer answered, "They do not realize how wealthy I am. I make $250 by writing an article; that is $250 which I spend at once by not writing. Let them figure it, and they can see I am a very wealthy man with very expensive tastes." "I do not see why economic laws should move a man if the man cannot move economic laws," Mr. de Madariaga commented. Then, on leisure:

> There is no outward leisure without inward leisure, and the inward leisure can only come to human beings who are at peace with themselves, and who are not worried by any prominent trouble. Well, most of us in the modern world are worried about prominent troubles, which are that we need movement, and we need speed. . . . Most of us cannot enjoy leisure.

Dean De Vane concurred, but put the matter in a more optimistic light. "There is not a man in this room," he said, "who does not normally work pretty nearly eighteen hours a day. . . . Our work and our leisure—really, it is a very hard thing indeed to call one one thing and the other another. The distribution of work has become as important a thing as the distribution of wealth. Now, I think, if you want to raise the suicide rate in this country, you will reduce the amount of work, and make it stick that a man may not work more than four hours a day."

Mr. Starr raised a labor man's distinction: The kind of work Mr. De Vane had been talking about, he said, is self-exploitation, undertaken voluntarily, and not to be confused with exploitation by an employer. Self-exploitative work—and here Mr. Starr agreed with Mr. De Vane—is practically indistinguishable from constructively-used leisure.

A question of choice of policy began gradually to emerge: Which course is more beneficial in an industrialized country— to put the first emphasis on raising the general living standard, or to put it on increasing the amount of the industrial worker's leisure time? Mr. Rockefeller, limiting himself to the situation of the United States at the present moment, said he felt that in view of the size and complexity of our national and international problems, he would rather see us go back to a forty-hour week rather than down to a thirty-hour week. Any increase in leisure time must for the present be sacrificed to the national interest. The reply of Mr. Heckscher was that we seem, to a surprising degree, to be getting both; that is, the history of shortened working hours over the past century has been equally the history of increased production at every level. Perhaps the world and ourselves would not necessarily be better off it we spent more time working than we do.

The example of the Soviet Union was now cited, as a sort of yardstick for our success or lack of it in handling work and leisure. Mr. Holland, on the basis of a recent trip there, spoke with approval of Russia's success in keeping people working productively on the land by a system of incentives. Mr. Heckscher pointed out that Russia, like the United States, has to an extraordinary degree put emphasis on limiting and reducing work hours; and Mr. Boeschenstein of Owens-Corning Fiberglas pointed out that as a result of this the Russians have their leisure problems, too: "You can see them wandering around with their families wondering what to do in the summertime, by the thousands."

Industrial society—as the conference seemed to be saying over and over again—tends to follow certain patterns regardless of the political systems within which it flourishes. Even in Russia, despite its best efforts, the flight from the land goes on; and Messrs. Rorimer and Fay, accepting this flight as a fact, spoke of the need for beautifying and humanizing our industrial cities. Mr. Fay cited Paris as a sort of ideal of a city that provides a setting for living and recreation, as well as work—indeed, perhaps to the detriment of work. "There is nowhere where one might wish more to loaf," said Mr. Fay. "I always felt a sort of grudge against the fact that I had to work there." On the other hand, "there are some cities . . . that are not planned at all and which are really a tragedy in terms of human lives."

Mr. Rorimer was more specific; he spoke of the inferiority in human terms of American cities to European ones. In New York, where the industrially-created atmosphere is such that all green plants have to struggle for bare survival, Mr. Rorimer had noted a saddening evidence of retreat—on a plot of ground beside the Waldorf-Astoria Hotel that was formerly brightened by grass, the management had now substituted pebbles, which do not need the constant services of a gardener. "It is a horrible thing to think about," said Mr. Rorimer. "Our cities in this country, with some few exceptions, because of the cost of maintenance . . . are not like those in Europe. And you come up with the conclusion that their salvation lies in pebbles." In short, because our concern for leisure is such that the gardener works short hours for high pay, the city cannot afford to beautify the place where people— the gardener included—might enjoy their newly-granted leisure. Here, surely, is a case of concern for more leisure time reaching the point of no return.

Thus in Panel III, the problems of industrial leisure were anatomized, the questions raised if not the answers given, and the worrisome conclusion reached that perhaps, in concentrating on quantity of leisure to the exclusion of quality, industrialized countries have lost sight of the forest in looking at the trees. United States failures in this area, the discussion had suggested, may not be due to a loss of national tradition but rather of an adherence to it: work and no leisure was the Puritan ethos on which the United States grew. The "patriot dream" in our second-favorite patriotic hymn speaks of "alabaster cities" that will "gleam undimmed by human tears"; alabaster is more nearly descriptive of spotless factories and dull high-rise apartment houses than of charming parks and playgrounds. Perhaps, the discussion had suggested, we have lived out the patriot dream too well, and need a new dream now. At any rate, Ambassador Malik, speaking out of the tradition of Christianity rather than that of industrialism, gave the others in the panel something to think about by asking the question, "Why is leisure a problem at all?"

To Mr. Malik, it seemed that the panel had depicted Western man as working eight hours for a living, and then wondering what to do with the remaining sixteen hours. To him, the picture seemed "abstract and false" because in addition to his economic activity, there are, or should be, at least seven other forms of activity that are important in his life. These, as he listed them, are family life; church; books; political life; local and national education; community life; and a personal cause, whatever it may be: "a commitment, a concern, an interest, a basic movement." So the real problem of leisure, as Mr. Malik saw it, is not the filling up of spare time but that of "the reinvigorating of family life, church life, good book reading, political life, the life of education, real communal life, and the fundamental purpose of life." But whether these objectives can be attained by any great number of people in a secular industrial society was a question about which many participants had grave doubts.

Panel IV, the self-proclaimed leisure-hater, after some initial sparring, was off again on its favorite point of contention, the

conflict between industry and culture. The session opened with
Mr. Blough and Sir Julian Huxley debating whether industrialism—of which this panel had recently finished formulating its
admirably clear and complete description—is a "way of life" or
not. Mr. Blough said it is: "It applies to everything you do and
it's all interrelated. An industrialized society is—well, it's the way
you educate the youth. You cannot have industry today without
education. It's that complicated, but it's also that simple. Everything in the United States that I know of is part of the total
picture—unless it is a ladies' literary society some place, and even
there, I think, they are affected by industrialized society."

Sir Julian countered that industrialism "affects your way of
life, but it isn't a way of life"; the increase in leisure time permits an industrial worker to develop quite another "way of life"
in his time off. Mr. Blough was unconvinced, maintaining that
the difference between time on the job and off it is not and
cannot be that sharp: "We haven't developed a leisure that is
so much different from what we have had during the last forty
years."

Judge Wyzanski mediated, as it were, between the litigants.
The point, he argued, is not whether or not industrialism is a
way of life in itself, but rather how it uses its powers to influence
in a good direction the way of life that surrounds it:

> Industrialized society is furnished with a great wealth of choice.
> The choices are not only those of the coercion of the iron law
> of wages or the coercion of the state power. They are all the per-
> suasive choices from religion, through philosophy, through the
> arts—all the creative aspects of man. And our blindness to our
> persuasive power is the greatest indictment of our society.

Now Mr. Wheeler of Pitney-Bowes led the panel into its main
debate by vigorously attacking the notion that industrialism's
"way of life" is an anti-cultural one. "As a matter of fact," he
said, "industrialization brings more opportunity to bring the
humanities into practical play of living than anything that has
ever occurred. Why? Because you have organization, as Roger

Blough has pointed out you must have. You have human beings working together as teams. They must cooperate and understand one another." Mr. Wheeler then suggested a way in which the men of the humanities—"the Ph.D's and the scholars and what-not"—are failing in their function. They do not communicate; they write in a private language, said Mr. Wheeler. "You read a great many of these papers and treatises and things and they are so verbose and so complicated that you almost give up before you start." Thus they fail to wield over industry and its attendant society the power of persuasion of which Judge Wyzanski had been speaking.

Rising to that challenge, Mr. Kazin attacked the idea of "communication for its own sake," which, he said, "results in terrible, terrible misconceptions of what thought and art are about." And the idea is prevalent all through American life: "Everywhere we put emphasis upon form rather than content"; teaching literature, for example, not as a subject of man's aspiration or man's gift of expression but in terms of the forms in which it is put; listening to hi-fi sets to gauge the scope of our loudspeakers rather than to be moved by music; transcribing books into movies or musical comedies with an evident disregard for the integrity of the original product of a writer's mind. All this, Mr. Kazin charged, is the result of industrial thinking, of making communication a thing in itself; and the effect: "industrialized art, industrialized taste, industrialized entertainment."

Sir Julian said he agreed with Mr. Kazin and went on to defend the scholars' complicated ways of expressing themselves. Complicated matters simply cannot be explained simply, he said; and to understand them, the reader must be willing to bring to the task both effort and self-discipline. "For instance, if you are to enjoy your leisure in exercise like mountaineering, you've got to discipline your body," said Sir Julian, "and by the same token, if you are to enjoy or profit from either *War and Peace* or a historical treatise, you must be willing to discipline your mind in preparation."

Mr. Wheeler complained that he had been attacked on ground that he was not seeking to defend; he had not meant symphonies, novels, or paintings, but only treatises on the problems of industrialized society, which, he still insisted, are "unduly complex. . . . They could be written a great deal simpler, if they are meant to influence the industrial society and the attitude of industry." Mr. Blough stood shoulder-to-shoulder with Mr. Wheeler:

> I would like to say that the art of communicating is a most important art and while the understanding may be a complicated thing, it does no good for a philosopher to attempt to communicate with our poor understandings in business about philosophy unless he puts it in terms which can be comprehended.

Mr. Blough went on to maintain that any philosopher, critic, or theologian living and working in industrial society, who fails to make the effort necessary to understand that society, thereby loses effectiveness. Turning to Mr. Houston, he pointed out that the very sheets of paper Mr. Houston uses in his work with the Eskimos on West Baffin Island is the result of an industrial process: "You rely upon an industrialized society. . . . Everything we do is a part of an industrial society. What I am trying to say is that we are all interrelated."

And now it was Mr. Kazin's turn to light into intellectuals like himself, but on grounds different from those of Mr. Wheeler and Mr. Blough. The failure of the American intelligentsia, he said, is not that they refuse to speak the common language out of arrogance or fear of contamination by industrialism; it is rather that they have been debased by being *too much* influenced by the thought habits implicit in industrialism. The trouble with the essays on industrial society that had proved a problem to Mr. Wheeler, said Mr. Kazin, was not that the papers were written on too high an intellectual level, as Mr. Wheeler had modestly implied. The trouble was the precise opposite: that the papers were sloppily thought out and expressed, couched in esoteric jargon in order to conceal their barrenness of thought and slipshodness of craft, and then buttressed up by the author's learned degree or his institution's prestige—exactly as a shoddy industrial product may be successfully merchandised by fancy packaging. And the reason for these failings, said Mr. Kazin, was that "in some way the image of making something and then selling it has been allowed to affect the way of thinking" of all of us—intellectuals included.

Mr. Kazin pursued his attack on his own breed relentlessly:

> More and more, we don't have philosophers in America; we have professors of philosophy. . . . There is very little original thinking. I am convinced of it in my field. I feel sorry for my country when I think of all the academicians who dress up their thought, by working in collaboration as if they were working in an assembly line, and kid themselves that they are doing some real thinking, when in point of fact they are merely dressing up, packaging, and even advertising their thought. . . .
>
> I am increasingly worried about the intellectual level of our intellectuals. . . . The trouble is that the domination by industry of the way we live externally has come to seem to many of us an expression of our total dissipation in it. I don't think that is really true. Exactly as a man in your capacity, Mr. Blough, can still feel nostalgia for an earlier America, which you expressed to me yesterday privately, so a man living in this society can today think thoughts which are, in the deepest sense, metaphysical. What troubles me is not that these thoughts aren't thought in America any more, but some way or another people who do feel these things feel that they are not in step, that they are not modern.

This brilliant summation of the worst cultural effects of industrialism seemed rather to take the panel's breath away; at any rate, it spent the next few minutes in a rather desultory exchange about the teaching of science and philosophy, as if it needed a breather. And then Mrs. Bunting of Radcliffe came back to the single word that had touched off the debate—the word "communication." Mrs. Bunting said, "I want to add just one point which I think we all understand but I don't think anyone has quite said. . . . The thing you are calling for, Mr. Wheeler, is just as necessary, even if it is not the same thing, as our great big academic theses. . . . Let's say the *History of West-*

ern Philosophy by Russell is not the same thing as Plato; that doesn't mean it isn't an awfully useful thing in increasing understanding. . . . And abstracts: an abstract is not the original article, but my lands, how useful it is!"

Mr. Blough re-emphasized his point about the necessity for philosophers, just as for industrialists, to understand the modern world, including its science and technology. He also introduced the disarming argument that the very presence in the room of so many distinguished intellectuals seemed to *prove* that industrial society can produce them:

> It is just as important . . . to know what Fermi was doing and what Einstein was doing as it is to know what Newton was doing. Those things can't be overlooked. I don't know whether Mr. Kazin, or Dr. Huxley, or Judge Wyzanski, or [Mrs. Bunting] will some day go down in philosophical or other history; but I am quite confident, and I have no reason to believe otherwise, that somewhere in the United States today—somewhere in England, somewhere in France, Europe, somewhere in Asia, Africa—there are people who mean just as much from the standpoint of new thought to the human race as the people we have referred to in older ages.
>
> So, my final point is this: We have had several phases discussed here this morning that interest me a great deal. One was that our present-day culture is dominated by industry; another was industry's effect upon our culture. . . . As far as my own view is concerned, [the second point] is a misconception. It isn't a culture which is affected by industry. It is an industrial culture, and to think of it otherwise is simply thinking of it in parts as distinguished from the whole.

So Panel IV had accomplished something concrete, and something not at all easy: It had opened up certain lines of "communication" between those representing industry and culture. (Again, the silent Mr. Diké must have been listening with fascination.) Mr. Chapman of Buenos Aires suggested that the new-found contact be applied to a consideration of industrial leisure; and while this leisure-wary panel can hardly be said to have adopted the suggestion, the attempt to accept it resulted in a rewarding final phase of the session—just as an attempt to tell a child the facts of human reproduction may lead to an interesting abstract discussion of botany and entomology. Sir Julian, speaking of leisure in its broadest sense, wanted to differ with the view that the function of leisure in industrial society is to keep the system going through the consumption of produced goods. He saw this view, and the mechanization of leisure that results from it, as the product of a bad tendency of industrial society "to externalize everything—to think in extrovert terms."

Like so many speakers in the other panels, Sir Julian saw leisure as a time for turning inward rather than outward, for exploring your inner being and finding out what you are. Judge Wyzanski chimed in with agreement; industrialism, he insisted, makes possible a wise as well as an unwise use of leisure—just as it makes possible a wise as well as an unwise use of the great power it creates. Thus the Judge led the way into a discussion of industrial power, in which, by virtue of his corporate position, Mr. Blough had to play two roles at the same time: (1) Mr. Blough the man, and (2) Chairman Blough the symbol of industrial power.

Such power, said Judge Wyzanski—*pace* Lord Acton—does not necessarily corrupt; the wielders of such power must learn, as there is increasing evidence that they *are* learning, that "there is a social responsibility which each of us has as to his brother. We are our brother's keepers, and there is no escape from the obligation."

It was at this point that Mr. Lilienthal noticed how fast and how far the panel had strayed from leisure:

> May I make a trivial remark? It's quite evident that . . . we are simply unable to discuss leisure. . . . Anyone who disagrees with Charlie Wyzanski invites decapitation. I'm about to lose my head, but in a rump session—not here. . . .

> JUDGE WYZANSKI: Rump is not what comes off in decapitation.

The idea that Mr. Lilienthal wanted to introduce, in contradiction of Wyzanski, was that industrial society does not increase the power of the individual over other individuals; in fact, he said, "I think exactly the reverse is true."

SIR JULIAN: I do too—I do too.

JUDGE WYZANSKI: I didn't mean power of the individual. I meant the total fund of power. . . . I don't mean it to increase the power of Mr. Blough. Mr. Blough has far less power than his predecessors had in the United States Steel Corporation. He can't do half the things. He is a constitutional monarch with the diffused power of the Queen.

MR. LILIENTHAL: Good.

All eyes turned to Mr. Blough.

MR. BLOUGH: I just want to add, while agreeing with this—I object a little to the word "monarchy," but—

SIR JULIAN: Constitutional? You don't object to that, sir?

Mr. Blough nodded his head in agreement; Mr. Diké rubbed his eyes, perhaps in wonderment at the ways of industrial society.

Finally on leisure in the closing moments, the panel turned up some good thoughts on that topic. Dr. Glasser suggested that in its avoidance of leisure, America, like Panel IV, is "a little bit grim": that our emphasis on the value of work goes too far. Sir Julian, taking a leaf from Dr. Glasser's book, pointed out that psychological findings insist on the necessity of "dreaming" for mental health. Mr. Kilgore of the *Wall Street Journal* suggested that perhaps if leisure is not scarce, it becomes devalued like a commodity that is in oversupply: "then it becomes unemployment."

Mr. Houston, drawing on the experience of his remarkable microcosm on West Baffin Island, stated some facts that underlined the problem of finding out just what leisure is—and, perhaps, the advantages of not trying to set it apart from the rest of life. Mr. Houston recounted that when he had tried to introduce the concept of a weekend to the Eskimos, they would have nothing to do with it; they reasoned that the weather on the weekend might not be good, and therefore they didn't want one.

When Mr. Houston arrived, hunting to the Eskimos was work; now that the making of art and craft objects has been introduced among them as a means of subsistence—an industry—the same hunting that used to be work has become leisure. By the same token, with a slight change of economic emphasis, hunting could be work again, and print-making leisure. Perhaps nowhere else in the conference was the ideal solution to the leisure "problem" so perfectly stated.

The Saturday-morning activities of Panels I and II have been saved for last in this account, because it was in those panels that there appeared the greatest disposition to summarize.

Mr. de Kiewiet, Panel I's bee-keeping chairman, announced at the outset that one of his bees had been buzzing in his ear before starting time. The buzzer was Raymond Aron, who had let the chairman know that, as a result of overnight thoughts, he wanted to make "some irreverent remarks about our discussion yesterday."

Mr. Aron's irreverent remarks were these: First of all, the theme of the conference was "The Individual in the Modern World." It seemed clear to Mr. Aron that, in such a context, Western Europe is more important than, say, Nigeria, in spite of the respect and esteem that he or anyone else might have for Nigeria. Yet in Panel I (and, Mr. Aron might have added if he had heard them, in most of the other panels), the American participants in thinking about modern society had tended to think about Nigeria. And this seemed to Aron to be "a very good revelation of the present mood of the American community"—a mood of journalistic crystal-ball gazing, of putting more importance on what will be or should be, rather than what is. Another mood that he had noticed in the previous day's discussion was that of American self-criticism, which, said Mr. Aron, made it difficult for a foreigner to intervene (and here again, what he said applied equally well to other panels). Mr. Aron was inclined to be critical of American self-criticism: "It is a permanent illusion of American discussions that if you were better, you would have more success in the cold war." This is not so, he thought; indeed, America's self-critical mood may be a liability in the cold war, because "when you are helping other people, when you are rich and other people are poor, if, beyond your richness, you have also virtue, it is much more difficult for other people to accept it."

Finally: It was wrong, said Mr. Aron, for the panel to have discussed the cold-war issue. That was not supposed to be the subject of the conference; and it is far easier to talk about "moral mobilization" than to know what it means, or to do anything about it. "We must aim at a good society," said Aron, "not because we will win the cold war, but because it is good to live in a good society." And the essence of a good society, in the sense of a free society, is that it have "no blueprint, either for itself or for the rest of the world"—that it have and that it live by certain values and certain moral convictions, but be pragmatic and empirical when it comes to the organization of economy.

Thus Aron, as a shrewd critic of the discussion itself, had given the panel plenty of food for discussion in its final session.

Professor Hauser of Chicago objected to the Aronian remarks on several counts. First, considering their importance to the individual as to every other aspect of modern life, Mr. Hauser thought the panel had been right to discuss both the situation of underdeveloped countries like Nigeria, and the huge fact of the East-West conflict. On the matter of "no blueprint," he thought that, in view of the high stakes involved, the United States would do well to impose "the kind of mobilization controls that may be necessary"—to impose, that is, a kind of blueprint. And such planning would inevitably involve greater public expenditures at the expense of private expenditures.

Mr. Gruen, a maker of blueprints by profession, took instant alarm at one Aron point: "The difference is not one of planning or not planning. The difference is between autocratic planning and democratic planning. In city planning, it expresses itself very clearly. . . . In architectural planning, there is a difference between the striking array in Berlin and the staring apartment-house arrangements in Moscow—the autocratic, inhuman plan, without any human or personal content." Mr. Aron allowed that he had been speaking of blueprints in a broader metaphorical sense, not of architectural blueprints:

When I used the word "blueprint," it was not to make the living of Mr. Gruen more difficult—

MR. GRUEN: Difficult? Impossible!

MR. ARON: The blueprint of a city is not the blueprint for the salvation of mankind. They are two different things.

Mr. Dunn backed up Mr. Gruen, saying that as a student of health problems he was very much aware of the need for community improvement to create more gracious living places—and that takes planning. No objection came from Mr. Aron, and the point appeared to be cleared up.

Now came more second thoughts. Dr. Escalona had worked up a sort of psychoanalytic critique of the previous discussion. "The question of why people behave as they do, whether it be in architecture or economics or conferences, is something about which psychologists have thought a little bit," she said. Why, then, had the people in Panel I behaved as they had? According to Dr. Escalona, as soon as the previous day's discussion had touched on the unintended and undesired by-products of industrial society, the group's mood had become problematic, even breast-beating:

That is what invariably happens if one is confronted with the discomfort of having intended one thing and brought about another thing, or the discomfort of recognizing the coexistence of some highly desirable and some highly undesirable things, in which one is responsibly involved. . . . It is more comfortable to be harshly self-critical, in problematic terms, than it is to look at the phenomena and try to see where we have failed to understand, where we still fail to understand. . . .

Perhaps the question that was transmitted to us by Dr. Diké yesterday is precisely the key question that we can't answer. As you will recall, the way it was put was, "We don't want you to tell us how to organize our society. We would like you to tell us how to avoid some of the mistakes you have made." I submit that, perhaps, one of the outcomes of this kind of informed discussion is to say [to Dr. Diké], "We don't know."

Thus admonished by Dr. Escalona, the panel spent the rest of its final session trying to "look at the phenomena and see where we have failed to understand." And, inevitably, the needle of the panel's barometer turned to education. Again inevitably, the discussion of education went over many of the points that had been made by others the previous afternoon. Degree-mania must be avoided; education of women must become broadened and made more in keeping with the times; the barriers between the various departments in our universities must be lowered; education must not be thought of as a panacea; and so on.

But Panel I had its own special emphasis in its discussion of education as a road to self-understanding. That emphasis was on a generalization of American education, a desegregation of education from other aspects of life—a metaphorical breaking down of university walls. This was first enunciated by Franklin Ford, professor of history at Harvard. Mr. Ford asked the panel to direct its attention to education conceived of as "the whole complex of efforts by which a society tries to transmit its culture to its young, and to prepare them to contribute further to it." This implies, of course, "fewer professional fences around the conception of education," and if some such fences could be taken down, Mr. Ford thought most people would be better-educated. Unfortunately, under the impact of population growth and the attendant huge growth in educational institutions, the American situation has gone the other way: the college degree has become enormously more important economically, the line between education and no-education has become sharper. But Mr. Ford, like McGeorge Bundy in his background paper, saw the opportunity for a reversal over the next few years. He saw the chance for an education more fully integrated into the individual's whole life, where the present rigid calendar notion of academic life would be broken down, where education might continue through adult life and might—as it has in some of the best-integrated societies of the past—merge with work and leisure so as to become almost indistinguishable from them.

Mr. Lovestone felt that something along these lines is already happening, and as evidence he cited the enormously growing attendance at night schools of all sorts among union members. Professor Hauser, going along with Professor Ford's ideals, saw existing formal educational institutions as the only agencies that could take the lead in the change; and, harassed as they are by enrollment demands—he spoke particularly of the millions of Negroes and Appalachian whites who have moved from the rural South to the urban North, and desperately need education to adapt to the change—such institutions face above all the problem of inadequate allocation of funds. This deficiency he laid squarely at the door of American business.

J. Stillman Rockefeller of the First National City Bank of New York, as a representative of business, let Mr. Hauser's charge go by default. Instead of answering it, he directed toward the panel—and particularly toward Dr. Escalona—the question, Is lifetime education possible? Is the human being so constituted that he can "go back to the books or go back even to the monasticism" at intervals during adult life? Dr. Escalona said she thought he can; that small segments of the population do, even now; and that the main factor in our society that makes such a regime seem difficult is our rigidity of thought about education, our tendency to classify it as an activity of youth—our emphasis on passively adapting to the existing environment rather than actively taking advantage of its possibilities. David G. Hill added that if it can be done, it must be; speaking from his experience as president of Pittsburgh Plate Glass Co., he said that "all of us in industry are experiencing the simple plain fact that a formal education will not last a lifetime." There is so much to be known these days that it cannot be absorbed in twelve or sixteen years, most of them years of immaturity.

Mr. Fuller of Shawinigan Chemicals, Ltd., complemented what Mr. Hill had said by pointing out that those adults who take advantage of educational opportunities afforded them—by industry or by their communities—are those who have acquired the motivation toward education early in life. Mr. Fuller's experience was that "the motivation, the desire to learn among the young people, if properly handled in the earlier years of their education, will carry on through their lifetime."

So the onus was back on the schools: They must create the desire to learn in their pupils, and the rest will take care of itself. The challenge was accepted by Professor Ford, who said, bluntly enough, that these demands on formal education made by the panel's industrialists emphasized Professor Hauser's question: "Where do the resources come from?" "Here," Mr. Ford added, "is where we may sound, for the moment, less visionary than you gentlemen." Did that sound a little like "put up or shut up"? It did. No one gave Mr. Ford a direct answer, or made a pledge to Harvard; but this hardly indicated that the import of the discussion had not taken effect. Perhaps one of the practical after-effects of the conference will be a deepened recognition by the industrialists present of education in all its phases as the keystone in the arch of our society.

Before the session adjourned there were two enlightening foreign views on the discussion; and then, from the chairman, in his capacity as an educator and thus a man assigned to build a better keystone, a plea for patience and sympathy.

To Sir Muhammad Zafrulla Khan of Pakistan, the first participant from the Old World to break the American monopoly of the talk for a long time, a good deal of the discussion had been perplexing when not incomprehensible—the reason being that the modern world of Pakistan is simply not the modern world of the United States, Canada, and Western Europe. Yet, Sir Zafrulla pointed out, "Our modern world is the world in which we are living, although it may be three centuries before your modern world." What, then, are the problems of the individual in modern Pakistan?

The problem of education, he felt, was one of overspecialization along class lines. The workmen—for the most part, farmers who are slowly becoming factory workers as industrialization proceeds—are educated in too limited a technical sense, in too *ad hoc* a fashion. On the other hand, in the classical education of the governing class, technical skills and handicrafts are neglected to the point of exclusion. "I wish," said Sir Zafrulla, "that when I started going to school, I could somehow or other have been taught the use of my hands, in some respect or other—gardening, carpentry, and so on." (Sir Zafrulla's criticism of education in Pakistan closely parallels that set forth by Mr. Diké in his background paper on education in Nigeria—like Pakistan, a recently-independent nation that had long lived under British rule.)

As to leisure, Sir Zafrulla said that the motive behind its use in Pakistan at present seems to be very largely escape and nothing else: "The cinema is the great attraction, and the attraction is not so much that one will amuse oneself in a very healthy way. . . . It has a sort of attraction, no doubt, but the main thing is that they will not sit down and face themselves." What is needed is some encouragement to the newly-industrialized worker in Pakistan, and in countries like it, to use at least part of their free time "to commune with himself; to commune with his family; to commune with his Maker." (*vide* Mr. Malik.)

The previous discussion here and in other panels had made it plain enough that, despite its century-plus head start, the West has not yet found a way to such contemplative use of leisure as Sir Zafrulla called for. Mr. Aron now seemed to imply that, despite superficial differences, the broad educational aims of countries like Nigeria and Pakistan and countries like the United States must be the same. Wherever the educational system be, it faces a double imperative: that of educating technicians to do the jobs that must be done in industrial society, and that of educating citizens who will "maintain the continuity of intellectual and moral tradition." Mr. Aron's last word on leisure was also, plainly, another challenge to education: "The quality of leisure will be the expression of the quality of society and the quality of the people concerned."

Mr. de Kiewiet, shouldering the loads that were so heartily being thrust on the educator from all sides, could be forgiven for calling attention to their weight. Both the number of students and the body of knowledge they must be taught are proliferating at a furious rate: In New York State alone, he pointed out, over the next ten or fifteen years as much new educational brick-and-mortar must be raised as has been raised over the last two centuries. As to the body of knowledge, J. R. Oppenheimer has said that it now doubles every ten years. Have patience with us! Mr. de Kiewiet pleaded. Give us your sympathy, and if possible, your cash!

> All of this adds up to a burden, a physical burden—lack of time, lack of personnel—that people in society sometimes do not understand. I would like, if you will forgive me, to convey to sympathetic people like yourselves some sense, not merely of the burden, but of the frustration that the organized educational institutions in this country suffer at the present moment when, willing and perhaps a little too gladly, they take on the burdens and obligations that are suggested to them. At the same time, they do not get the resources or, sometimes, the basic understanding to make it possible for them to make their contributions in the fullness and the magnitude which, I think, is indispensable.

In the cafeteria, Panel II returned to its *"meistersinger* arrangement"; the morning was devoted to brief statements by each participant answering the question, "What do you consider to be the crucial problem or problems facing the individual in the modern world?" The result, while it could not possibly be a summary of the whole conference, was a kind of microcosm of it. Most of the problems that had been discussed in more or less detail by the various panels were brought up, and the diversity of the problems raised drew attention to the breadth of the conference's concerns.

Two participants, Mr. Scheff of the Flint Glass Workers and

Frazar B. Wilde, board chairman of Connecticut General Life Insurance Co., spoke of specific practical problems of work and economic life.

Mr. Scheff felt that the basic problem is worker security; that is, steady employment or a guaranteed annual wage and a reduced work week. "I made the statement yesterday that what was good for the people in this country would be good for the people of the world," said Mr. Scheff. "I haven't changed my mind about that. . . . I think that we can accomplish our objectives and do something for the good of humanity."

Mr. Wilde acknowledged, "These remarks are far from philosophical. They do not go to the root of the larger problems. They are a businessman's observation in a specific field." The problem that Mr. Wilde addressed himself to was the crucial one of the worker displaced by automation. Unlike many of those who raised broader problems, Mr. Wilde proposed a solution: the retraining of such displaced workers for other jobs under corporate auspices, to be encouraged by a federal tax credit to corporations for this purpose. As a man who has lived and worked all his life in New England, where changing economic and technological patterns have overthrown a whole economy in his time, Mr. Wilde obviously spoke from the heart.

Two participants put their emphasis on particular educational problems. Mr. Stanovnik said, "I see no major problem for the moment other than the problem of how to educate man, how to make it possible for him to know more about science. The more he knows about science, the less dependent he will be on the spontaneous forces of nature." That first, everything else afterward—a view that certainly had the virtues of clarity and resolution.

Mr. Hrones of Case Institute also spoke of technical education, but in a different context. The problem of training engineers, he said, is that technological progress moves so fast these days that one education will not begin to last a lifetime; and the solution lies in emphasizing not the particular engineering techniques and concepts current at the time of the student's education, but rather a broad base in the sciences and in classical mathematics that will enable the engineer to grow and change with his times.

Two others made conspicuous use of the word "leadership."

Mr. Chapman of the New York Public Library felt that man's greatest problem—"whether he's a scientist, an educator, a businessman, a union leader, or a politician"—is that of not simply knowing, but of understanding. Leadership requires specialization, but does not exclude broad comprehension—which, today, is too often lacking in our leaders. Mr. Chapman's recommendations were that education for leadership be aimed at producing a broad cultural understanding to set off the necessary specialization, and toward that end that the habit of reading be encouraged more than it is now.

Mr. Fitzroy of Richmond University Center said:

> Quite independently of Mr. Chapman, I came [last evening] to the conclusion that the need was for politicians. I mean politicians in the best sense. I mean these individuals in our social structure who can engineer the compromises that are necessary if social change is to take place without revolution. I include the President and the senators who are sitting down in Washington this morning, questioning a handful of industrialists. I include the councilmen here in Corning who are concerned about the possible development of a slum area.

But having arrived at that decision, Mr. Fitzroy recounted, he had concluded that perhaps he was being naïve. He had asked several other participants to tell him what they thought the basic problem was. The first said, "In America, racial segregation." The second said, "Acceleration. Things are moving too fast." The third said, "Man works too much. He must learn to loaf." (The reader of the preceding pages will be able to make some judicious guesses as to whom Mr. Fitzroy had been questioning.) The fourth said, "The population explosion." The fifth said, "The problem is segregation." The answers having come full circle,

Mr. Fitzroy decided that he had been right in the first place: the need is for enlightened leadership. Where are the competent and necessary leader compromises of the future to come from?

Another pair of participants emphasized the problem of leisure. Mr. Paget the management consultant said that in his view the putting of free time to constructive use is our critical problem, and one in which the services of not only educational institutions but also the churches and the communities must be actively enlisted. Because "on the wise and understanding use of this leisure time may well, it seems to me, depend the success or failure of what we call our present culture." And Sir Oliver Franks put it this way:

> I suspect that the problem Mr. Scheff was speaking of—unemployment—will be resolved not by finding more jobs. There may not be more jobs. It will be resolved by people doing less time in their work. The work will diminish. . . . In industrial society people have, to a great extent, found their security in the sense of belonging to and contributing to their society in their work. If work time progressively diminishes, then I think it becomes more difficult to have that sense of full contribution and full security.

To sum it up in a few words, the problem appeared to Sir Oliver as "how to make work satisfying; how to make leisure purposeful."

To move on to those who framed their statements in more broadly philosophical terms, Miss Rukeyser, the poet, spoke of creativity and its uses. She put her problems in their elemental form, that of questions. But it would be wrong to think of them as philosophical questions—they were a poet's questions:

> For the sake of what do we risk our lives, or work all our lives long, or ask others to make way for machines? How can we work with the forces that make life creative? How can we work against the waste and destruction of people's lives, their relationships, and their creativity? How can we become aware again of the forgotten forces? How can we help to create a present that will allow this change to go on in our own lifetime . . . so as not to destroy the lives of people as we do, but to nurture people and meanings?

How can we help to create a present that means a continual birth for ourselves and our culture, and an exchange of life with all other cultures?

To three of the members of Panel II, the problem centered on the relationships between cultures.

Tengku Dzulkarnain, dean of the law faculty of the University Islam Sumatra Utara, Indonesia—and a participant who had had little to say during most of the conference—now had a great deal to say in a few words. The notion had been repeatedly expressed that what happens in the United States and in Western Europe today is bound to happen in other countries of the world tomorrow. Mr. Dzulkarnain did not think that this is so. Industrialization may eventually come to a country like Indonesia, he said, but it will be a long process, and its result may be something very different from Western Europe or the United States. "When the same events happen in two countries, the reaction of the people will not be the same," said Mr. Dzulkarnain. "This is why I want to warn you not to generalize. . . . Speaking politically, I see this as the reason why many Western countries—the United States not excluded—have failed in foreign policy."

Mr. Allam of Cairo listed the leading disadvantages of industrial society, as he saw them and as they had been enumerated by other participants: unemployment, increased leisure improperly used, materialism, deterioration of mental and physical health, lack of comprehension—and saw the chief means of combatting them in looking outward rather than looking inward:

> The world is smaller today than it ever was, and year by year it is getting smaller. I think we have to try to get some insight as to what is going on in other parts of the world, and how the people in these other parts are affected by us.

Professor Herskovits of Northwestern supported Mr. Dzulkarnain and Mr. Allam from a Western point of view. To him, the chief needs of the West, and of the United States in particular, are to fight specialization—to work toward a society in which work, leisure, and education will flow together rather than remain capable of being put in separate compartments—and to develop a quality that he called "cultural modesty": that is, an understanding that "just because we have machines does not mean we have the answers to human problems; just because we have solved the problem of subsistence and leisure does not mean that we can tell other people that our values are necessarily the supreme values." As a final point, Professor Herskovits thought industrialized societies must work toward fuller use of their human resources, by which he meant, specifically, a fuller participation of women in the work and direction of society.

Professor Stone of Sydney, Australia, like Professor Aron in Panel I, was skeptical of blue prints for the future, seeing an essential characteristic of free society in its lack of them. He put the problem as it appeared to him in terms of awareness: If scientists, historians, social commentators, and educators could learn to "acknowledge and exhibit the specific features of a science culture," then Professor Herskovits' cultural modesty might emerge, and the gap between our social ideals and our social practice be narrowed.

Three participants allowed themselves to be overtly optimistic, however guardedly, about the future of the individual in industrial society.

Mr. Leithead of Cluett Peabody made a paradigm of himself: He had come from a rural environment to a citadel of industrialism, and he had no hesitation in saying that he was glad to have made the change, if only because he didn't like milking cows at 4 A.M. Referring to Professor Herskovits' statement that the blood pressure of South Africans went up when they moved from the bush to big cities, Mr. Leithead retorted, "I can only tell you that mine went down. I was very anxious to get away from the farm." He was convinced that the necessary adjustments of man to industrial society can be made in time, so long as "we have the freedom to make these adjustments in our own way."

Mr. Larrabee the author-journalist quoted Robert Frost: "If there is any divine purpose in history, it is that it shall always be equally difficult for man to save his soul." In Mr. Larrabee's view, the scientific technical revolution is irreversible, and it is a major turning point in human experience, and it neither increases nor decreases the chance for a man to save his soul. The problem of saving it for industrialized man is the problem of remaining oneself while still contributing to society—in David Reisman's terms, which Mr. Larrabee quoted, of remaining autonomous while being other-directed. As to the probable spread of the West's way of life to the rest of the world, "It is our conviction that what will work for us is likely to work elsewhere"—a belief that, for Mr. Larrabee's own part, is "simply an act of faith in a statement of mixed hope."

And Professor Guerlac, as a science historian to some extent committed to a hopeful view of a scientific civilization, gave an admirable demonstration of one kind of cultural modesty by putting much of the blame for our present dilemmas on the shoulders of scientists. His assumption was that industrialization is "a necessary but not sufficient condition of human happiness." How, then, to make it sufficient? Through the fostering of greater respect for the abstract values behind industrialism, and the setting of higher standards of taste by our leaders—goals which, in Professor Guerlac's view, are not always well served by our scientists, industrial leaders, or educators.

Finally, what unity there was in the striking—and, undeniably, individualistic—diversity of the Saturday-morning statements in Panel II may be suggested by comparing the two of those statements not already reported: those of Dean Coburn and Dr. Alexander.

Dr. Alexander, the man of medical science, said:

We all agree that we live in a rapidly changing world. If we want to characterize it, it is industrialization and technology. It reduced the whole format of human life. It reduced the efforts necessary to satisfy man's fundamental biological needs. This resulted in interesting social and psychological problems. . . .

The question now is, How to use the energies which are no longer needed in the same degree for economic goals? . . . I would summarize this way: That the problem which Western man today really faces is how to build on the solid foundation of economic achievement a second story of civilization.

Dean Coburn, the man of God, said:

It seems to me that the central problem we are faced with, whether in this conference or as part of the human race, is the problem of meaning. That to be a man is to ask the question "Why?" . . . If men find meaning, then they live. If they don't find meaning, then they've lost stature as men. . . .

If our technical societies help to set men free so that they can really pursue the truth, that is going to help make men truly free, ultimately. It's when partial understanding of the truth is given the authority over all search for truth that we get into trouble, it seems to me. . . .

I don't want to pretend that religion has any easy answers. I think the religious dimension opens up an area of understanding. Professor Herskovits talks about cultural modesty; I would like to suggest religious modesty. . . .

If this society that we are in sets men free in terms of response to truth wherever it is, then we can afford to trust truth, and truth within the more ultimate framework of faith. Then, I think, life can be affirmed positively, and men can go about their business with not only all the difficulties of monotonous work, but with all the difficulties of suffering, pain, sorrow, tragedy, death—and affirm that the whole enterprise is good.

CHAPTER 7

᧞

A CLOSING PERSPECTIVE

᧞

THE VALUE OF A CONFERENCE like this," one of the participants said between sessions, "depends upon whether you think people can communicate with each other with words." (Indeed, the serious problem of the questionable value of words for communication had been raised in one of the formal sessions by Pendleton Herring.) Surely this is true. In a conference so brief as to permit little scope for the more intuitive forms of communication, it was words or nothing. Putting on such an affair represented an act of faith: faith not only that the air-conditioning would work and that the participants would arrive on time and in good order; but more than this, faith that the participants would say something worth while—would not, for all their influence and learning, talk a lot of nonsense.

While there were many failures of communication at the Second Corning Conference—all of the participants spoke fluent English, but there were moments of misunderstanding so profound that the common language seemed useless—in the end, the faith of the planners was soundly rewarded. For the editor, a summer spent immersed in the conference transcript has been a sort of trip around the modern world of ideas. The conference provided a comprehensive glossary of current thought. It was descriptive while it was not prescriptive. All of the major ideas that influence modern society came up at one time or another, and most of them were tested by being challenged. There was usually a sense of people condensing material, saying less than they knew rather than more.

The total effect was to project a huge, close-up image of the society we live in onto a wide screen in unsparing realism. Some of the individual participants emerge from the dialectic as almost allegorical figures. Mr. Diké of Nigeria, smiling and eager to learn, yet proud, firm, and unshakable on what he knew, was emerging Africa; Mr. Moraes, suave and subtle and somewhat aloof, was neutral India; and Mr. Dzulkarnain, who remained silent until the end of the conference and then said flatly that United States policy in his corner of the world has largely failed, seemed all too convincing a representative of the mood of such a country as Indonesia. Not only figures but events were somewhat allegorical. The unexpected eruption of East-West tensions at the Friday-evening dinner meeting came painfully close to being an unrehearsed re-enactment of a United Nations session.

Apart from the drama of its familiar confrontations, there was a different sort of drama in the conference's unfamiliar ones. Under what other circumstances might Mr. Blough of United States Steel have sat down to discuss the effects of industry on culture with Mr. Kazin, the literary critic? Such a confrontation seemed to represent something new and important in American life—or perhaps, something that has been lost in the course of our increasing specialization of work and must be regained. Did Messrs. Blough and Kazin go home changed? Will literary criticism and the management of United States Steel show the effects?

A note of questioning would seem to be the proper one on which to end this account. As has been said, there was no plenary session. (The absence of one was, perhaps, a small but telling blow against the American tendency, deplored by more than one participant, to abstract, to digest, to oversimplify by summing up.) At the conclusion of the Saturday-morning session, the participants were conveyed by bus to Spencer Hill, outside Corning, to watch the ground-breaking ceremonies for Corning Community College (an event of local importance that, perhaps because of its symbolic meaning, they all endured with excellent grace); then they were conveyed to the Knoll, the residence of former Ambassador and Mrs. Amory Houghton, for a farewell lunch. That afternoon, they began the trips—by automobile, train, boat, private or commercial plane, and in Mr. Houston's case, of course, dogteam—that would take them home to their respective corners of the world.

If their thoughts en route followed from their words at Corning, those thoughts may have been in the form of questions forged out of the give-and-take of the roundtables and tempered by the conference's pooled resources of knowledge and experience. The basic question was an old, though not a simple, one. If the conference had adopted a motto to state its central concern, the motto might have been Hamlet's words to his disappointing friends Rosencrantz and Guildenstern:

> . . . It goes so heavily with my disposition that this goodly frame, the earth, seems to me a sterile promontory; this most excellent canopy, the air, look you, this brave o'erhanging firmament, this majestical roof fretted with golden fire—why, it appears no other thing to me than a foul and pestilent congregation of vapors. What a piece of work is a man! how noble in reason! how infinite in faculty, in form and moving how express and admirable! in action how like an angel! in apprehension how like a god! the beauty of the world! the paragon of animals! And yet, to me, what is this quintessence of dust?

The conditions of May 1961 were new, but the problem itself was old. How to redeem this sterile promontory and make it a goodly frame? How to release this quintessence of dust to be in action like an angel, in apprehension like a god?

PART II

(NOTE: Some of the papers appear here in somewhat abridged form.)

CHAPTER 8

৶৵

THE INDIVIDUAL
IN MODERN SOCIETY

৶৵ KEYNOTE ADDRESS:
CHARLES HABIB MALIK

I

The derivation of man from and the reduction of man to material, economic, and social conditions is the great heresy of this age. Whether Karl Marx created this heresy or whether he only expressed in a radical manner an already pervasive temper of thought is a fit topic for a profound separate historical-cultural investigation. Whatever the truth of the matter, what is indubitable is that the Marxist interpretation of man has become increasingly dominant in recent years, and not only in the Communist realm. Who is not thinking and talking today of economic development, of the undeveloped, or underdeveloped, or less developed, or developing peoples, of social and economic justice, of economic and technical assistance, of the "revolution of rising expectations," of raising the standard of living of the masses, and of hunger, poverty, and disease as the primary enemies of mankind? In all this talk it is material-economic conditions that people are principally thinking of. According to this outlook the essential difference between people is the economic difference. What is important about a man, whether he comes from India or from France, is not his race or color, or culture, or religion, or learning, or moral perfection, or personal character, but his so-called economic status or class. The economic wealth you dispose of, the degree of material security you enjoy—whether in the form of money you have individually earned, or saved, or inherited, or of legal arrangements you have entered into with your employer, company, or corporation, or of governmentally guaranteed security in socialist states—this economic-material basis is the decisive distinction between man and man. And when thinkers or statesmen, say at the United Nations, compare different nations or peoples, they usually fasten on their economic development alone; everything else is forgotten—their culture, their religion, their outlook on life, their fundamental ideas, even their form of government. The one mortal sin today is not atheism, paganism, bigotry, tyranny, cruelty, oppression, immorality, or falsehood: The one mortal sin is to be behind materially, whether as an individual or as a nation.

We are face to face, then, with an incredible infatuation with the sheerly economic, with a species of idolatry of the material and elemental. Where Karl Marx has not won politically, he appears to have won ideologically. This Marxian onslaught has reached such proportions that when statesmen today talk about winning the cold war they usually stress the economic factor alone, passing by all other factors in silence. What people *are* intellectually, morally, and spiritually is unimportant; what you *are* and what therefore you may do for them in these realms is unimportant; what is important is the economic and technical assistance whereby you help them to build a "sound economy" and meet their material needs. Beat the Communists in this field, and people will oppose communism and you will have won the cold war.

One can quote endless passages by responsible men in which problems are finally reduced to their material-economic basis, with the evident presupposition that, if only one met these problems on this basis, all would be well. Here is a passage from a well-known author: "We cannot compete with communism in

Asia, Africa, or Latin America if we go on doing what we have done so often and so widely—which is to place the weak countries in a dilemma where they must stand still with us and our client rulers, or start moving with the Communists. This dilemma cannot be dissolved unless it is our central and persistent and unswerving policy to offer these unhappy countries a third option, which is economic development and social improvement without the totalitarian discipline of communism." *

It is not necessary to discriminate precisely the extent to which I would agree with this passage, or with similar statements of the same general point of view; it is sufficient here to say in passing that the whole realm of ideas, of mind, of spirit, of fundamental outlook, or basic attitude is dangerously neglected by this position. Furthermore, I want to make it plain that I am not here denying that certain "client rulers" should not have been supported; that certain rotten economic and social systems should have been overthrown; and that therefore there is here a valid field of "competition" between communism and the West. In these matters I hold radical views of my own also. Nor am I denying the importance of the economic factor in the immense world struggle. What interests me here is not the rightness or wrongness of policy with respect to this or that government or social-economic order: what interests me is the metaphysical presuppositions of this whole emphasis on the economic and social with respect to the nature of man. Man is the integral product of his material, economic, and social conditions; if there is anything the matter with him, it is due to some defect in these conditions; therefore, correct these conditions and you have done your duty by him, and he will emerge an angel: it is this radical materialization of man that I deny and that I desire to refute.

II

How has this materialistic metaphysics arisen—I do not mean historically, but existentially in the mind of man? How is it pos-

* Walter Lippmann, *Washington Post & Times Herald,* May 9, 1961, p. A13.

sible that certain "good thinkers" and certain "responsible states-men" either hold it explicitly or presuppose it by their thoughts and actions? I suggest that what happens in the soul of man is something like this:

The world has become physically one, as a result of fast trans-portation and instantaneous communication. On the other hand, here are these one hundred nations of which the United Nations is composed: they display so many sovereignties, a dozen religions, a score of cultures, a score or more of languages, a score of social orders, many different forms of government, and a dozen stages of economic development. Despite the fact that the world has been physically brought closer together, it is obvious that in these several realms there is no unity about the world at all. In fact, the more the diverse peoples and cultures of the world get physi-cally closer together; namely, the more they see and rub shoulders with and know one another, the more they tenaciously hold to and consciously become jealous and proud of their distinctive cultural heritages. The mind then is bewildered: It wants unity—that is indeed its innate tendency—but it finds only physical unity, the most superficial and the most external of all unities. This silly unity (that we are all now physically neighbors of one an-other, that we inhabit the same planet, etc.) does not satisfy it—and no wonder. Goaded by its unabating quest for unity, the mind then hits on the next best thing: All these human beings are, after all, animals; they all need food, clothing, and shelter, and a minimum standard of material existence; here then is an obvious principle of unity—*man is an economic animal*. In this way the whole of humanity is neatly levelled down onto this one single plane—the plane of the levels of economic development. Everything else is viewed as derivative from and dependent on this. Culture is a function of the economy, religion is a function of the economy, morality is a function of the economy, the system of government is a function of the economy, etc. And when the thinker or statesman who is thus engaged in this unifying, simpli-fying, or levelling-down process happens also to be one who does not have fundamental convictions of his own, or who had them once but has "outgrown" them since, or who has them but is ashamed of confessing them, or who has them but is afraid that they prove too "divisive," or who dreads being "persecuted" on account of them, or who belongs to a racial or religious or some other kind of minority, then he clings all the more firmly to this wholesale materialization of man. At last a principle has been found which will equalize all men, and he will not have to stand out; here is a materialist brotherhood; in this all-embracing sea of matter all men—and therefore he, the timid, lonely, frightened, or rebellious one—can safely swim without discrimination and without scandal or offense. Any other principle of unity will either leave him out, or leave large segments of humanity out (and, as a "humanitarian," he wants to include *everybody,* the whole of the "human race"), or bring upon his head the persecution of the world. Nothing then is safer, more equalizing, more comfortable, and more "needed," than the seamless sea of matter. As fish in this sea we are all "brothers."

III

Philosophically, precisely what is materialism? Materialism is not just belief in the existence of matter—namely, of something accessible to our senses; in this sense, everybody, including the most outspoken idealists, such as Bishop Berkeley, is a materialist. Nor is it just the doctrine that there is a substratum, whether or not we sense it, and whether or not in every case it is the same kind of substratum, out of which everything is composed—say, the hard, round balls, the atoms, of the classical atomic theory, or the "probability waves" of the recent versions of that theory; again, in the sense that everything is composed of some kind of substratum, everybody, including the saints and the theologians, is a materialist, for God, under any theory, has some substratum. Nor is it just the belief that man cannot exist without food and drink and air, and this body which is composed of flesh and blood and bones, and a general material solid support—say the earth—on which he can lean; again, in this sense, everybody, including the most radical ascetics, such as the hermits of the desert, is a materialist.

Materialism rather is the denial that there is a higher and a lower in existence and that the higher is independent of the lower and can never be reduced to it. The precise metaphysical formulation and refutation of this doctrine, including a survey of its historical development, is outside the scope of this lecture. But when the whole—any whole—is looked upon as only the sum total of its parts—that is materialism. When the highest and most distinctive in man—his mind, his spirit, the fact that he can be touched and transformed by something that is holy and divine— when all this wonderful side of man is reduced, as an epiphenomenon and without any remainder, to his bodily functionings— that is materialism. When mind, spirit, truth, ideas, principles are denied an absolutely original potency—that is materialism. When nothing that is fixed and firm and given and complete and perfect and full of being is allowed, when everything is dissolved into the fluency and flux of elements and things—that is materialism. When man is interpreted as made up only of insatiable and uncontrollable desire—that is materialism. When quality is overwhelmed by sheer quantity—that is materialism. When, surveying the majestic orderly evolution of the past, the mind derives, as by magic, the higher integrally from the lower, the more perfect integrally from the less perfect, the more advanced integrally from the more primitive, the different integrally from the same—that is materialism. When the whole of human life is viewed as inherently without rest, without repose, without peace, without grace, without fullness of satisfaction—that is materialism.

IV

Now as these things constitute, alas, the very warp and woof of modern civilization, is it any wonder that materialistic communism, with its exaltation of human desire, with its derivation of all ideas and all norms and all valuations from the sheer economic struggle, with its interpretation of history as the product only of conflicting class interests—interests that can never be reconciled except through violence and the destruction of one class by another, with its inciting of all that is primitive and elemental and unformed to rise up against all that is more perfect, more developed, more sure of itself, with its doctrine that in the end there is nothing, save atoms in motion—is it any wonder, I say, that materialistic communism has found in this spiritual climate of modern Western civilization a perfect soil for its development?

On a strictly materialistic interpretation, the problem of the individual in modern society is fairly simple. Societies are more or less economically secure. There is a widespread material revolution whereby the less developed and secure are feverishly exerting themselves to greater development and security. The so-called "population explosion" is compounding the urgency of this development. This revolution expresses itself in two ways: (1) Asia, Africa, and Latin America are seething with revolutionary programs for development and industrialization. (2) The laboring classes in Western industrialized societies are clamoring more and more for their right share in the material wealth of their own country, whether this wealth is produced by their labor or by the processes of automation. The theory is propagated in Communist countries that the government is their government, and that the total produce of the economy is justly distributed among them. On this view, everybody is caught in the grip of a tremendous, creative, universal, original force of nature: to live in an economically and socially just society and to be materially secure. *Everybody is on the road to material security and socialization,* with communism as the ultimate goal. To the question, Who are you?, the answer is: You are precisely *where* you are on this road to security and socialization. Since the whole of creation "groaneth and travaileth" after this socialist-communist-materialist ideal, to find out who you are, determine first where you are on the road to this ultimate goal. Being *is* socialism-communism-materialism;

therefore, you *are* to the extent you *are* socialist-communist-materialist. This applies not just to you as an individual, because, after all, you, as an individual, do not count; for what can you, as an individual, do, what can you produce? This applies primarily and principally to your society. Societies *are* to the extent they have to be socialized, with communism as the ultimate goal.

If, then, you ask, what is the individual in modern society? the answer is: Determine first the economic "stage of development" of the society in which he lives, and that determination will tell you what and who he is. Societies are more or less developed, more or less industrialized, more or less capitalist, more or less socialist. Individuals are one or the other of these "economic" designations. You can then run down the peoples and countries of the world one by one, and when you have determined the degree, the rate, the possibilities and the final objective of their development and socialization, you have said the last word about them.

As to such things as depth, truth, and kind of culture, of religion, of morals, of intellectual apprehension—all these things are either nonsense, or they have an exceedingly relative validity, depending as they do on "subjective valuation," or they "come afterwards." They "come afterwards" either in importance and value, or in the sense that, once you have assured the material base, these things will "naturally" well forth from the genius of "the people." You do not need to worry about the intellectual, moral, and spiritual, once you have made sure of the material. At any rate, you cannot "compare" individuals on the basis of these "subjective" criteria; whereas, on the "objective" criteria of development, standard of living, and the extent to which their societies have been socialized, they can be readily "compared."

Thus when you speak of the individual in the modern society of Japan, or China, or India, or the Middle East, or Russia, or Europe, or Africa, or the United States, or Latin America, you are ignoring the specific cultures, religions, moralities, forms of government, and fundamental outlooks on life and existence of these various countries, and are concentrating wholly on the degree, rate, manner, and possibilities of their economic development and socialization.

This materialistic interpretation is not only logically possible: It is today a prevalent interpretation. You find it in 90 per cent of the books on what are called "conditions in Asia and Africa." These books of course examine the governmental structure, but always as a function of the economic development: Governments are *tools* for raising the standard of living of the people; they justify themselves only to the extent they serve the revolution, only to the extent they help in the forward advance towards economic security, material abundance, and socialism.

Nothing is sadder than when the Western mind, in thinking of or going to these lands, finds it possible only to challenge or help them materially, only to pass on to them the canons of an economic critique of their existence. Such a mind, forgetting or not knowing the infinite spiritual riches of the West, is a travesty of itself.

V

I reject the Marxist criteria of interpretation. I believe they are nauseatingly superficial and false. They have become fashionable only because the Communist Party, which adopted this interpretation as its official dogma, rules now in Russia and China. In seizing and maintaining power, the Communist Party has done so, not by persuasion, but by force. We are dealing everywhere with the rule of a small minority which came to power by ruthless intrigue and revolution and which maintains its power by police state methods. Behind the vogue of the materialist interpretation, in the astounding dominance it has recently acquired, lies the sheer material-military might of a great power. Now what has been established by force can one day just as easily be disestablished by force. This is especially so as in the establishment of communism as a political force, and therewith in the spread of radical materialism, there was nothing inevitable whatsoever. On the contrary, the thing arose and developed for the most part by accident and default, and at a dozen different points during the last forty years, the force of communism could have been countered by sufficient force to cause it to collapse. The rest of the world was simply divided and sleeping. Today the whole world is interested in what has been established by force, but what we are primarily interested in here is what establishes itself by its inherent truth and reason. I find no inherent truth and reason in the Marxist-materialist interpretation. So much force, arbitrariness, dogmatism, and sheer accident cling to this interpretation that I cannot take it seriously at all: I look upon it as a passing phase in history. I therefore pass to more profound and more lasting ways of interpreting the individual in modern society.

VI

Three criteria appear to me to be natural and inherent to the situation: (1) How much the individual is conscious of his unique, human, personal individuality, with its inner personal freedom. (2) How he is actually related in his existence to his society, and especially to the politically organized aspect of that society, the state. And (3) the extent to which and the manner in which he feels that he and his society or state bear a message of salvation, or at least mean something, for the whole of humanity. His individual self-consciousness, his precise relation to society and the state, and what kind, if any, of "world movement" he belongs to—these appear to me to be the three essential moments of a genuine understanding of the individual in modern society. The first determines whether he exists as a human indivdual at all; the second establishes his relation to society and the state; and the third characterizes his relation to the world.

On the basis of these criteria, we may roughly distinguish seven types of society and seven corresponding types of indivdual. These are but types, and their fitness to any particular case would necessarily be more or less loose. I also recognize some interpenetration among these types, and some intermediate instances outside them. Moreover, the terms I use are generalized from some existing societies and cultures, and should be understood only in the technical sense I use them here, namely with the limitations of their definitions and of the qualifications I explicitly introduce in this section. In any one case I could have given the definition first and then looked around and found that that definition applied more or less to such and such existing societies. I preferred the inductive approach.

VII

There is first what I might term "African society." Here the individual is wholly assimilated to his tribe and he is not conscious either that he has individual rights of his own or that he belongs to a larger grouping (say the human race or a world movement) than that of his own tribe. The individual hardly exists, society is everything, and, except where communism or some world religion has deeply struck, there is no consciousness of the world. The ongoing political transformation of African society does not alter this basic pattern. So-called African nationalism is only an extension of tribalism with a strong racist (anti-white) tinge. The status of the individual so far as our three criteria are concerned has not changed.

A second type of society is that in which the individual is wholly assimilated to his group, without individual rights of his own, but where he feels, or is made to feel, or his rulers feel for him, that he belongs to a worldwide movement destined to conquer the earth. This is "Chinese society" as I understand it today. The individual is compensated, as it were, for his loss of personal rights and freedoms by the sense that, although society or the state is everything, he nevertheless forms a part of a universal and world-conquering process.

VIII

I think in Russian society the individual is much more sophisticated, and that is why I view Russian society as a third type.

Here the state is certainly the overriding power, but the individual, owing to the fact that the old Russian traditions have not all been destroyed, still enjoys a certain degree of freedom in his relations to his church (if he has any), to his family and friends (especially among the peasants), to his literary circle (if he happens to be an artist), to his own national group (if he happens to belong to one of the innumerable national minorities in the Soviet Union), and even to his own university associates (if he happens to be a professor in a university). We must never forget that Tsarist Russia was a fairly advanced country even by European standards; that Russia is fundamentally an offshoot of Europe; that what the Soviets did was for the most part only to revolutionize the country industrially, economically, and politically; and that for the great artistic, intellectual, and spiritual products of the Russian soul we still have to go to pre-revolutionary Russia. Of course the Russian is also conscious today of the fact that out of his country radiates a movement with the transformation and domination of the whole world as its aim. Here, too, the carrying of a message compensates for the loss of personal freedoms and rights.

Indian society displays innumerable loyalties not altogether circumscribed by the state. There is thus considerable freedom in India (and Pakistan) so far as prescription from the state is concerned. The individual is not wholly assimilated to society, whether in the form of the state or of the caste. But there is no consciousness of a universal *Indian* movement, except for the vague and essentially negative desire to "mediate" conflicts wherever they exist. There is a "peace movement" in India, and the Indian individual is quite conscious of it; but peace as such is something purely formal, devoid of content, while it is the content of peace that counts most; and in any event, because peace depends not just on the will of the "mediator" but on the wills of the two parties between which the "mediator" is to "mediate," this peace or pacifist movement, real as it is in India, is nevertheless essentially unstable. It is clear, then, how Indian society, and the consciousness of the individual in that society, differs markedly from African or Chinese or Russian society.

IX

Moslem society is a somewhat intermediate society. The self-consciousness of the personal individuality of the individual is not as strong as in some Western societies; yet it is not altogether absent. The individual's assimilation is either to his state or to his religious community, or to both.

State, religion, and nationalism go intimately hand in hand. The problem of freedom, in the sense of the possibility of fundamental personal change, hardly exists. On the other hand, there is the distinct sense of belonging to a world brotherhood and a world movement. The unity of this world movement is more a unity of participation than a unity of joint action. Islam is a universal, total, world outlook, rooted in, but departing considerably from, both Judaism and Christianity. The Moslem is conscious of this distinctive universalism, and he feels himself a being apart. At every point he measures other outlooks by his own. Essential to Islam in its purity is freedom from any racial prejudice and the sense that Moslems are, both in a mystical and a real sense, all brothers.

The intermediate character of Islam is further revealed by the fact that, whereas the mode of application of our three criteria of interpretation is fairly uniform in the case of each one of the six other societies, in the case of Moslem countries these criteria of interpretation apply differently from country to country. Thus, individual self-consciousness, the relation of the individual to society and the state, and the way Islam is regarded as a world movement, all these three criteria differ considerably in their application as one moves in the Moslem world from North Africa, to the Arab Near East, to Turkey, to Iran, to Pakistan, to Indonesia; and even in the Arab Near East they differ from country to country. Any proposition concerning any one of our three fundamental criteria does not have a univocal application all over the Moslem world. We are dealing more with diverse "Moslem societies" than with a single "Moslem society." And yet there is a fundamental sense, even with respect to our three criteria, in which they are all Moslem. It is this difficulty which determines what I called "the intermediate character" of Moslem society.

X

I think the individual in society in the Latin world, and especially in Latin America, is a sixth type still. Except for minor dictatorships here and there (and in certain respects even under these dictatorships), there is plenty of freedom vis-à-vis state. Individual self-consciousness is carried in certain instances to the point of anarchy. But side by side with it there is the consciousness that Latin culture embodies a universal message, to wit, Latin humanism and the Catholic Church. By Latin humanism I mean principally freedom from racial prejudice (in this respect Latin culture is Mediterranean like Islam) and the peculiar legalism of the Latin mind; I also mean that universalism which everyone recognizes in Don Quixote. To a Latin American, say to a Brazilian, the universalism of Catholicism is different from the universalism of communism to a Russian. The Russian Communist feels that he, his Party, and his state are themselves the carriers of this message; its success depends on them; that is the peculiar new word that Russia wants to utter to the world today. The Brazilian Catholic, on the other hand, does not view Catholicism as a Brazilian word. This is not a new message that the Church in Brazil and the Brazilian state are carrying to the ends of the earth; rather is it an old message for which a completely independent and supra-national body, the Roman Catholic Church headed by the Pope, is responsible, and the Brazilian Catholic's sense of universalism arises, not because he and his state are responsible for that body, but because they participate in it. It is the belonging to an age-old already existing universal movement that confers upon the Latin Catholic the consciousness of universalism, and not his carrying a new message expressive of what might be termed "the Latin soul at this stage in its development." This is then how the Latin American individual exists today in his self-consciousness, in his relation to his state and in his sense of any universalism to which he may belong, or of which he may be the bearer.

XI

A seventh type of society with a seventh mode of existence of the individual occurs in Western Europe and in the English-speaking world. How may we characterize this society and this individual? The competence of the state is prescribed by law. Thus the state is quite limited in its functions: Law is above the state. Outside this competence individuals and groups enjoy unlimited freedom, with only the sanctions of custom serving as checks. The scope of this freedom is very vast indeed, vaster than in most societies. The principle that the people rule themselves, not just in the sense of passive consent, but in the more active sense of free decision, in free elections, after free debate, is of the essence. Thus, in the final anaylsis, the determiner of law and policy is the consensus of a free people, and not the dictates of a ruling clique arrogating to itself a separate wisdom from the political instinct and sense of responsibility of the people. In a well-organized free society there can be no fundamental conflict between the people ruling themselves and the people requiring and accepting the leadership of their leaders.

Virtually every individual (certainly more by far than in any other society) is conscious of his individuality; namely, of his rights, freedoms, and duties; and this consciousness expresses itself in freedom of thought, conscience, criticism, expression, and association. There was a sense of universalism, no matter how limited and external, in the age of imperialism (the *mission civilisatrice* and the British imperial sense of law and order) ; but with the disintegration of the empires, this particular sense has considerably atrophied. The West has for the most part withdrawn unto itself to defend its home and hearth. It preaches today independence, freedom, and neutralism, whether from conviction or from a guilty conscience or from a sense that these doctrines would tend to dull the edge of the otherwise sharp thrusts of communism and anti-Westernism all over the world.

The critique of so-called bourgeois existence as too individualistic, too self-centered, too irresponsible, and, in any event, as too inadequate for the harsh demands of the modern world, is justified. I mean the type of existence whose highest aim (usually called "dream") is to be settled in a comfortable apartment in town or in a nice villa in the suburbs; to raise a family, whether responsibly or irresponsibly; to add endlessly, whether by hard work or by exploitation or by speculation, to the bank account, whether one then lives a frugal, ascetic, and morally spotless life, enjoying only the thought of the security that the thus-amassed wealth affords him, or one squanders his substance by flitting from one evanescent excitement to another; to be a solid citizen, in the sense of paying his taxes, abiding by the law, belonging to the neighborhood club, and participating in the usual round of civic activities. When it realizes this dream, the bourgeois life depends thereafter for its opinions and convictions on what the newspapers, magazines, radio, television, cinema, and latest bestsellers happen at the time to advocate; it keeps on viewing the world only in general, only geographically, as composed of such and such "areas" or "parts," only as something that one's government or foreign office is elected or appointed or "paid" to deal with; it looks upon other peoples and nations externally, legalistically, "internationally," as alien and different, to be kept at arm's length; to develop such a timidity of soul as to become incapable of taking any risks, of striking out on any real adventure, or joining any real fundamental movement, of responding to any real fundamental challenge, whether of the body or of the soul.

This is surely not all that Western existence is capable of: this is indeed a caricature of that existence. With its untold spiritual resources, the West can do infinitely better than that.

XII

The three fundamental criteria of personal self-consciousness, of the degree of freedom the individual enjoys vis-à-vis his society, and of his consciousness of a world meaning in which he partipates, would seem to disclose that on a world scale we have seven types of society and seven types of individual. The so-called "individual in modern society" *is* these seven types of individual in these seven types of society.

There are of course other societies and other individuals, such as in Southeast Asia and in Japan. But these display on the whole mixed types, and we will adequately grasp them if we have adequately grasped the seven basic types.

Although there is some interpenetration (e.g., between Chinese and Russian societies, which would justify naming them "Communist" or "Marxist" societies, and between Latin American and Western societies, which would justify naming them simply "Western" societies), still we may regard these seven types as more or less independent dimensions. They constitute an intelligible and defensible framework of reference for the interpretation of the individual in modern society.

Sub-societies also abound under each type (more under some than under others), and a thorough investigation will be needed to discriminate them.

If our analysis is sound, it follows that the notion that there is an univocal thing called "modern society" with an univocal being called "the individual in it" is a myth. *There is no univocal modern society and there is no univocal individual in it.* The reason for this myth is precisely the materialist fallacy to which I referred at the beginning. The levelling down of everything onto the plane of matter, of the body and its desires, of the material standard of living, of the sheer economic process, of the masses toiling and the exploiters exploiting, obviously produces the false impression that you are everywhere dealing with the same type of being. All monism is awful, and none more so than the monism of materialism. In the truly significant respects which characterize the very humanity of man—namely, in the depth and creativity of his individual personal self-consciousness, in the extent and limits of his freedom vis-à-vis his group, and in his awareness of a universal world message of which he is the bearer and custodian—in these decisive respects economic-material development is at best neutral, and, under certain circumstances, by replacing the humanity of man, it could easily destroy it. And it is precisely in these significant respects that you have seven societies and seven types of individual.

To understand the individual in modern society, therefore, you must beware of every oversimplification, every silly generalization. You must go deeply into the concrete content of the life of each type of individual. The sentimental idea bandied about that we are all alike, that we all have the same needs and interests, that we are all "human beings," that we are all "brothers" one of another, has arisen either from some tendentious teaching or because we come in contact with each other on the most superficial plane—on the plane, usually, of tourists in foreign lands, or of smiles and civilities at cocktail parties in international gatherings, or of the commercial exchange of goods, or of that most artificial of communications called "diplomatic intercourse," or of that primitive sense, from which nothing really as to the nature of man can be concluded, that we all face today a common danger in war and therefore we all have a common interest in peace.

For my part, before I can believe any such nonsense about man, I should like to know exactly what the African or Chinese or Russian or Indian or Moslem or Latin American or Westerner thinks and believes in the depths of his soul (and there are means of ferreting out what there is in those depths) about himself, about his state and society, about time and history, about other people, and about the supreme being. It is these things that count, and not the level or sub-level of his economic development.

When we honestly attend to the detailed, concrete contents of the soul of each type of individual, especially with respect to these basic structures, we shall find that the differences are far more significant than the similarities, and that the similarities are often "used and exploited" in the interest of the differences. People will make use of that which brings them together with you, such as your money or your goods, precisely in order to bolster and strengthen that which separates them from you, such as their distinctive outlook on life.

Man is very deep. He is a veritable abyss. In him dwells a devil, often in the guise of an angel of light. The real problem is not his material and economic development, because he could possess all the material comforts and all the economic wealth of the world, and he could live in a just society, and the devil in him could still be there. In fact it is just then that the devil could ensconce himself most comfortably. A simple act of the spirit could bless or could curse a whole society, a whole civilization. The real problem is how to expose the devil when he shines forth like an angel of light, and having exposed him, how then to exorcise or at least subdue him. This problem is beyond any materialism, any economic development, any political independence, any "modern society," any "individual" and any "type" of individual, and silly monism. And that problem is only the beginning. The real problem begins *after* the exposing, the exorcising, and the subduing. The real problem is how and with what to fill the thus "empty, swept, and garnished house." It will be found that that which fills the "swept house" cannot come as an afterthought: It must have been there from the beginning.

XIII

Western civilization is in real trouble today. It is beleaguered from without and undermined from within. Without, international communism is planning day and night for its "burial," and neutralism is at least indifferent to its fate. And within, some of its finest minds are doubting its age-old values, and are beginning to look to strange, new gods for its salvation.

The individual soon develops a guilty conscience. Perhaps his wealth was unjustly garnered; therefore, he must share it. Perhaps the materialists are right; therefore, he will reconsider the ground on which he stands. And so he turns to the neutralists and tells them, "I will share with you my substance and my know-how"; and he turns to the Communists and tells them, "I will burn incense at the altar of your god."

Western man is not going to save himself and his civilization that way. For "thus said the Lord, Stand ye in the ways, and see, and ask for the old paths, where is the good way, and walk therein and ye shall find rest for your souls." (Jer. 6:16) Salvation and rest lie only in "the old paths, where is the good way."

If then we "stand in the ways, and see," we may rediscover the old path of the spirit, the path without which there would never have been a Western civilization today. This is the path where man is weighed, not by his body, nor by his desires, neither by his cleverness, nor yet by his might, nor even by his power, but by the depth of his spirit, and by whether in its depth it reaches the Lord its maker. In these ultimate matters one only says his word and goes. What is my word before, as it were, I go? It is simply this: No matter how strange it may seem, no matter how unfamiliar and discordant and even unintelligible it may sound to our ears, accustomed as they are to the fantasies of idealism, humanism, rationalism, and materialism, and no matter how much I say it with genuine fear and trembling, let me assure you that the bewildered and beleaguered individual in modern society can only find rest for his soul by the simple and humble return to the Living God, the creator of the ends of the earth.

What the individual in modern Western society needs most of all is to realize that he is the heir of a tremendous heritage.

Where is anything comparable to the depth and truth of the cumulative tradition of Greece, Rome, the Near East, and Western Europe? The sufferings, tears, insights, visions, and convictions of four thousand years—and what four thousand years!—pour integrally into this stream. This is the pearl beyond all price in the keeping of the West.

The decisive thing is that tradition is unbroken. Others have had a broken and checkered history—whatever its contents. The mind of the West is still so free and strong that it can study and teach David in himself, Aristotle in himself, Cicero in himself, Augustine in himself, Leibniz in himself, Kant in himself, without the distorting lenses of a tendentious ideology. The past is not violently suppressed and supplanted: It is open for all to see. This sense of ease with respect to the past—and, I repeat, what a past!—this freedom with which it is received without diminution and criticized without fetters, this infinite tenderness with which it is preserved, is a sign of the greatest vitality and strength. Those who have something to hide or suppress or be ashamed of are fundamentally insecure; those who fear nothing and face everything are absolutely sure of themselves.

Modern Western man must therefore realize what a great honor and what a tremendous obligation it is to be free—*free to be* the deepest that there has been. Let him only *be* that, in all responsibility, and in all gratitude. His is the possibility of a personal self-consciousness infinitely rich and infinitely true. His is the actuality of such a rule of law that there can be no question of society or the state mocking his person and his dignity and therefore encroaching upon his freedoms and his rights. Therefore his must be the necessity of bearing the most wonderful epistle of freedom unto the ends of the earth. Itself the matrix from which all universalisms have sprung, Western civilization's greatest need today is to articulate anew and for this age its ancient universal message. Modern Western man must therefore shake off all shyness, all timidity, all doubt, all embarrassment, all paralysis, all defensiveness in order to free himself to pass to the offensive—the offensive of love and helpfulness; the offensive of value and excellence; the offensive of man and reason; the offensive which affirms that the greatest things in life can only come through sorrow and suffering; the offensive of the spirit which is contrite and the heart which is broken; the offensive which knows how much it has trespassed and therefore is thankful for how much it has been forgiven; the offensive of One who creates and redeems and who has spoken. This is the offensive of being and peace. This is the offensive of freedom.

Not only his own fate, but the fate of other individuals in other societies, depends upon the individual in the modern society of the West. If he rises to the highest which his own tradition permits and requires, he will help in saving himself and the world. If, faltering and unsure, he fails his tradition and turns to other gods and principalities, then I dread to think of the future. For, as the literal heir of the ages, he is given much to guard and consider. And it is written, "unto whomsoever much is given, of him shall be much required." (Lk. 12:48).

CHAPTER 9

ON LEISURE IN INDUSTRIAL
SOCIETIES

RAYMOND ARON

The two concepts of *work* and of *leisure* are complementary.
Leisure is the time which work leaves free; he who is not obliged
to work has leisure. From this complementarity there follows a
consequence not without import: The meaning of leisure in a
given civilization depends on the meaning given to work.

If work becomes identified with physical effort such as manual
labor—activity which is arduous and therefore held to be de-
grading—only leisure appears worthy of a man of status. All work
is servile, and the freeman or the nobleman does not work: He
makes war or he meditates, he is a warrior or he is a priest. On
the other hand, if work is the essence of existence—if all men
must work, either because the human condition has been degraded by sin, or because humanity is fulfilled through the transformation of nature, or finally, because work is forcedly imposed
on all since it corresponds to the needs of the collectivity—then
leisure takes on a meaning which is negative rather than positive.
It is non-work, necessary for the worker so that he may recover
and return to his task; it is a disability imposed on everyone by

157

biological rhythm and organic weakness. In the first perspective, work belongs to the non-human side of existence; in the second, it is leisure which marks the fall, the incapacity of man to live his humanity permanently.

Western societies have valued work more, probably, than any historical society. The formation of modern society, whose primary objective seems to be the development of productive forces, is inconceivable in the absence of a moral and social value attributed to work as such, whether exertion is exalted as a virtue or whether success is considered a sign of election. In spite of this valorization, work, in most European countries, has nonetheless always retained a negative element, a survival of the idea of the punishment of God: "You will earn your bread by the sweat of your brow." Leisure has therefore never been entirely stripped of its positive content. If work was harsh, leisure brought rest, and although it was not noble, at least it was not as hard.

Does work, in the current phase of industrial societies, have a positive or a negative meaning? I am tempted to answer that the concept has become *neutral*. Work is the exercise of a trade which ensures one's livelihood. One works in a factory, in an office, in a university, on the stage of a theatre or before the microphone of a radio station—wherever the individual has found a job, an occupation which brings him income. The memory of crisis and of unemployment, combined with tendencies inherent in any market economy, has given an almost sacred character to the search for jobs in a number sufficient for all. Society must give jobs to everyone; it matters little whether the results are useful or not, whether the product is a satellite or an advertisement for perfume. For the economic machine to run full blast all men capable of working must find employment, receive a salary, and spend the money received. Work is the condition of expenditure, and expenditure the condition of full employment, and full employment the condition of work offered to everyone.

Since work is now neither good nor bad, neither the punishment of God nor the fulfillment by man of his humanity, leisure in turn is neutral. Leisure is that part of the day, of the week, of the year during which the worker is not on the job, in the factory, the shop, or the office. Now it happens that the progress of productivity has made it possible to increase considerably the duration of leisure, the number of hours each day and of days each year during which man is not at work. What does this leisure time, empty or full, mean? What could it mean? What should it mean?

Leisure has a different meaning for everyone according to the nature of the work to which it is counterpart. Certainly it is first of all essentially rest and *relaxation*: During the evening of each day or at the end of each week, the manager forgets his problems, the teacher his students, the worker his tools. But even this general proposition requires some commentary or reservations. The manager does not forget as completely as the worker, if he forgets at all. He needs to forget, to free his mind from an obsession or his nerves from excessive tension, but he does not always succeed. On the other hand, the worker has no difficulty in forgetting the lathe or the assembly line.

The antithesis is not between mental and manual work; it is between work in which the individual is completely committed and work which is nothing more than breadwinning undertaken by the individual with more or less indifference or boredom. Mental work, of course, falls in the first category more often than manual work. But at a certain skill level, manual work excludes neither interest nor personal commitment. On the other hand, some teachers or second-rate professors sometimes find no satisfaction in their teaching. They count on their leisure to work— that is to say, to read, write, listen to music, or to travel and discover the world.

A full, balanced life presupposes that work is a source of joy. But we shelter no illusions: It is not yet so, and perhaps it will never be so. In a large industrial society, there exist millions of occupations which can hardly be sources of joy, either because they require physical efforts which are themselves strenuous, or more frequently, because they are monotonous: easy in themselves but tiresome in the repetition of the same gestures. Technical and psychological organization of the company and the shop can bring about frictions and tensions among workers, and between them and their supervisors or engineers. It is not conceivable that all workers in modern industry could have the happy feeling of finding self-fulfillment in their work. They demand or should demand of leisure not only rest, not only entertainment (no longer thinking of their job), but *joy* and *enrichment*.

It seems to me that workers, whether manual or intellectual, whose job interests them without fulfilling them, demand of leisure *diversion,* at least initially. The world of the office is a closed world, enclosed by an administration often too vast to be understood in its entirety by the employee. The worker is not unhappy in his work if he has the good fortune to have tolerable relations with his fellow-workers and his supervisors, a respectable salary, and sufficient prospects for promotion. But rarely is office work at the lower or middle levels such that the employee feels himself fulfilled, proud, or creative. He does not live for his work either. A sort of equilibrium develops: The diversions of leisure help him forget his work, but they are experienced as diversions, not as the authentic end of existence.

A further stage is reached when diversions are understood as something else, this something being designated by one or the other of the three terms: *enrichment, maturing, education.* Reading good books, or listening to good music, represents a distraction in relation to the daily worries of the job or of the home. These diversions involve also the acquisition of culture and frequently acquisition in joy. The word *maturing* refers to another phenomenon. The writer or the artist allows his work to mature in leisure. It is in traveling, in chance walks and encounters, that a book develops, takes shape and form. Non-work is sometimes for the intellectual time gained, not lost. In this sense, the intellectual is the person for whom work and leisure tend to become undifferentiated. Doubtless the writer who listens to music is not working on the books he expects to write, but music contributes also to making him what he is, and from this point of view leads indirectly to the development of the work.

I would not want to push too far this rapprochement of work and diversion for the creative intellectual. The distinction remains, even for him. We all know some intellectuals who have "produced" little because they preferred diversions to the actual effort of creation. Sometimes more cultivated, richer in culture, they had fewer works to their credit because they had not consented to limit their curiosity and their discoveries, as is required by the increasing specialization of scientific and academic life.

The professor, the writer, the artist continue their education whenever the obligations of their job and of their work allow them some leisure. At all levels of society, and at all levels of intelligence, the time of non-work can and must be the time when the individual *learns*—he learns what is going on in the world, he improves his professional competence, he acquires also some acquaintances and knowledge useless to his trade (could one have the pleasures of friendship if it were not for leisure?). He completes his culture and he allows his curiosity to wander. Each of us knows no more than a small part of cumulative wisdom, even in his own discipline. Why should the specialist resist the temptation to glance from afar to regions which will never be familiar to him but whose outline he may vaguely discern? Leisure can also be utilized as a sort of liberation. Industrial society imposes specialization for the sake of efficiency. Leisure authorizes dispersion for the sake of pure pleasure or enrichment.

Education during free time is not necessarily without an ulterior purpose. Those who have not had from the beginning the good fortune of regular and prolonged studies can fill their leisure with work similar to that of students. It would clearly be desirable to increase facilities offered for the education of adults desirous of educating themselves outside their work.

Brief as they are, these analyses suggest some lessons which have no pretension to originality but which run the risk of being sometimes forgotten. It would be vain to decree dogmatically what should be the leisure activities of men in industrial society. Men fill their leisure in function of what they *are* and what they *do*. All seek first and foremost rest and diversion, diversion being a condition, an element, of rest. They seek diversion at the concert hall, before the television set, at sporting events, in the reading of Peter Cheney or Tolstoy, according to their taste, according to their occupation, and according to what they have learned in their youth. The leisure activities of each person are the counterpart—complement or contradiction—of his occupation, and they are also the image of his personality. The leisure activities will be mediocre if the personality is mediocre. They will sometimes seem mediocre even when the personality is not, if the pressure of the occupation is such that relaxation is possible only at a lower level of intelligence and sensitivity.

It would be in no way paradoxical to conclude that education in our time must prepare for leisure at the same time as for work (I believe the organizers of our conference have understood the reciprocal bonds between these three notions). The man who works five days a week, and is left to himself during the three weeks or the month of paid leave, is on vacation nearly one day out of three; and during the days of work, he has two or three hours of leisure in the evening—that is, hours not devoted to the strict necessities of family life. It would be almost tragic if this liberation should appear to millions of men as potential boredom or a burden to bear and not as a marvelous opportunity for enrichment, escape, and culture.

But, we repeat, the use which will be made of these free hours or of these weeks of freedom will depend only to a very limited extent on what society or the state offers today. It will depend primarily on the characteristics of the occupation and the personality of the individual. It is excellent that there is in many areas a television channel which presents an "educational program." The number of those who will watch this program will be determined only to a small extent by the quality of the program or the ability with which the educational content is rendered "amusing" in the eyes of the viewers—it will depend especially on the mood and the tastes of those to whom it is directed. This mood is a function of work, these tastes are a function of the education received as well as of the gifts and innate preferences of each individual.

These fundamental givens must not be forgotten when we tackle the problem of the relation between the individual and the collectivity during leisure, and the problem of the role of the collectivity and of the state in the organization of leisure.

In modern society the individual works (plies his trade) outside the family; he enjoys some leisure at home. These general propositions require reservations and shadings because they include exceptions. The merchant, the artisan, or the farmer often works at home both in the physical and economic sense of this expression. He resides at the place of his work; he works in the place of his residence; his wife and sometimes his children participate in professional as well as domestic activities. On the other hand, the young enjoy leisure outside the school, the shop, the family. Even some adult workers do not always pass their leisure hours at home. There is a social life in the evening; workers can meet outside of work at a café (in France) or at each other's homes.

The fact remains that the typical man in urban industrial societies leaves home to go to his work, which is less individual than collective work, and which takes places outside his family residence. The same man most frequently spends his daily leisure hours at home. However, this formula, which television has made accurate for an increasing number of workers in an increasing number of countries, is not applicable to the young, who starting from a certain age cannot find the desired freedom for leisure in the family circle. It is inapplicable also, generally, to the weekends and to the weeks or months of vacation. Certainly, most often the family—parents and young children—usually remains together during these days or weeks of leisure, but some families could get together in groups, or on the contrary each could seek isolation. In brief, what is the actual role and what is the desirable role of the collectivity in the content and organization of leisure?

In societies of a Western nature, the content of daily leisure activities is essentially determined by the diversions offered by the collectivity, private or public, and especially by television. Individuals choose among the programs offered them when there are several programs. These are not independent of the preferences of the public, since the return on advertising and therefore the profit of the company is a function of the attraction exercised over the television viewers. But the preferences of individuals are "conditioned" by the programs as much as the programs by the individuals. (All these remarks refer to the American experience.) The question therefore arises of knowing what is the best organization of what one calls mass media, since these at the present time cannot but exercise a considerable influence on the content of leisure and at the same time on the idea which millions of viewers will form of the world.

In this respect, a comparison between television in the Soviet Union, Western Europe, and the United States—a comparison which has often been sketched out but to my knowledge never carried through scientifically and systematically—would be fascinating. Juridically, television (and radio) is a state monopoly in the Soviet Union, a public corporation recently exposed to the competition of a network financed by advertising in Great Britain, a state service theoretically open to all opinions in France; finally, in the United States, both radio and television are in the hands of private companies whose explicit goals are to make money through commercial advertising. From the legal status there flow multiple consequences as regards the style of television, the nature of programs, and the influence on the masses.

Radio and television have as goals, in theory, to amuse, to inform, and to instruct. As we could have expected, we find once again the same functions which we were tempted to attribute above to leisure. The problem is evidently to know what proportion should be devoted to amusement, to education, and to information. It is tempting to answer that it is for the individual to choose himself the part which he desires to grant each of these functions, that the collectivity has no other duty than to put at the disposal of its citizens all the means necessary for the accomplishment of one or another of these functions. The individual is the freer, the greater the margin of choice left him by society. The margin is the greater, the greater the number of programs at any given instant. According to this interpretation it would be the American citizen who is the most free in the world by far in regard to his daily leisure and television.

Even if one accepts this doctrine—diversity of amusement, individual choice among offers—there would be many reservations to make on the authenticity of the freedom which it effectively allows the individual. Advertising does not constrain the buyer but it influences him, it creates a climate, it creates an obsession. Is it legitimate to invoke the classical conception of individual freedom, conscious and rational, while the means of communication tend to inhibit, to paralyze, to constrain the capacity of personal decision?

But there is more—even if the American formula of diversity and individual choice corresponded in fact to the ideal of liberty, it is not evident that the collectivity must content itself with a role which is, so to speak, passive. Or, more precisely, it is at least conceivable that the state should want to favor the informative and educational functions of television, that it should want to forbid certain procedures perhaps efficient in attracting viewers but in other respects deplorable. It is possible to plead that the state must not leave the last word to bad taste and to the mediocre mass tendencies partly maintained if not created by the entertainment offered.

The controversy—should television entertain or instruct, should it respond to the desires of the public or have as a goal the formation of the public taste?—could be continued almost indefinitely with no lack of arguments for either side. In fact, however, it is a question of finding a balance between total submission to the exigencies of advertising and the techniques of psychological manipulation, on the one hand, and the authoritarian determination by the state or public corporations of what the public will have the right to see and hear, on the other.

I must admit that I am truly horrified by certain aspects of American television: the time taken by advertising, the interruption of programs at the most moving moments by announcements, the complete freedom given to private companies to compose their programs as they wish and to offer at times the worst spectacles of violence, simply because the viewers are avid for them. I do not exclude the possibility that this judgment expresses a European prejudice; it is difficult to be entirely objective about such things. But to tell the truth and to help stimulate discussion, I will say frankly that the state seems to me to have, with regard to the means of mass communication which inevitably determine the content of leisure, a responsibility which goes beyond the simple guarantee of choice. The state is not simply a menace to this liberty; it can also be a defense against *hidden persuasion,* against the exploitation of what is least noble in human nature. French, English, and German television seem to be in this respect superior to American television. For the time being the French television viewer does not have the choice of channels, and the Britisher has the choice between two channels, but in neither country does programming go to the extremes at times reached by some American programming.

Television in totalitarian countries shows us another aspect of the problem and another risk of state intervention. Aside from entertainment, radio or television can be a means less of *information* or *instruction* than of *indoctrination.* Since large numbers of workers will watch the television screen in the evening, it is not impossible to use persuasion with a view, not to sell Gillette Blue Blades or Chesterfield cigarettes, but to spread the conviction of the superiority of the Communist system and of the corruption of the capitalist countries. The similarity between commercial advertising and political propaganda is a banal proposition which psychologists have put forward and explained for a long time. The similarity of these two techniques has entered the common consciousness and become expressed in the language. In America one speaks of "selling" a projected law or a political program as one sells a perfume or a medicine. The Soviet Union pushes the sale of political truths to the point of totalitarianism, as the United States pushes the sale of consumer goods to the point of obsession. The Europeans are less liberal than the two Great Powers in the use of these sales techniques. Public television is in Europe politically pluralistic and liberal, but it is less pluralistic than in the United States, more liberal than in the Soviet Union.

Television illustrates the new character which the private-collective antithesis takes in our epoch. The individual looks at television in his home with his family, but does not, for all that, escape society. Materially he seems to be alone with his loved ones in his home. Psychologically, by the images which he sees, the impression which he receives, he is really more socialized than he was previously when he passed the evening with some friends or neighbors. The society which penetrates his home through the intermediary of television is global society, more distant from the narrow locale in which the individual lives than were the local collectivities within which he found himself once during his hours of leisure.

It is through work that each individual acquires his income. During the hours of leisure the individual undergoes influences which form in part his ideas, his feelings, his understandings of the world. Let us not go too far. The attitude of each individual depends on his occupation, on his place in the professional hierarchy, on the level of income. It depends also on the family, the education received, religion, the multiple groups to which the individual belongs. He receives, often in a passive manner, the impressions transmitted through entertainment, by the means of communication. The studies which have been made do not reveal yet a great efficacy of leisure as regards education or indoctrination. Let us limit ourselves to saying that the instruments of leisure are likely to be effective in certain circumstances.

The opposition between the private individual and the collectivity is combined with two others: that between the individual (or the collectivity) and the state, and that between the liberal state and the totalitarian state. Television is juridically a state enterprise in France, but it is not put in the service of indoctrination. There is for the time being only one channel, but for technical and not political reasons. The French state will offer, once it is able to, a certain choice to the public; meanwhile, the difficulty is the inability to simultaneously satisfy the requirements of all viewers. According to their education and their occupation, these viewers do not find their amusement in the same shows. In other words, in this respect, the essential point is not the legal status of the means of mass communication, but the intent which those who control the mass media use them.

It is the content of the program which accentuates its private or collective character. The television viewer of a football game may well be alone before the television screen, but he is virtually participating in a collective manifestation; he is with other millions of television viewers. On the other hand, if he listens to a symphony he is in a certain sense alone with the imagery of sound even if millions of people absorb in themselves the same spiritual substance at the same time. Let us finally understand that the solitude of each person is not the characteristic quality of superior entertainment. The spectators at the theatre compose a more authentically collective public than the listeners of music. It does not follow from this that theatrical entertainment is inferior to musical entertainment. We are simply noting that certain ways of enjoying leisure favor solitude—reading, music—while others are in their meaning social, even if the radio or the television serves as an intermediary. In this sense the work of a writer is individual, that of a factory worker, socialized.

We arrive thus at a last aspect of the life of leisure on which we would like to say a few words. Does the individual fashioned by industrial society use leisure to flee not only his job, but the city and the crowd? Or does he aspire once he has left the factory or the office to a warmer, closer community which answers an unsatisfied need of his mind or of his heart? It is clear that such a question cannot have a general answer valid for all members of an industrial society or for all industrial societies. Let us indicate some of the tendencies which are apparently typical.

One tendency which seems almost universal could be called "the flight from the city and the search for nature." The *dacha* of the Soviets, the farm of the Americans, the summer cottage or the country property of the French are expressions, for once similar, of a same desire, a same need. The man of the cities, of the offices, of the factories, does not want to live his days of leisure in the framework in which his work unfolds. Even those who do not have a residence outside the cities go out on the highways to the country. The *dacha* and the farm suggest equally that family solitude is most frequently desired at the same time as the rupture with the customary locale—society remaining present through the intermediary of mass communication, but introduced or excluded at will by the man of leisure alone in his home. It depends on each one that the amusements accepted be private or collective, that they enrich or that they debase.

But other tendencies are equally visible. Young people often feel the desire to meet together in groups during their leisure time. Nor is there any lack of adult men and women, even with children, for whom the company of friends and neighbors constitutes an indispensable element of leisure. It appears that two contrary tendencies, more or less strong, exist: the search for a private life and the search for a social life in and through leisure. Probably, once again, the strength of either tendency is proportional to the nature of the work. The businessman or the professor rests from an overactive social life, whereas the worker or the employee whose human relations during work are infrequent and strictly professional wants to be with others when he escapes from the solitude or the anonymity of his work.

From this pont of view the efforts of the totalitarian regimes like the Third Reich and Fascist Italy to organize collective leisure for workers and employees become understandable. These organizations clearly had a propagandistic purpose, since they could affect only a small number of persons, and were evidently meant to demonstrate in a spectacular fashion the solicitude of the state for the lower classes and the accession of the "poor" to the pleasures previously reserved to the privileged. Trips, boat rides, beach vacations, which were considered the symbols of the amusements of the rich, were finally, by grace of an enlightened and authoritarian state, offered to "all."

But if we eliminate from consideration political intent and demagogic setting, the fact of collective and organized leisure activities remains. Now, the free citizens of the West sometimes choose such leisure activities voluntarily, taking the initiative of movements in groups or answering the appeal of different concerns, commercial or not, which offer such opportunities for vacationers. Certainly, economic reasons explain in part this socialization of leisure, but they do not explain it entirely. We would be wrong if we failed to realize that certain individuals in industrial societies demand of leisure an opportunity for community, just as others demand a chance for escape and solitude.

Must one catalogue political activity under the rubric of leisure? Certainly not, if it's a question of candidates for elective office, or of party regulars who obtain their income from politics itself; but free voluntary political activity undertaken by so many convinced persons outside of their hours of work is one way of filling the hours of non-work. It gives to the loyal party follower a means of being himself, of working for a cause and not for money, of finding himself among friends. If the totalitarian parties sometimes exercise such an attraction, it is because they correspond to certain needs that professional life does not satisfy. Then, too, they undertake to organize diversions for their faithful. These people have found in the party a community which takes charge of them for all of the time external to their work. The diversions themselves aim to indoctrinate, to confirm the individual in the faith to which he has adhered, and even more, to tie him tightly to the community of his choice.

The politicization of leisure is an aspect of socialization. This politicization is perhaps more dangerous in liberal regimes than totalitarian regimes. In the West it is a one-way proposition: only the parties least favorable to representative government try to take over leisure. Only the Fascists and the Communists attempt to monopolize the leisure of their militants or their sympathizers. In the East, politicization is evidently pushed further, but it is but one aspect of the general politicization of existence. And individuals react to it with the skepticism evoked by the excesses of propaganda and with the search for that solitude which appears all the more precious, the more difficult it is to enjoy in the overpopulated cities.

Two ideas, it would appear, must dominate the consideration of the problem of leisure: the complementarity between work and leisure, and the impossibility of statements having a general validity precisely because of the reciprocal relation of occupational and spare time. What the individual demands of leisure depends on what he has and has not found in his work, and on what the education he has received has made him. A fully human life is enriched, constituted by non-work as well as by work. Education must also prepare for leisure. The human being fulfills himself also through leisure.

Today for millions of men leisure has a double function, a double virtue: It brings them echoes of the entire planet, it gives them the opportunity to discover a fragment of the vast world. Information and travel permit the individual to escape the narrowness of a small social milieu. He is able to know concretely that other societies, other peoples, other customs exist, which are not necessarily inferior to the society which is his, the people of which he is a member, or the customs which seem normal to him because they are his.

Never has humanity from one end of the planet to the other been as united in one single system as it is today. Never have the representatives of so many states met regularly in solemn assemblies. Never, before the twentieth century, has humanity known a single and same history on an earth whose modern means of communication, of production, and of destruction reduce its dimensions. Man at work occupies but *one* place, within *one* plant, *one* enterprise, *one* country. The man of leisure goes forth to the discovery of many peoples, many continents, many races. In this sense leisure *could* prepare humanity for the age in which we are entering, that of universal history—on condition that men, being sufficiently educated, should be able to profit from the denationalizing permitted by travel through time and space, travel by air or by hitch-hiking, travel in thought or in the images of the viewer in his armchair.

The opportunities are equal to the perils. The traveler runs the risk of losing himself. Or he could discover himself in discovering human diversity.

CHAPTER 10

❧

WORK AND THE INDIVIDUAL
IN THE MODERN WORLD

❧ ROGER M. BLOUGH

Work Is To Do

"Work" is pre-eminently a human matter. It concerns all humanity, and an inquiry into work is at once intriguing, baffling, and of high importance.

Work is central to living. It is as old as man and his religion. It is as new as an optical maser. It engenders the growth of nations. It is employment and unemployment. It is the freedom to work and freedom from work. It is necessity, security, frustration, and personal satisfaction. It is biological in its urge. It is everywhere —at home, in the field, at the shop, at school. It absorbs man's waking hours and besets his rest. It is alive with preconceptions and misconceptions—of which this paper undoubtedly has a goodly share.

Elusive are the descriptions of work. It may now, less than before, be defined as drudgery; yet some work may be so disagreeable and unrewarding as to be indistinguishable from drudgery. Work cannot be denominated exclusively as creative activity; yet there is much of creativity in work. It may be defined, in

173

physics, as energy transferred. And while this definition serves the physicist and is therefore useful for measurement in terms of physical change, it does not suffice when the human equation is added. The writer who spends an hour before rising in the morning pondering the next turn or twist of his handiwork is as much at work as in a later hour when words find their physical way to paper.

Work may possibly be defined as exertion undertaken other than for the enjoyment of the exertion itself, but this tends to becloud the pleasure, per se, in work.

Work may be thought of as change and, while this concept is useful to analysis, it falls short of ready understanding.

Work can be conceived of as molecular activity in animate or inanimate objects, and this serves usefully to point to the omnipresence of work and further the analysis, but this concept lacks comprehensiveness when measured against such things as motivation.

Work may be something a machine does and a man does, but certainly the two and the results of their efforts are not comparable.

Work has religious and philosophical connotations; and, although these aspects are all important, there is more to work.

Can it be said that "work is motivation in action"? This might apply to the slave who works to avoid punishment or to a drudge who works to avoid starvation. It might apply to the symphony conductor, who works at once for monetary rewards and by reason of a compelling desire for expression. But surely work is more than motivation to satisfy an immediate want.

Thus work is indeed intriguing and its definition elusive. It is as essential as food and rest. It is change; it is motivation; it is the satisfaction of a want; it is a means of nourishing self-respect—yet it is more.

Work is individuality in action. It is human expression. It is being one's self—effectively. It is—when well accomplished—the source of most enduring and widespread contentment.

Work is to do; it is ceaseless and seething energy amplified in its brighter human dimension by a but dimly discerned celestial fire.

Work in Earlier Years

Since one of the characteristics of man is his contemplative nature and since work has been such an omnipresent condition through all recorded time (and from all indications will be so for some time to come), it is only natural that much thought should have been given to work. Thus it is said that in ancient Greece and Rome work was considered a burden and without dignity. It was for slaves. Even free artisans and craftsmen were considered less than enviable. The honorable thing was to develop the arts and philosophy and to engage in politics—although at least in the present day these worthy callings would hardly constitute leisure.

This description of ancient disdain for work, though accepted in the writings of some, does not commend itself. For even the supervision of slaves must have involved a considerable amount of work.

A reasonable assumption might be that some forms of work were more distasteful and therefore to be avoided, if possible. Other forms of work could be performed by only a relative few. To conclude that the Greeks, for example, avoided work would be stretching credibility; to assert that they chose what work they could well perform might be closer to the fact. That choice in selection of work did exist and does is a happy circumstance; some of us would turn in a surprisingly negative performance as flute players in the New York Philharmonic.

To say that a Demosthenes, or later in Rome, a Cicero, was unacquainted with work or disdained it as demeaning is to strain any conceivable definition of the term. There is considerable evidence to the contrary. Marcus Aurelius, himself a tireless worker, wrote:

In the morning when thou risest unwillingly, let this thought be present—I am rising to the work of a human being. Why then am I dissatisfied if I am going to do the things for which I exist and for which I was brought into the world?

Ancient concepts of work as contained in the mores of many cultures and in religions are historically fascinating. Among the teachings of the Talmud it is said, "Great is work for it honors the workman." The ancient Hebrew concept saw work as a command from God: "Be fruitful, and multiply, and replenish the earth, and subdue it . . . ."

Later, the Hebrew concept evolved so that it looked upon work as punishment for Original Sin, attributable to the early fall of man: "By the sweat of thy face shalt thou eat bread."

With no discredit to this doctrine, one may find some grain of truth as well as comfort in Mark Twain's witticism:

> Let us be grateful to Adam, our benefactor. He cut us out of the "blessing" of idleness and won for us the "curse" of labor.

Regardless of the origin of work, all through the Old Testament there is evidence that work—plain physical work—was considered not only proper but an evidence of some righteousness.

It has been said, however, that Jesus' attitude was one of indifference to work. Support for this is claimed by reference to His words:

> Consider the lilies of the field, how they grow: they toil not neither do they spin.

Yet Jesus Himself was a carpenter. It is also quite clear that when He said to His disciples, "Go ye into all the world and preach the gospel to every creature," He was issuing a call to strenuous work and to hardship as St. Paul subsequently learned.

Whatever the concepts of work of the Romans and early Christians, whatever the truth of the assertions that work was considered without dignity and never an end in itself, work certainly became accepted as natural for "fallen man." This was borne out by the Benedictines. Lynn D. White, the classicist, tells us that St. Benedict's "insistence on the spiritual value of manual work makes Benedict the pivotal figure in the history of labor. . . . The provision of Benedict, himself an aristocrat, that his monks should work in fields and shops therefore marks a revolutionary reversal of the traditional attitude towards labor; it is a high peak along the watershed separating the modern from the ancient world. For the Benedictine monks regarded manual labor not as a mere regrettable necessity of their corporate life but rather as an integral and spiritually valuable part of their discipline."

Somewhat the same attitude toward work was manifested by Martin Luther. Work was good in and of itself. Work, for Luther, was a form of religious service.

With the doctrine of Calvinism and predestination came a new attitude toward work. Ceaseless effort and a proper valuation of the results of effort, not work for the purpose of acquiring leisure, but work for the sake of work and to be of greater service, was the teaching. And this concept included a religious sanction for profit, savings and investment in tools of production—for economic progress. It became a part of the Puritan spirit that permeated the New World, a base for the growth of the private capitalistic economy.

Dimensions of Modern Work

Before delving into the "how" and the "why" of work, its motivation, and its consequences for individuals and for nations, it is well to visualize, if only in one nation, the comprehensive and increasing dimensions of work.

To gain a perspective of work, it is useful to consider the growth of population and the changes in the work force since the turn of the century in the United States. For the world at large the multiple aspects and the dimensions of work have some degrees of difference, but also some similarity.

In the thirty-year period before 1900, the population of the United States almost doubled, increasing from 40 million to 76 million. In the next thirty-year period, from 1900 to 1930, population grew by 47 million people and increased to a total of 123 million. In the next thirty years, from 1930 to 1960, the increase was 57 million—to a total of 180 million.

In 1900 the total labor force was about 27.6 million. (Here we unfortunately but necessarily omit the indispensable lady of the home, not because well-performed home management is not highly skilled work as well as being one of living's most desirable rewards, and certainly we do not wish to be unchivalrous. However, statistical data provide their own limitations.) By 1960, the labor force had risen to more than 70 million. But since 1900, the nature of the work force has changed materially—and certainly the job content has changed. Moreover employment and unemployment have received much greater attention.

It is estimated that in 1900, 5 per cent of the civilian work force was unemployed; in the seventeen years from 1900 to 1916, inclusive, unemployment averaged 4.8 per cent. In the fourteen years from 1947 through 1960, unemployment averaged about 4.6 per cent of the civilian labor force. In 1960 it was 5.6 per cent. By contrast it is significant to note that after reaching 15.9 per cent in 1931 and 23.6 per cent in 1932 unemployment reached a peak of 24.9 per cent in 1933, and remained intolerably high at an average of 18.6 per cent during the 1933-1940 period. In all of these unemployment statistics, due allowance must be made for the degree of accuracy in collection, changes in definition of the word "unemployed" and general refinements of reporting. Moreover, there are probably many more women included now in the work force. If anything, today's unemployment data for the United States tend to have a bias on the high side in comparison with those of earlier years or with data from abroad.

In numbers of people, which is certainly an important consideration, unemployment rose from 1.4 million in 1900 to 3.9 million in 1960. The President's Economic Council estimates that a normal unemployment figure is about 4 per cent. In 1960 this would have been 2.8 million people out of 70 million in the work force.

It is to be expected that the normal—if there is such a thing as normal—number of individuals in the work force moving from place to place and seeking new jobs, or waiting recall to old jobs, or seeking employment for the first time, would increase as the total number in the work force increases. Thus the *number* of unemployed was greater in 1960 but the *proportion* of unemployed to the total work force is comparable to the ratio that prevailed during the early part of this century, and much lower than that of the 1930's.

So the fact is that thus far in this twentieth century, the creation of new job opportunities has kept pace fully with the rapid increase in the population and the continuous expansion of the work force. And interestingly, the fact also is that this has occurred in the midst of the greatest period of mechanization and advancing technology that this nation has yet witnessed.

It is also interesting to observe that after only nominal membership in 1900, the growth of unions rose fairly steadily until the 1930's when they grew rapidly. This rapid growth continued until it leveled out in the late 1940's. In 1960, of the total civilian work force of 70.6 million, about 21 percent or 15 million were members of labor unions. The effect upon work patterns, the work content in jobs, levels of employment costs and the many other effects of the presence of unions are entire subjects in themselves and important as they may be must remain, in the interest of reasonable selectivity and brevity, outside the scope of this inquiry.

The Transition to Industrialism and the Nature of Work

An extremely interesting inquiry would be to determine the source and general nature of the jobs which were created between 1900 and 1960. More than 40 million additional jobs came into being. The number of new jobs, of course, greatly exceeded 40 million, because during this period employment in agriculture dropped from 10.9 millon to 5.7 million, and many jobs in other types of employment became obsolete. How does one go about creating a job? And does the history of successful job-creation since 1900 suggest at least one answer? Population increase would of itself increase the number of people working but there is much more to job-creation than that.

Since non-farm white-collar workers rose from less than 30 per cent of those employed in 1900 to almost 47 per cent in 1960, it is evident that something significant has occurred—the nature of work has changed. Likewise, since the 37.5 per cent of all those employed in 1900 engaged in some type of farm employment dropped to only 8.9 per cent in 1958, a marked change in job content is obvious. Even the job content of work on farms also vastly changed.

It is also significant that in the short span of ten years after 1950, the number of service workers increased from 12 per cent of those employed in non-farm occupations to 13 per cent. The number of white-collar workers rose from 43 per cent to almost 47 per cent in 1960, and on the other hand, blue-collar workers declined from 45 per cent to 40 per cent. So the trend of increase toward white-collar employment is marked.

The character of both blue-collar and white-collar jobs has been altered. Both types of jobs now involve greater use of and responsibility for equipment. The jobs call for less physical and more mental effort—and there have also been changes in compensation. As the poet Ogden Nash once put it: "People who work sitting down get paid more than people who work standing up."

Thus it becomes clear that there flourished in this century a mechanism for creating and transforming work.

The significance of this transition to greater industrialization—which can readily be discerned in the growth of equipment, machinery, new types of plants, and so-called automation—is this: It was accompanied by a remarkable increase in the number of jobs in new kinds of work. If only population had increased—and nothing more—we would have 26 million farmers today instead of only 5.7 million.

The significance of the increase in the number of jobs is not lost when the length of the work week is taken into account. In 1909 the average work week in all manufacturing totaled 51 hours, and in 1960, about 40 hours. Thus technological improvement much more than accounted for the reduced work week and brought a marked increase in the number of jobs while changing the nature of work and relieving workers of many burdensome tasks.

One interesting datum * shows that in 1900 the source of energy in the United States was about 5.5 per cent human, 21.5 per cent animal, and 73 per cent inanimate. By 1950 this had changed to 0.9 per cent human, 0.6 per cent animal, and 98.5 per cent inanimate. This simply confirms that a much greater proportion of "work" is now accomplished through mechanical effort, and of course the aggregate amount of energy expanded and work accomplished is many times greater than it was in 1900, but that is another story.

What has happened in the United States has also undoubtedly occurred, to a greater or lesser degree, in other countries. For job-creating factors were present in varying degrees in all industrialized countries, although individuals have organized in somewhat different ways in order to accomplish their work. And the manner of organizing for work itself is of great importance.

Organized Work

In the dim past, man realized the usefulness of working with others and of employing even such primitive tools as the early plow to amplify his work.

Effective work is organized in a much more complex manner today, but in basic principle the organization is the same—a group of individuals working together and effectively using tools. By working together in groups, individuals can do for themselves what they cannot accomplish alone.

Most of the individual work in our nation must be done by

* *America's Needs and Resources.* Twentieth Century Fund, 1955.

people who are part of a group. Working together is not only the more effective way of working; it is the only way most of the work we do can be accomplished. Only people working together can build a passenger ship, a suspension bridge, an atomic reactor, or an automobile. Only an organized group can operate a railroad, an airline, or a department store.

This is not to say that organization for work is without its unrelenting and continuing problems, many of which are created by the size of the group and the complexity of the work to be accomplished. As C. Northcote Parkinson points out, "Work expands so as to fill the time available for its completion. . . . The thing to be done swells in importance and complexity in a direct ratio with the time to be spent. This fact is widely recognized, but less attention has been paid to its wider implications, more especially in the field of public administration. . . . The fact is that the number of the officials and the quantity of the work are not related to each other at all."

Not necessarily proving Parkinson's Law—and not overlooking the fact that in the United States, government functions and responsibilities have, with popular approval, been increasing—but indicating what he had in mind, perhaps, is the increase in government employees as compared to the increase in the remainder of the work force. In 1920, federal, state, and local government employees totaled 2.6 million. In 1960 they totaled 8.5 million. The increase in government workers, over the forty-year period was 225 per cent, compared to an 81 per cent increase in the number of non-government workers.

With the entry of many organized groups, large and small, into the private business and industry of the nation, a condition of competition was created. There are many facets to competition and many different concepts of competition in this country and elsewhere, including differing opinions as to the effectiveness of competition, most of which are beyond the scope of our inquiry.

What is relevant, and important, is that in a free society this competition between groups for success in their work is continuous and inescapable. It is competition for survival of the group as such by means of its ability to satisfy consumer needs.

Thus competition, itself, is work. There is rivalry between children at play. Competition is present among the numerous forms of religion. It is in art and in the multiple forms of art. It is especially present between groups which produce similar products for the market place. Competition among groups is a characteristic feature of any advanced industrial society which is based upon the individual having a choice in his work and in his purchases. Choice becomes the hallmark of individual freedom only where there is competition.

While individuals organize to compete, and, in most instances, are fitted for competition in production only if organized, and while organization helps to solve some problems, it also creates many others. Here we may consider only a few, and all of our inquiry must center on the individual.

Free Organization and the Search for a Better Way

First, a few observations regarding effective organization to do work. The intriguing things about any organized group, per se, are related to its purpose, its size, its leadership, and the measurement of its effectiveness. A group may be formed at the instance of government, or it may be private in origin. Either way, it is in effect a work group. While there are many reasons, and valid ones, why governments must organize groups to accomplish specific government objectives, in any individual-oriented society emphasis is necessarily and properly placed on the freedom of individuals to organize themselves at will and select their own form of organization. To the extent that government unnecessarily absorbs opportunities to do work which private groups might accomplish, to that extent the private sector of work is diminished; and this, in a free society, raises policy inquiries of first importance.

As there is freedom to organize, so there can and should be freedom in the selection of the work any organized group will perform. Likewise, in a free society, competition will provide its own disciplines and will measure the success of the group in working at its task. Its activities will, of course, be subjected to community scrutiny and some regulation, but its over-all effectiveness as a group and its usefulness to society will stand or fall in comparison with and in competition with other groups.

Given freedom to choose its task, it may well be that the group chooses to produce sewing machines, or photographic equipment, or even glass products. Its success will be a measure of its usefulness. But in a larger sense it is a part of the organizations which compose our society—a society at work. As an organized unit it is an inseparable and integral part of a production process by which people in society as a whole seek to better their lot. So that whatever physical function a particular group may perform, in a very real sense it represents a search on the part of a segment of society for a better way. The search may be for a better type of steel or a better automobile, or a more adequate form of credit, or an atomic-powered submarine, or a better food for man or beast. The group succeeds and benefits its own members and others only as it performs the primary responsibility of advancing that search.

These working groups, small or large, succeed by their production methods through technological improvement, through the better use of tools, but never without effective coordination among individuals.

Work in groups is naturally a mental as well as a mechanical process. It is market research as well as laboratory research. It is psychology and sociology as well as technology. It is, as someone has so aptly said, "imagineering as well as engineering." It is the use of the wheel, the strength of steel; it is the understanding of men and the understanding of materials, the better to harness the total energy of mind and matter to obtain the greater fruits from work. It results in more things for more people.

Inevitably, more tools, more "mechanization," more "automation" are employed—because more and better goods can best be produced with the aid of machinery, rather than by men alone, however great their number.

Some of these groups have performed so well that production is now entering a more advanced phase, employing mechanisms which, it is said, replace human effort. It would probably be more accurate to say that these new mechanisms are modifying the mental and physical effort which has heretofore been involved in production. This, of course, does not mean replacing a mind with a machine, although superficially it may seem so. For the machine must be designed, directed, and maintained by human minds and hands.

Thus, the group, as part of its search for a better way, must be continually examining its production process. In all of this there is an obligation on the part of those who create employment to design the individual's job so that it will represent a more adequate use of the individual's natural aptitudes and abilities. For the individual is the heart of the matter. His observation, judgment, reason, and his adaptability and versatility are indispensable.

In all of this organization for work, therefore, there need be no deterioration of the individual, no lack of pride in workmanship, no loss of creative opportunity; but there can and should be a continuous search not only for the better product or the more useful function, but also for the environmental betterment of the individual himself. For in the larger sense, he and the associates in his own group and in his society are the objects of the search for improvement. An economist Frank Chodorov has said, "There will not be a good society until there are good people."

A Creed of Human Relations

In the organized work group of which I am a part, we have tried to articulate this Search for a Better Way in a statement we call "Our Creed of Human Relations":

We believe in the dignity and importance of the individual employee and in his right to derive personal satisfaction from his employment.

We believe each employee working toward attainment of the general business objective is an important member of the Corporation's team.

We believe each employee is entitled to receive—recognition and respect as an individual, constructive leadership, adequate information about his job and the business, prompt and fair consideration of his occupational problems, encouragement to contribute his ideas for improvement, opportunity to develop and advance, equitable compensation, and safe working conditions.

We believe each employee has the responsibility to—make the most effective use of his skill, effort, equipment, and time in the performance of necessary work—provide loyal and faithful service to other employees and the Corporation—and cooperate fully toward attainment of the general business objective.

This creed, we believe, expresses our concept of the relation between work, teamwork, and the individual—a relation that forms the nexus of one group's total philosophy of work.

Some years ago an attempt was made to learn the opinions of thousands of individuals in our company concerning the human relations among us. This was done in the form of a questionnaire sent to front-line supervisors and others in a management group of 25,000 people. The answers to the questionnaire were sent anonymously to a university for tabulation and analysis, thus assuring candor in the responses. Happily a great preponderance were reasonably satisfied with their work environment; but many found something to criticize, or one or more changes to suggest.

Among the things with which the individuals were most concerned were the personal recognition and respect they received, and the sense of belonging to the group. A number desired more information concerning work group affairs and wished to be taken into confidence. They wanted more information with respect to plans affecting their work. They felt a need of opportunity to be heard, to express ideas and opinions, although only about one in ten offered this suggestion. They wished more adequacy of definition, both of their duties and their authority. They wished support from their superiors in the exercise of their function, and an occasional word of appreciation. Interestingly enough, those dissatisfied with the treatment received at the hands of their colleagues outnumbered those dissatisfied with the respect and recognition they received from their superiors. Many said they would like to be more useful, and a number were searching for more guidance.

There was great support for the idea of promoting from within and for not bringing in new people to fill job opportunities. With it all, there seemed a desire to make the most effective use of skill and effort, equipment and time. Certainly all associated in the group may be said to have been concerned with individual recognition and respect, the opportunity to develop and advance, constructive leadership, equitable compensation, adequate information, and safe working conditions. All seemed to want to contribute their ideas for the success of the enterprise.

This study, however, offers only a partial answer to the question: How does being a part of a working organization affect the individual?

The Worker in His Work

Whatever description of work one may adopt, there is for most people, although clearly not all, an internal reaction to work, conscious or subconscious, which affords a sense of well-being that can be described as pleasurable. In the words of Thomas Carlyle:

> Older than all preached Gospels was this unpreached, inarticulate, but ineradicable, forever-enduring Gospel: Work, and therein have well-being.

An insight into the value to the individual himself of having work to do can be gained by the effect upon him of having no work to do. For instance, one of the tragedies of a depression is the effect that unemployment has upon the individual worker. For most people, being "laid off" is a personal depressant. Not only are the individual's standard of living, and even his necessities for living, at stake, but so are his personal relations with former associates in his work, with the community in which he lives, and even within his own family—all of which may seriously deteriorate. He loses confidence in himself. His life appears purposeless, insecure, and without direction. Thus prolonged and involuntary unemployment, aside from all of its other social effects, has its personality results just as does the accomplishment of effective work.

Another way of testing the personal benefits of having work to do arises with the ill, the handicapped, and the retired. Who finds greater satisfaction in his work than a blind individual, or an ex-soldier who has suffered a great disability, when, by training or retraining, he finds a suitable and rewarding occupation? And how frequently is retirement simply an opportunity to do a form of work one has long been ambitious to try?

It may be fashionable to say that no one loves labor for itself. It is also true that there is an almost universal disinclination to do unrewarding or fruitless work, and when the effort which must be expended in the performance of a given task exceeds the satisfactions—material, psychological or spiritual—to be obtained from the successful completion of that task, the willingness to do such work diminishes as the incentive dwindles.

But for most people enforced idleness is more onerous than the requirement to do what most of us in this nation are doing. We can agree with Voltaire: "Work keeps at bay three great evils, boredom, vice and need."

There is also an element of truth in the assertion that work in an organization involves some irksome submission to routine and to the direction of others, and that this may cause some resentment. Being required to do anything by circumstances, or doing it at the request of our associates, is never as pleasant as doing it on one's own initiative. The existence of any external discipline, whether it be circumstances, people, governmental authority—even such a simple discipline as obeying the traffic laws—

may cause a reaction which makes living less pleasurable. Thus, it may be said that no one "loves" work or the rigors of work or the associates who signify work in the worker's mind.

If all this be true, then the circumstances under which work would be the most pleasurable would be those which afford the greatest range of initiative and where external and internal organizational conditions are associated with a minimum of feeling of discipline. The art in modern organization is to combine the discipline which an effective organization must have to accomplish its work with the freedoms of initiative and expression important to the individuals composing the group.

To work is to express one's individualism. To the degree that the external discipline or authority is a necessary factor, to that degree the individualism must adapt itself. To the degree that work is voluntary, purposeful, responsible, and accomplished in a free atmosphere, to that degree it is less of drudgery and more rewarding.

There are other reactions that help to compensate for any natural emotional resentment against work as a part of an organization. One is the sense of belonging to a group of reasonably congenial but healthily aggressive fellow workers. One is the feeling of doing something useful, particularly in the absence of discomfort or fatigue or hazard. An additional compensation is a feeling of satisfaction in the workmanship and of pride in the product, together with a feeling of being appreciated. Pride of achievement can be as gratifying when arising through synchronized machine production as when it comes from manual craftsmanship, for satisfactions arise through mastery of a technology, a new skill the worker did not know or did not need in earlier days.

Work in organizations can provide all of these satisfactions, as well as providing the necessities of existence. If the work is successful it will provide more than mere existence—it will provide a better home and economic means to find relaxation and pleasure in the pursuit of hobbies and travel.

To work well is to perform a responsibility; to assume responsibility identifies an individual as mature, even though the individual is a boy of ten years selling papers for his own account.
To work well is to develop the real dignity of the individual.

Genuine dignity in a worker emerges as the individual gives
strength to the group and gains strength from the group. For
only in his strength and in the strength of the group is there
mutual respect and security. He is first a free man, free to join
the group and free to leave, free to produce and to distribute,
and to enrich his own economic and social values.

The very joining and leaving is a constant and dynamic process. Those who leave a group usually seek an opportunity elsewhere. Those who join seek work for all the reasons we have
pursued.

In the United States there are more than four million industrial and other enterprise units from which he can choose. And
there are many millions of professionals, sole traders, artists and
artisans, and other single, non-group-associated individuals. Even
so, the very existence of numerous small and large organized
groups is essential to the preservation of single individual effort—
whether by lawyer, doctor, poet, or painter. There are more than
35,000 ways of earning a living in the United States.

Work Is a Multi-Colored Spectrum

Work is a multi-colored spectrum showing one hue to the
day laborer and another to the college president. If the laborer's
work were suddenly made to consist solely of mental problems,
ideas and concepts, and constant dealing with people, his feeling
of inadequacy and frustration would probably exceed any satisfaction from his occupation. On the other hand, if a college president were forced to follow a mechanical ditch-digger with a
shovel in his hand, his sense of usefulness might come to a
dead end.

Psychiatrists tell us that strong guilt feelings often are associated with working at the "wrong" occupation; the improperly

placed individual may feel very uncomfortable and inadequate. This is undoubtedly true, but the answer to this lies within the individual and is certainly not an indictment either of his work or of organized work.

Quite the contrary feeling arises when the work done is somehow a thing of value and especially is this true when it is of value to others.

But it is frequently said that repetitive work is deadening and that the modern white-collar or blue-collar worker who deals with a repetitive action leads a very dull life indeed. This satirical concept pictures work as repeatedly twisting a wrench on identical nuts as they pass on an assembly line—a portrayal made famous by Charlie Chaplin many years ago. That concept, I suspect, is as out of date as is the unreal script which inspired it.

Comparisons are frequently attempted between the individual craftsmanship of recent centuries and the alleged robot nature of work today. Cracking stones with a sledge hammer, washing dishes continuously, planting rice or corn, or pulling weeds by hand, shoveling coal into a boiler or innumerable other forms of work may have had some virtue and still do. But few people today would select the older types of work in place of the modern job they have. Of course, the expert artisan, the fine carpenter or silversmith was no robot then—nor is he now—but his work cannot be compared properly with the least rewarding work of today. In any case, workers are not being turned into machines; rather, with technological advance, they are presented with the opportunity to master skills which challenge their capacities— skills which test all available human ingenuity. Work in a modern manufacturing plant or office need not be dull.

It is often said that there is a continuing contest, in large organizations, between those who manage and those who are managed, with the latter rebelling against the exercise of authority. On some matters it is futile to generalize, and this seems to be one of them. It can, of course, be observed that there are many unresolved problems related to work involving new equipment or changes in crew size or installation of incentive plans, or matters of that kind. In any event, there are usually two sides to the question. It may also be that the so-called "problem" between managers and employees relates more to the elemental resistance against change. Most of us prefer to do things as we did them before, to follow our habitual way. This resistance to change may be in the managed or in the manager. Or it may, on occasion, be found in both.

It is interesting to note that this resistance to change becomes less of a problem in completely new work, as in a new plant built in a new location. In this case, where changes are numerous, an entirely altered situation arises. The environment is different, the machinery and equipment modern; there are new crews, new work habits, new standards of accomplishment. While performance standards and changes from old work habits may be resisted in this new environment, at least there is a fair chance that the necessary changes will be met with more understanding. This is especially true where the motivation in the form of incentives or otherwise is found satisfactory.

Resistance to change is human and understandable, but it is well to remember that competition in group work involves constant change.

New forces come into play, new or more competitive products, new forms of taxes, new equipment—all of which constitute change and compel working under different circumstances. Changes in customer needs and demands also necessitate changes in work to assure acceptance of products in the market place. The entire process of change is inexorable and natural. It constitutes a discipline which is at once harsh and cleansing in its reaction upon the individual or the group that does not work well. It is beneficial over-all, since it eliminates the unnecessary and the unwanted.

In the midst of technological and institutional revolutions, resistance to innovation can be a form of slow-motion suicide— for individual groups or for nations. If desirable change is not accepted, the competitive world will by-pass any craft, or department, or business unit, or entire industry, or even any nation that resists it. There is no compensating counterbalance for undue resistance to change.

The art then, in working with people, is to achieve useful change in an acceptable fashion, an art exceeded only by the higher art which inspired the innovation to which the adjustment must be made.

Technological Advance, New Jobs and More Jobs

Group work and technological advance have gone hand in hand. One builds upon the other. But since the Middle Ages there has always been the fear that growing technology and industrialization will create a jobless labor force instead of creating jobs. Part of this fear comes from temporary job dislocation which is a very real and disturbing circumstance to those involved. Part of the fear arises from mistaking cyclical change, with its periods of reduced employment, for the results of technology. And part of the problem arises from a lack of understanding of the inevitable and much deeper spread of joblessness in any group or local area if it does not keep competitive technologically. Moreover, there is of necessity a job-changing and work-saving mechanization in the process of job-creation, in making the new tools and manning the new tools which produce better goods for wider markets.

One cannot be dogmatic about work, but we have seen how in the United States the number of jobs has kept pace with population and has increased in the last sixty years by the very appreciable total of many more than forty million. We have also noted the marked and, for most people, pleasing change in job content. All of this occurred during a period of national growth characterized by intense mechanization and by no relative increase in unemployed workers.

While there are of course many factors involved, it would seem irrefutable, therefore, that national growth, investment to mechanize work, and more jobs are all interdependent. This is to say that in our modern world national growth reflects the rate of mechanization and in turn growth in mechanization finds reflection in national growth.

If this relationship is valid, then one would expect that where there is greater national growth and employment there also would be greater growth in mechanization. Observation appears to confirm this: there are numerous examples of greater mechanization and greater national growth among nations with high, although not always evenly sustained, employment.

For example, it appears, based on data available for the period 1950 to 1959, that in Western Germany and in Japan output and investment grew faster than in France and England, and the growth in the number of jobs tended to follow these trends.

We do not here consider the "why" of more or less rapid growth or technological advance, but simply the relation of growth, investment, and the availability of new jobs. It is of course true that in these countries both increased mechanization and employment were affected by many things, including post-war necessities and a pent-up reconstruction demand. There are other reasons why the data cannot be regarded as wholly conclusive. Nevertheless, they do not appear to belie observation that the process of mechanization sustains and increases employment and, while changing job content, does not in the over-all siphon away work which previously existed.

For the United states, comprehensive data are available which enable us to make certain supporting, if not wholly conclusive, observations. This can be done by comparing the data on productive employment and investment during the decade of the 1930's, before World War II, with the decade of the 1950's after that war.

In the course of compiling the gross national product data, sufficient detail has been provided to permit a determination of investment for new productive purposes. This is done by subtracting from gross private domestic investment the expenditures for residential non-farm construction and the amounts for depreciation—which represent expenditures intended to maintain existing production facilities. The remainder can be regarded as business expenditures for additional construction, for equipment, and for inventories—all of which are new job-creating investment.

INVESTMENT AND EMPLOYMENT—United States*

	1930-1939	1950-1959
INVESTMENT (in billions)		
Gross Business Expenditures for Non-Residential Construction, Equipment, and Inventories	$49	$418
LESS: Capital Consumption Allowances (reported depreciation)	77	303
Net New Business Expenditures	$28†	$115
EMPLOYMENT (in millions)		
Net Increase in Number of Persons Engaged in Private Production	2.3†	6.3

* Source: U. S. Department of Commerce
† Net Decrease

In the 1930's such expenditures were a minus quantity. In other words, as the Table shows, the capital expenditures of business were not sufficient to maintain existing facilities as measured by the depreciation on them. From 1930 to 1940 private productive employment actually decreased by about 2.3 million (or 5 per cent) despite an expansion in the available labor force of about 6 million.

In the 1950's, in contrast, such new job-creating expenditures aggregated $115 billion, and employment increased substantially—by 6.3 million, or over 12 per cent.

From these same data an estimate of the amount of investment per new job created can readily be made. The $115 billion figure for the 1950's, divided by the 6.3 million increase in employment, gives $18,000 as the amount required, on the average, to provide a new job.

The data further provide a means of approximating the source of the new investment. Thus corporate profits not paid out in dividends amounted to $85 billion, covering about three-quarters of the net new business expenditures of around $115 billion. This means that about $13,000 of the $18,000 average could come from reinvested profits and the balance of around $5,000 was available from savings invested by individuals all over the United States, including funds accumulated by workers from their wages.

All this leads up to this simple fact. It takes "people" and "work"—quite a lot of work—to generate the savings and investment needed to create and equip a new job. Using the 1950's as a sample period, 50 to 56 million "people" were engaged in generating, through production, corporate and personal savings which were invested in tools and thus provided 6.3 million more jobs. Under the conditions prevailing during the 1950's one could conclude, without stretching the data unreasonably, that the annual work of more than 80 people was required to create one new job at the relative rates at which savings were generated and invested in new equipment during the 1950's. Hence, in a free country, will not work for the future depend on the savings of corporations and individuals which are necessary to pay for the new tools of work? Is there any way to provide work for free men other than by people working and saving?

This may lead to another question: Can government create new jobs, and, if so, who pays for them?

During the depressed 1930's, virtually all the net additional jobs added in this nation were government jobs. They almost doubled, increasing by about 2.8 million. During this same period, both government expenditures and debt increased while corporate and personal savings available for business investment declined. At the same time, unemployment in the civilian labor force was very high, averaging about 18 per cent. In the 1950's the number of people employed by government increased by 2.9 million, about the same as the 1930's, but contrary to the 1930's persons engaged in private production increased by 6.3 million and savings rose.

The added government jobs were financed in part out of taxes —more out of greater taxes on individuals than from corporate taxes—not because of a decline in corporate tax rates, but rather because taxable corporate profits were relatively less. The ability to pay individual taxes arose, of course, out of production, that is, out of work.

Beyond this, there were further sizable increases in government debt. To some extent this borrowing to pay for government jobs was financed in an inflationary way and thus represented a resort to a hidden form of taxation—an erosion of the buying power of dollars including those that were vitally needed for mechanization and creation of real, private, productive, new work.

To summarize, therefore, mechanization and technological improvement in general, while changing job content and eliminating some jobs, has proved to be a job-creating mechanism of great proportions—and is inextricably intertwined with national growth. Moreover, in a free country the future creation of jobs is directly correlated with invested savings, both corporate and personal, and this in turn depends upon the freedoms and incentives in work and the effectiveness with which work is performed.

Motivation

Organized work, and for that matter all work, relies on motivation. This may consist of the struggle for survival, the motivation of monetary or other material rewards, the desire for physical security, the motivation of position or prestige, the satisfaction in being a part of the organization, or the satisfaction in work itself.

There is the motivation of team play in a group, the kind of approval and satisfaction that comes from belonging to a winning combination which, for example, has broken a record. This is amply demonstrated by plants that increase their production quite markedly under the stimulation of this motivation—and fail to do this where there is negative motivation.

There is also the motivation in pride of workmanship, an enduring type of motivation. Another is the patriotic motivation during periods of national emergencies. Adherence to ideologies is another. These motivations have been and will continue to be effective ones.

There is also the motivation of which H. L. Mencken wrote:

> You ask . . . why I go on working. I go on working for the same reason a hen goes on laying eggs.

Mountaineer George Mallory had a form of motivation when he tried to conquer Mount Everest because, as he said, it was there to be climbed.

Beyond these motivations, however, in the well-developed civilizations of the world at least, there is need for supplemental motivations.

One of the aspects of motivation is the hope for some reward, monetary or otherwise, in relation to the measure of the value of one's work—a kind of measurement of fairness.

There is also the complex motivation which arises from ownership interest. This is exemplified in small businesses of which there are hundreds of thousands in this country. Among those in the civilian work force probably one-third are in single proprietor or partnership businesses. For example, there are about a million retail establishments in the United States which do less than $50,000 of business annually. Common ownership in larger or small business serves to maintain and build upon a community of interest among those engaged in the common effort.

It is interesting to note that probably fifteen million Americans own shares in American corporations and, of course, many others have an indirect interest through their participation in insurance companies, investment trusts, and many other types of organizations.

Perhaps one of the strongest motivating forces in any work situation is habit. Habit is at once valuable and restrictive—valuable because it is an important determinant in the quality of the work performed, restrictive because of the difficulty in changing any work habit when a better way is found.

There is also the motivation associated with appreciation.

Recently several management men in a front-line organization were discussing appreciation for work well done. One man said: "The appreciation I want from my boss is additional work to do; then I know what I have done is satisfactory and I have a chance for advancement."

Probably one of the greatest motivations in anyone's work is the desire to have his work recognized so that he will enjoy a better status in the eyes of his fellow men. To some this means as much as economic rewards and the satisfactions inherent in successful completion of a task.

In addition to these rather elemental reasons why men work, there is another motivation. It exists whether the worker is part of an organized group or whether he works alone. It derives from a basic desire to serve his fellow man, to serve, sometimes, without necessarily knowing why—even though he frequently suffers disappointment in the manner in which his service is received. Whether he serves in a productive group, or a college faculty or board of trustees, or a town council, or in some federal post in Washington, the individual becomes, in his own thinking—if he thinks about it at all—a more useful and contributing member of society. His desire to serve is a form of self-expression; it is individualism.

We have been discussing men working in groups to accomplish their tasks. Perhaps it would have been more precise to use the words "unique persons," instead of "men." For each man is unique. Each has different capacities, strengths, weaknesses, and depths of character. It is from the expression of these individual qualifications and characteristics that great individual work has come—yet these very diversities are also the touchstone of inspired team play.

Uniqueness and individual freedom in work are not, as sometimes supposed, antithetical to effective organization and teamwork. Quite the contrary. Successful teamwork demands that each position be played individually and well. Otherwise the team fails, as any baseball manager can attest. Thus the procedure with respect to rate or flow of production, or synchronized functions, is an over-all effort.

Working Groups in a Complex Society

Since 1900 the voluntary groups of individuals organized for production have become increasingly complex, both within themselves and within the "society of groups," if that is a useful term. Many groups today compose to a degree at least a kind of self-contained community in which the individuals composing the group have a marked common interest in addition to their interests as members in the community at large.

Rapid growth in the size of groups, technological change, the increasing millions of individuals employed, large-scale production, and market diversifications have had their effect on the evolution of these voluntary groups.

This evolution is evidence of private initiative and enterprise coupled with man's steadily advancing search for means of organizing and working together to accomplish stated objectives. As such, existing forms of organizations may be looked upon as a marked achievement of recent history.

How best to work as groups within the larger responsibility of society is an unmapped terrain. For the future the success or failure of these groups of fellow workers will depend not only upon their general effectiveness but upon their acceptance within society as a whole—of which in the aggregate their members compose by far the greater part.

Clearly, however, it is incumbent on those within the voluntary production groups to assist in the strengthening of other groups, such as those in education, science, culture and social welfare, for these groups, in the broader sense, are equally productive. Certain interrelations between, for example, those who compose an educational institution and those in commercial production are becoming increasingly clear. The desirability of mutual support and the free exchange between these groups is also becoming increasingly clear.

In all of this the guide line for progress is the preservation of the integrity and individuality of the person per se, and the freely formed groups which are not directly involved in production can be most helpful and effective in this area.

Whatever form of organization may be necessary to insure progress in a highly complex world, it is yet to be demonstrated that any need exists for a type of organization which fails to insure freedoms for the individual or which shears the strengthening effect of work from man as Delilah weakened Samson by trimming his locks.

Perhaps the best insurance is to recognize those attributes of organization which contribute to acceptance of responsibility. For, inherently, acceptance of responsibility depends upon individual qualification. And a free society depends upon the preserving and increasing of what may be referred to as a blood bank of qualification. Only through self-expression in achieving individual excellence can the individuals in a group meet this test of qualification.

Western civilization has in recent centuries achieved its dimensions in the hard self-discipline and the endless sacrifices of its individual members. In its truer expressions of self-government, of private initiative, of multiple forms of organization—both in the commercial and non-commercial areas—the basis for advance is the individual, his personal qualifications for work and for life.

Industrialization, as it is known in the Western world, is simply then the manifestation of free men at work. It is the handmaiden of free men.

Industrialization is bound to grow. For the free individual characteristically is unceasingly engaged in a restless search for improvement. He ceases to be satisfied with the more burdensome way when he perceives the better, easier, more productive way. This constant search and the role of industrialization in fostering that search are as real as the existence of Mount Everest, the Statue of Liberty, or atomic fission.

Industrialization is simply man's way of utilizing more creatively the technological aids available to him. Industrialization moves apace by fits and starts, momentarily delayed here, rapidly advancing there. But given a reasonably peaceful world, the eventual world-wide sweep of industrialization is as inevitable as the persistence of ever-higher human aspirations.

The larger question then is how work shall be accomplished and what effect it will have on the human spirit, the propagation of individual opportunity, and the preservation of human dignity.

Work in Newer Nations and Competition Between Nations

It will undoubtedly convey no new image to speak of widening competition in a shrinking world. But with modern communications and transportation systems, and with the United Nations and the multiple forms of interchange, there is an impact of world affairs on all nations never before experienced. This impinging of the world upon every single nation has special relevance to work.

We have seen something of the development of work concepts in America, their relationship to early religions and to the later Calvinistic and Puritan concept. We have noted the necessity and advantages of organized work and the way it has been organized. And we have considered the effect of work on the worker himself.

It may well be that the rise and fall of any society is related to its concepts of work and to its willingness to change those concepts to make them more effective. While there are many complex, ethnical, religious and national habits relating to peoples and to their work, it can be said with some degree of accuracy that the changing of a given concept of work to a newer concept— for example the usefulness of organized work, the manner of accomplishing organized work—and the rapidity of that change, will determine the mode and rapidity of the industrialization of a country.

If one may be permitted to refer to the success of the United States in production, it would be to emphasize as a contributing factor our ability to organize larger business units while preserving the smaller, and our methods of accomplishing work—all in an atmosphere which permitted the acquisition of the tools of production but at the same time preserved individuality.

The utility of tools was well put by Carl Snyder.

> It is obvious that we cannot have any general gain of wealth, comfort and enjoyments for the whole nation save by a definite increase in the product per worker; no other way. But this, we now know, does not usually mean any fabled gain in the "efficiency" of the workers. There may be a little, but only that. It may be doubted if, on the average, the workers of today are more industrious, skillful, or "efficient" than those of a century ago. Practically the sole gain in product is through improved machinery, new processes, new inventions and discoveries. This is precisely what is meant by the Industrial Revolution.

It is well to repeat that while the productiveness of a less-developed country will be enhanced by additional capital, machinery, and equipment, the most important thing which any emerging nation can hope to secure from a more industrialized country is a new concept of work.

This does not necessarily mean that the workers in the less-developed country need to work harder, although that may be involved, but it does mean that with certain work and thrift concepts they, as individual workers, can enhance their effectiveness, generate the capital that is imperative if workers are to obtain and use better tools and thus gain for themselves a better means of living.

The point is that the secret of growth and productiveness of any nation is not the acquisition of machinery from outside its borders, useful as that may be. For machinery is perishable and is soon obsolete. The secret is to acquire new concepts of work, particularly organized work, and the source, in work, of the machinery and equipment.

One may not weave too fine a skein in support of one cause or another to explain effective industrialization. It is certainly true that physical climate may be a factor, raw materials may be

involved, as well as the aptitudes of the populace. But it is strikingly and repeatedly demonstrated that organized work is vital
to production. The supplying of this concept of work is therefore
of first consequence—but it also creates its own reactions.

Many countries, for example, welcome the help toward greater
industrialization that foreign capital and work methods can give.
But they frequently request that the ownership of the new enterprises be on a partnership basis. Some do so in order that their
nationals may have a hand in formulating their own advances
in their own societies and that individuals in those countries may
be afforded full opportunity for self-development.

This may be thought of as a feature of nationalism, and that
may be. But it is also, to a degree, individualism asserting itself.

If, therefore, the problems of less industrialized nations weigh
heavily upon the nations themselves and upon those who would
assist them, let measures be discovered and introduced which have
created industry elsewhere. Let improved work attitudes and improved organization of work begin to operate at its own creative
level. This is much easier to say than to do, but it is the only
way for those who wish to be both industrialized and free.

The work of industrialization moves forward, regardless of
who does it, or how it is accomplished, or the many problems it
presents. And as it proceeds, questions are frequently raised
regarding the ability of a free society to survive in competition
with a less free society. This question really subjects to inquiry
the relative effectiveness of one form of organized work in comparison wth another. If the concepts which we have been discussing have any validity they lead inevitably to the conclusion that
great flexibility—in working organizations, in the size of the work
units, in the freedoms for the individuals involved to choose work
—comprises the most effective way to accomplish work regardless
of competition between nations. Where competition does exist
between nations and among groups of nations, these concepts
should be all the more valid.

Increasingly we see arising broader-than-one-nation institutions. They arise for special purposes such as defense as in NATO or to create economic improvement as in the Common Market. These arrangements affect work and rely upon it. In fact, they arise for the same reasons that individuals form groups, that they as nations may accomplish with others what they cannot successfully accomplish alone. As in the case of individuals, it is essential that nations choose their own arrangements and be responsible for their own results.

How far this combination to seek common objectives among nations will proceed is problematical. But if economic organization in free societies be any guide, the trend toward multi-nation institutions may continue. If it does, it will affect many things, including work groups. In fact the anxiety of independent work groups to get on with their work may be one of the motivations of nations to establish the various multiple-nation institutions. In the long view, what is elemental in this relationship between production groups is to a degree elemental in the emergent attempts to establish multi-nation relationships.

It may also be that when the developments of the next century become history, the most absorbing phase of that history of nations will be that which relates to their methods of work. For while the motivations of the people as a whole are many, the adoption of less successful or more successful methods of work must certainly be influential in the success of any nation.

It has been said that bad money drives out good. By like token, it may be said that good work drives out bad, in that it is competitively more acceptable. Good methods of organizing work simply out-distance poor methods of organizing work—just as the first Ford car is out-distanced by its modern progeny.

Those who may be concerned, therefore, with the competition between nations or among groups of nations, should first inquire into the work habits of men: how they organize to accomplish their tasks, the usefulness and freedom of groups at work, and the ability to acquire tools for work—freely and rapidly.

In all of this search the focal point is the reality of individualism, the *raison d'être* for human freedom. To the degree that industrialization permits the expression of human freedom it will endure, and to the degree that industrialization suppresses voluntary action and constricts the human spirit, it will deteriorate, dragging into degradation its victims.

This is the lesson of history as it relates to work. And this is the way that organized work may serve the tide of man's rise. This is the operation of equality of opportunity and not the leveling of personalities. This then is industrialization—the way the needed work of any nation can be accomplished. This is the way for those who seek industrialization and freedom.

An Evaluation

We thus conclude where we began—work is pre-eminently a human matter. In our increasingly busy world of work and constantly changing values what are we busy about and what do we value?

Are we busy about more homes with more family comforts in the home, more forms of transportation and more travel, more schools and higher standards of instruction, more hospitals and clinics and better health, more houses of worship, more athletic events, more cultural centers of music and art? We are indeed; but is there anything substantively mischievous about the quest for widespread better homes and work-lightening appliances, and should this quest preoccupy the present-day Jeremiahs whose unwearied strains petition us so unremittingly?

Are we not also concerned, and rightly so, with the discovery of how men of all lands can best live together in reasonable harmony under voluntarily adopted law and not by the dictation of brute force? Do we not try mightily in thousands of research centers to create and to innovate for bettering life even while, of necessity, learning the means of defending life? Are we not concerned with the soaring population that creates the need for work but multiplies the trials and errors in securing its accomplishments?

Do we not—and naturally—in the midst of these inevitable struggles have grave misgivings regarding our times, the magnitude of our seemingly unsolvable affairs and our effectiveness as a society—in work patterns and in human relations? And do not many of the thoughtful feel a state of serious apprehension in which real and imaginary evil crowds out the many virtues surrounding our work and our existence? Do some not say with increasing resignation,

> The world is too much with us; late and soon,
> Getting and spending, we lay waste our powers. . . .

Yet in the more understanding and helpful moments, do we not remember those who *do* think of work as something more than better plumbing and refrigerators, who *do* understand that there are no elite in industrial production and that tomorrow's vice-president is today's first line foreman, that interpreting a new advance in science in terms of its relation to human sensibilities is important *too*, that the unleashing of human capability is the object of organization and the object is not organization for, by, and of itself?

It is true there are those who do feel lost in an industrial world—in a world of work of which they see only a fragment—and who tend to feel a spiritual bruise within themselves even while others facing the same circumstances are continents apart in reaction and in evaluation. This must be recognized, but only for what it mostly is—the opportunity among free men to be dissatisfied and to do something about their dissatisfaction, especially about work. For this dissatisfaction is not the deepest hurt; that can come only from those things which cannot be corrected.

If we may then evaluate work as we know it in its better aspects, is it not creativity and is there not the opportunity of making it more so? Does it not provide many more with personal participation and private ownership of their own productiveness? Are not the standards of work and the conditions of its performance constantly being raised? Is not the individuality of man and his personality enhanced by the improving nature of work content in the modern circumstances of work? Does the individual himself not have more time and more means for cultural interests and eleemosynary and public matters? Is not the nagging hunger of men for improvement and individual achievement somehow better satisfied than before?

Are we not, in a word, observing so many examples of service by individuals within groups and alone which are beyond the call of duty, instances of extraordinary performance, of the sparkling non-conformity of excellence, that these examples tend to become almost commonplace—just as the average human height has increased?

At least in one view, the frustrations and the fears of the few are exceeded in the work patterns we have considered by the satisfactions and the achievements of the many—by the increasing excellence of the common man, if such there be, and of the uncommon man.

The gropings and the searching for the better human way will and must continue, but let the enshrinement of individualism be the lode star. For this is the fulfillment of human work.

CHAPTER 11

ـﻪﻰ

A REPORT ON RECENT
EDUCATIONAL HISTORY

ﻪﻰ McGEORGE BUNDY

IT IS AN HONOR to be asked to give the report on Recent Educational History for the Corning Educational Conference of 1975. The framers of this meeting quite rightly believe that the last fifteen years have seen extraordinary and unprecedented improvements in American education, and I rejoice in the chance to analyze these matters before this notable audience. What makes your invitation a particular distinction, of course, is the happy change that has occurred in our habits of conference in the last fifteen years. The 1950's, as the older members of this audience will recall, were clouded for professional academic men by a preposterous proliferation of panels, discussions, conferences, weekend retreats, symposia, and other semi-formal gatherings—all sustained by an assertion of noble purpose and paid for by people unable to think of any better way to spend their money. All this has changed so radically today that this is the first invitation for a speech of this kind, which I have had since the Eliot Centennial at Harvard in 1969. This is a gain for both the audience and the speaker.

In the last fifteen years, as always, higher education in this country has lived in the context of society as a whole, and it is therefore only right to remember, as we begin our review, that like everything else American education since 1960 has been deeply affected by the national response to three great challenges. The first and greatest of these, of course, was the challenge to find a stable expectation of survival in a world desperately divided in its politics, and terribly threatened by its new ability to make weapons of staggering power. To say that the world is safe today would be wrong, but clearly it has survived, and on the whole its chances of continued survival have improved. The second great accomplishment, for the United States, has been the resolute and varied attack upon the basic problem of space—this is, of course, not the relatively trivial problem of "outer" space which was so noisily debated in the latter years of the 1950's; it is rather the matter of sound use and development of our own acres, limited as they are, and pressed upon as they necessarily have been by the growing needs of a growing population and the special demands of the new kind of civilization we have been building.

And finally, of course, all of us lived, in these years, through a redefinition and reassertion of our purpose as human beings. At the end of the 1950's, this question was often called the problem of "national purpose," and in a sense, because of the faltering and uncertain government of those years, the focus set by the adjective was useful. But more deeply (as most of us knew then, and as we all have come to understand in later years), the crisis of the mid-century was a crisis, both individual and general, in the human condition. Our rediscovery of the high purpose of man as a living, loving, thinking, and acting moral entity, as I am almost ashamed to reiterate, is the decisive accomplishment of our society since 1960. That this rediscovery is not uniquely American is only another way of saying that it is right and important, and I wish I dared to steal your time at this meeting on education for an attempt to assess fairly the various contributions to the new orchestration of man's place on earth which have been made in these last years from every society, across all the national borders whose persistence reminds us of both great traditions and unfinished business.

In all of these things our colleges and universities bore a large part. It is curious, and amusing, to recall that right through the 1950's there was an unresolved debate among American academic men as to the proper role and function of the university in relation to such great issues as the political division of the world and the menace of the new weapons. Many deeply honorable and devoted men asserted that these matters must be left to others, just as they tried to turn the face of many of our oldest and strongest universities away from the urgent academic questions of space and numbers. We know now how wrong they were. It may well be that at particular moments—as perhaps in the early months of the first Kennedy Administration—there was an excessive and somewhat undignified exodus of individual professors from particular universities toward public life, but the follies of this particular children's crusade should not be allowed to obscure the general proposition so clearly established in later years: that the higher learning in any high society is inevitably, properly, and deeply connected to the hardest contemporary problems which that society faces.

And, of course, this connection runs both ways, as we can easily recognize if we look for a moment at the part which the universities did and did not play in the hardest of the three great changes—the reassertion of man's purpose. Here, of course, the initial difficulty was that the universities were expected to do too much, not too little. Characteristically, in the 1950's, men filled with a sense of moral urgency denounced the universities for failing to provide a beacon or a banner. In and out of college halls eloquent men described the uncertainties and the lack of direction of the day, and in their closing paragraphs they placed the blame, or the challenge, or both, at the doorstep of the university. Of course this was not all wrong, because institutions devoted to learning in all its senses must never be inattentive to questions of man's ends, and many of us can remember that in many of our newer learned disciplines there was a suspicion of any concern with these subjects, for fear that cloudy and sloppy "moralism" would obstruct rigorous thought and dispassionate experiment. The universities of the 1950's could certainly have done more for matters of "ultimate concern" than they did.

Yet what we should have known even then, and clearly see now, is that just as no one part of the society can be isolated from its great practical concerns, so no one institution or set of institutions can be asked to assume sole responsibility for the great final questions of man's purpose. As our sense of direction sharpened and as men came to understand with new clarity the common meaning and hope of human existence, they drew their strength not from universities and colleges alone, but rather from each other, and from scores of especially gifted and persuasive men in many different callings.

The re-emergence of clear and direct communication from man to man and trade to trade may have owed something to the style of candor and immediacy which came into American politics in the early 1960's after a decade of circumlocution. It may have owed something also to the growing up in that decade of a generation which had experienced and outgrown all of the subtlest and least appetizing arts of paid persuasion through televised advertising. Or perhaps it was the very process of serious confrontation with the great political realities I have already mentioned which changed the tenor of discussion. And all of these, certainly, were reinforced in these years by the accelerating and wonderfully exciting expansion of our reasoned understanding of the way the human being works, as a biochemical phenomenon.

But, again, I must not stop to deal with these great questions in this paper. It is enough for me to make the immediate point that the universities were a part—but only a part—of the main. To have survived, with gradually growing hope of further life;

to have learned how to live effectively, and for the long pull, on our limited and infinitely precious earth; and to have gained clarity in our sense of what we are and why—these are not small matters in the life of any society, and what we need to have firmly in mind as we turn to the more specific problems of educational life in the last fifteen years is that if any one of these three great achievements had not occurred, we should have a much more sorry tale to tell.

Your invitation has generously given me the right to discuss any part of the record of accomplishment of the last decade and a half in American education, and in many ways I wish that my own qualifications and experience were such as to justify a concentration of my attention upon what happened in our primary and secondary schools in these years. For surely here was the focus of what our incurably hyperbolic historians call "the educational revolution." What has happened in the colleges and universities is certainly remarkable, but as we look back to 1960 we must recollect the great advantages, in strength and opportunity, which the college and university people had. To put it in its simplest and narrowest form, they had the advantage of their own close attention, as the men presumably best qualified by training and ability to think constructively about the nature of learning and the social organization of the learning process. Moreover, they were relatively rich, relatively unoppressed, relatively influential, and relatively intelligent, so that their progress, great as it is, must take a pale second place to the splendid achievements of the American school system as a whole. But in the field of school teaching I am equipped only to praise, not to analyze; I must press on to my own sector of competence.

Yet just in passing, and perhaps in part as an overture to my main remarks, let me suggest that like other great constructive revolutions, this one in the schools owed its strength to many different forces. One of them was the dramatic revival of immediate interests in the processes of local government which came with the real attack on land use, transportation, and the face of the city. Another was the spreading discovery that the full recognition and encouragement of talent is not inconsistent with general social harmony among citizens of a free society. Third, we may list the gradual breakdown, from an overweight of unreason and irrelevance, of notions of distinction by blood or color. Fourth, we have the remarkable pressure of simple supply-and-demand in making teachers equal to citizens, and some teachers more equal than others. And a university man like myself must give a little credit, at least, to the reunion of learning which had already begun in the 1950's and which re-established a lively and mutually reinforcing connection between leading scholars and the first-year classroom. And finally there was the change in teaching methods which was in part the product of lively stimulation from imaginative philanthropists and in part the necessary result of our own internal revolution of rising numbers and rising expectations. Surely all of these forces had influence, at least in some degree, and surely their combined result—most dramatically visible in the new school systems of the growing South and West—is a sure guarantee of the future quality of American life as a whole. The best is not behind us.

But I really must turn to the universities, and fortunately it is a pleasure. Who would have supposed, in 1960, that we should easily reach so many goals that then seemed bold to their proponents? Then we had perhaps five or ten universities of truly international quality; we now have twenty-five. Then it seemed as if the small college might be dying a natural death, but we now understand that its apparent anemia was only the preliminary to an extraordinary rebirth of usefulness of influence. In those days we asked ourselves in tones of anguish where the teachers of the next generation were to be found; we know that the question was unreal. In the new life of our colleges and universities there is always help for those who will learn how to seek it. (This may always have been true, but a truth not acted on has no great meaning.) Perhaps the most surprising thing, to those who were engaged in academic administration in the 1950's, would be our splendid discovery that as new institutions grow in strength, old ones are not weakened. Yale and Princeton have not vanished from the mountain tops as Washington, Vanderbilt, and Brown have joined them. Even Harvard has recovered from the damage which was done by its noisy and overnoticed Washington branch in 1961. And while for a brief period in the middle 1960's it appeared that the entire university system of the State of California might be consumed by a civil war, we now know that these were merely the growing pains of shared greatness, and groups of eastern deans have even learned to think that this greatness is good.

But I think perhaps I have already talked so much in terms of praise and affirmation that it may be better, as we now look more closely at what has happened in our colleges and universities, to consider the things which they are *not* doing as they were doing them fifteen years ago. I think, indeed, that if I were to try to explain our accomplishments to an American still living in 1960 I should find it best to begin by telling him of the way in which distinctions and categories which he took for granted have been gradually blurred—and even discarded—in our best institutions today. At least four of the distinctions which were central to the structure of the American college in 1960 have ceased to have any real importance.

The first and in many ways the greatest of our accomplishments has been to rub out most of the distinctions separating the student, the teacher, and the research scholar which bedeviled our thinking about higher education in the first hundred years of the American university. Since I myself, as a younger man, was among the noisemakers in the first stages of this happy change, you will perhaps forgive me if I expand, and even boast a little on this point. You will recall that by 1960 these opposed categories—and perhaps particularly the categories of "teaching" and "research" —had begun to make a fractionated shambles of the American university. In spite of all that older and wiser men could do and say, fashion seemed to favor what was called research as against what was called teaching. In part this was, of course, the inevitable result of the fact that reputation can spread more widely by way of the printed word than by way of effective work with students. In part also it was the result of the horizontal institutionalization of specific branches of learning, across the universities and colleges of the country—a topic on which I shall have more to say later. And in part this division grew from the remarkable expansion of the federal government's interest in scientific research in the years after the World War II. With a timidity from which it has fortunately escaped, the federal government initially felt it essential to limit its activities to "research," leaving "teaching" to others. It was imitated, and perhaps in some measure even anticipated, by some of the great philanthropic foundations (which even today have only an imperfect and intermittent understanding of the way a university really works). Foundations which sought the credit for supporting "research breakthroughs" were not always sensitive to the impact of their philanthropy upon the internal structure of university life.

But the main responsibility for this radical disjunction of two things which we have now learned to put together must be placed upon the universities and colleges themselves. After all it was their business to understand first, and to sustain most intensely, the notion that in the life of a university man learning as a whole is what counts. It was for the universities to remember and to reassert that there is in the end no sharp line between the learning of a freshman and the most abstract inquiry of the most isolated professor. By the very nature of a university (and I apologize for repeating these truisms now), these widely different activities are part of one way of life; and it follows, with the most inexorable logic, that the institution which separates them sharply, or seems to place one above another, must gravely damage itself.

I will not weary you with a description of all of the kinds of damage that were done by this false distinction. Let us recall simply that the separation of teaching and research flaws both kinds of activity. Learning is one, and if learning by a student is not connected to the process of inquiry as a way of life in itself, it is not really alive. On the other hand the work of the investigator takes its full meaning only from the learning by others of what it is. These notions were understood, even in the bad old days, by the best of our teachers and investigators. It is the saving grace of universities that their best men will always transcend the worst pattern of organization and the most radical errors of customary belief.

But the true importance of proper understanding is that it releases a liberating force for ordinary men, and I do not think there will be argument among us as to the improvement which has occurred as we have abandoned this great false distinction. No longer do hundreds of our better men miss the joys of working with students because they have been led to think that "teaching" is beneath their dignity. No longer do thousands of men without the gift of great imaginative investigation torture themselves, and clutter the learned journals, with work of astonishing triviality and indistinction. Our new freedom and understanding have liberated even those who were temperamentally best adapted to the sort of reality there was in the old distinction. The man whose heart really does belong almost wholly to research no longer feels a moral pressure to give a reluctant fraction of his time to forms of teaching which he does badly. In the university community as we now know it, all kinds of work are equally honored; all are understood to be a part of the whole, and all are interconnected in so many ways that efforts to protect a misconstrued "balance" are no longer necessary.

Hardly less important than the impact of this emergence from folly upon the scholar himself is its meaning for the student. Our undergraduates and graduate students no longer think of themselves as passively exposed to "teachers." Instead they are members of a learning community. They are younger; they know less; they are, as a group, somewhat less gifted intellectually than the members of the faculty. But they are not cut off, or separated by a polar distinction; they are participants in common activity. It is no longer a rarity to have freshmen who play active roles in laboratory investigation. It is no longer queer for seniors to help in the learning of freshmen. We no longer distinguish sharply between the book which is read as part of a course list, and the book which is read because it is an essential element in a joint inquiry from which a professorial essay may emerge. As the students have become simply junior members in an organization with a common purpose, we have begun to find it hard to understand the massive literature on what was called "motivation" which burdened the desks of academic men in the 1950's.

The beginnings of this radical realignment of categories were evident in the late 1950's, and those of us who were then young Turks would not have been amazed—though we would surely have been delighted—to hear in 1960 that so much could be accomplished in this direction so soon. But I think we could not have contained our astonishment if we had been told then of the change which has occurred in the place and meaning of the Department in American academic life. For in 1960 the department—whether of chemistry, or economics, or psychology, or philosophy—the department was the decisive unit of organization and action. We would never have guessed that it would so soon become insignificant. For it seemed plain, in those days, that the departments had laid their iron hand upon the final sources of power and influence. Did they not control budgets, promotions, and new appointments, subject only to the frail consent of harried and outmaneuvered administrators? Were they not the source of the magical and persistently dominant degree of Ph.D? Did they not, in their constantly tightening network of alliances across the major institutions, embody all of the strength and many of the attitudes of the most ferocious of craft unions, so that all philosophers in leading departments of philosophy were banded together against outsiders everywhere? Were not the departments, in short, the necessary and inevitable strongholds of the little men who have always needed more strength than they themselves can bring? How astonishing then that they should so soon become unimportant.

What did it, obviously, was the true and irresistible course of the higher learning itself. The brilliant results of scientific investigation and creative scholarship which characterized the first six years of the 1960's simply smashed the old lines of division. What could be made of the notion of a department of history, as distinct from psychology, when it became wholly clear that Professor William Langer had precisely identified the wave of the future when as president of the American Historical Association he told his colleagues in the mid-fifties that future historians must also be modern psychologists? How could there be a department of chemistry, as distinct from physics, when over a period of years it became more and more plain that the first-rate chemists were first rate physicists first? How could there be a rational separation of economics and politics after the great and path-breaking works on economic development as a political phenomenon which dominated the best departments in both fields in those same years? How could departments matter, as centers of academic power, when it became the rule and not the exception for the very ablest men to insist upon the right of affiliation in whatever part of the university they were welcome? In the end it was learning itself which did to the departments what a few extraordinarily farsighted individuals, like James Bryant Conant, had tried to do with money, and with especially prestigious professorships, a generation before. The brightest of the young men found the departments foolish, and the best of senior scholars, seeking the company of these bright young men, were forced to agree. So the real powers of the departments were gradually eroded, and while they remain, in most of our older universities today, as useful instruments of decentralization and of administrative tidiness, they spread no terror in the heart of any student or assistant professor.

The mention of administration brings us to the third of the lost distinctions of the last fifteen years—the distinction, so painfully prevalent in 1960, between the administrator and the professor. You will remember the vogue in the 1950's of what was called Parkinson's Law, under which, as it applied to the life of universities, one could expect that administration would multiply, while scholarship and virtue declined. And indeed administrative staffs did increase very rapidly in those years. Most of the time, I think, these increases were a practical necessity (but here, of course, my own bias as a former administrator may be apparent). The process of admission, the management of financial aid, the unending search for funds, the proliferation of connections with the government, the substructure of the all-powerful departments themselves—not one of these was inevitable in itself, or deeply essential to the very process of university life; but all of them seemed urgent at the time, and those who skimped on administrative effort in any of these areas were not, in the short run, the wise ones. So the distinction was real, and its dangers were evident.

We must not be too hard on the universities of those days for their failure to find a rapid answer to this problem. The distinction between the administrator and the professor faded away only after many strange and unexpected events had occurred. Perhaps the most important was the final demonstration, in the admissions crisis of 1963, that the problem of placing properly qualified young men in college could be fully solved only if the enormous admissions staffs of the "prestige" colleges were themselves assigned to professorships in new institutions. Since it speedily appeared that most directors of admission were longing to be professors, the experiment was tried at once—and since it further appeared that most directors of admission are better professors than most professors, the experiment was successful.

This was only the most striking demonstration of a general proposition which many administrators had felt in their hearts for years—that in any well-run place the distinction between an administrative officer and an officer of instruction is essentially unreal. Administration too is a part of learning, unless it be badly done or unnecessary, and as this truth was demonstrated in a few unusual places, in a time when good men were very hard to get, it began to spread with extraordinary speed. And for the numerous professors who had always had some interest in managing affairs, it was a satisfaction to find that what they had been taught to spurn as "administration" became a fruitful part of their whole lives when it was merely one more element in a unified professional existence.

The greatest change of all—though still the least complete—was the gradual weakening of the line between membership and non-membership in the university community itself. In 1960, of course, you were either a teacher on the payroll, or a student, or (in a much more distant and less significant way) an alumnus—or you were nothing. Moreover when you ceased to be a student, either by taking or by failing to take a degree, you went your way, and if you went off the teaching payroll, by resignation, failure of reappointment, or retirement, your connection with the life of the place became either exiguous or nonexistent. This perhaps was the most wasteful of all the patterns of action of our universities, and the one which most obviously did violence—as we now so easily see—to the notion of learning as a proper, continuing, and central activity of man. Why should his graduation have cut off a promising chemist from any connection with our laboratory? Why should a man's graduation from law school and entry upon his profession make him no longer a member of a law school?

These questions, which could be reduplicated in varying intensity up and down the university, could not be answered effectively until money and leisure, in fruitful combination, produced both the possibility and the desire for continued connection across a really wide sector of the adult population. Then it began to appear that the university, properly construed, is not merely a place of full-time effort by young students and old professors—it is also a home, for hours, or days, or weeks at a time, of all highly civilized men. Our older universities have found this truth hard to pay for; only a happy few, so far, have had the luck to find the extraordinary new resources which this new concept requires. But our public institutions, connected as they are to the full political force of public opinion, have been able to win new appropriations, and the more adventurous of them have begun to show us how radically the whole nature of the university can be transformed, and how sharply its purpose can be clarified to all its members, when this wider concept is accepted. Of course the criterion of continued membership is seriousness, and there can be no room in this promising new development for sloppy, or second-rate, or merely casual work. But these reminders are not necessary for an audience in 1975; they belong rather to the tired and irrelevant debates in which the real meaning of this opportunity was being missed during the 1950's.

Well, gentlemen, I have talked too long, and so I have not time for even the most cursory review of the detailed history processes by which these four great changes came to pass. It is enough to say, in summary tribute, that we are about equally indebted to two pairs of leaders—first, those who began our two great new federal universities in Washington, D. C., and in the Pacific mountains during these years; and second, those in the two of our best established and greatest institutions which at the same time were not afraid to remake themselves. It was the fruitful combination of revolution among the strong and innovation among the new which was basically responsible, as we can now see, for the happy turn in our higher learning which we have gathered to celebrate. No one could have predicted, ahead of time, whether the new or the old would do better, and it was a happy thing for our society, in the early 1960's, that both bets were made at once.

In conclusion, let me remind you once again of the context in which these educational changes occurred. There are morals to be drawn here, not only about the inevitable connection of the university to the society, but also, in greater detail, with respect to the way in which the social changes of these fifteen years had a fruitful impact upon the interior structure of university life. But these morals should wait for another essay.

But my analysis so far is too narrow. It may be adequate if we stay within the walls of learned life, but did I not begin by asserting the crucial significance, for our whole educational system, of the great general events of the last fifteen years? So let me end by just a few words of reminder on this same point. Our survival, our mastery of space, and our new understanding of man's purpose have had enormous immediate impact on university life. Consider only how the battle for survival ended forever the gap between clerk and knight which was so bad for both—or how the new morality has, among other things, reunited "the two cultures" first defined by Lord Snow (and of course we have all joined in applauding his recent re-election as president of the International Association of Philosopher-Kings). Consider—more broadly—how the academy has been charged with new energy by its central—though not controlling—part in the acceptance of change itself as a necessary part of existence. What our predecessors preached without quite believing, we have learned to live by —without a need to preach.

One word more: In our celebration of this history—our own and happy—let us not forget that history (as distinct from historians) has no place for discontinuous functions. All this in which we now take pride had its beginnings in the years that looks so gray in retrospect. As the Rennaissance was born of the Middle Ages, and the Middle Ages from the "dark" ones, so our renewal was foreshadowed in a dozen ways, I am sure, before the fact. The identification of these foreshadowings is a task for professional historians, not retired deans, but their existence cannot be doubted. It may even be that in some earlier Corning Conference—some standard ritual in honor of the stable virtues of the day—a hint of all these things could now be found. For nothing as strong and clearly good as what we have seen in our years can be without a place in thought and word before it comes to pass.

CHAPTER 12

ৎঃ

DEVELOPMENT OF MODERN
EDUCATION IN NIGERIA

ৎঃ KENNETH O. DIKÉ

I

IN NIGERIA, as in all the other West African countries, Western-type education originated with the Portuguese adventurers to the Guinea Coasts in the fifteenth century. It must be admitted, however, that during the first four centuries of their contact with the West Coast the European adventurers confined their activities almost entirely to trade; education, in the formal sense, was merely incidental to commerce. In the fifteenth century, when crusading zeal was ever-present in Europe, commercial and religious issues were one and indivisible and in the early years of the West Africa trade, the Christian priest invariably traveled with the trader, either to check the advance of Islam—at that time the hereditary foe of Christendom—or to extend the Christian message to unknown lands.

From the earliest years of Portuguese enterprise in West Africa, education was regarded by both ecclesiastical and civil authorities as being of fundamental importance to the spread of Christianity. A certain amount of instruction in the Christian faith was obviously essential to genuine conversion, while only the ability to read could make possible a deeper and truer understanding of the new religion. Missionary education also had an obvious secular value in facilitating commercial contact between Portuguese and African.

A few examples will suffice to indicate the type and content of education then prevalent.

On October 29, 1553, a Jesuit father, Cornelio Gomes, wrote from the capital of the Congo that he had made it a rule not to baptize children unless he was sure that facilities were available for their instruction in the Christian faith. He had baptized one child whose father, he knew, lived near a school where the boy could be taught. Father Gomes had gone to the Congo planning to establish a college for between five and six hundred boys who would be chosen from the sons of chiefs. Within the college would be a school for catechists, the best of whom would be taught Latin and then more advanced subjects, with the object of training them as priests and legists. Soon afterwards the king of the Congo wrote to the king of Portugal asking for three hundred copies of a book to be used in this college, but a little later he withdrew his support and it is uncertain whether the project was carried through. It was revived, however, by a later king, Alvaro II, in whose reign some books of Christian theology were translated into the Congolese language for use in the missionary schools.

In accordance with the decrees of the Council of Trent, a seminary was established on the island of São Thome (off the coast of Nigeria) in 1571 to train boys from the diocese which included the coasts of modern Nigeria for the priesthood. Some members of the Itsekiri tribe (in western Nigeria) were trained in this seminary during the course of the following two centuries. It is also clear that missionaries who visited Warri (the Itsekiri capital) from São Thome in the sixteenth and seventeenth centuries taught many inhabitants of this coastal kingdom to read, so that Portuguese books were in demand there.

The missionaries who went to the kingdom of Benin in 1515

obtained the Oba's (king's) permission to teach his son and the sons of some chiefs the rudiments of the Christian faith, as a prelude to baptism. At the same time they taught the boys to read. When another mission visited Benin in 1539, they found a Christian Negro, held prisoner by the Oba, teaching boys to read.

These examples indicate that missionary schools were first and foremost the instrument of evangelization; and these schools spread throughout the West African coastlands, from the area of the Senegal and Gambia Rivers, to the kingdom of the Congo. Secondarily they helped to facilitate trade contacts with the natives. The few literate African traders were products of these schools and it was through their activities in the commercial sphere that Africans began to learn the business methods of the West. On the whole, then, the early Christian missions and their schools declined in the seventeenth and eighteenth centuries when the transatlantic slave trade was at its height. Once again West Africa clung to its age-old system of religion and education. Even in the sixteenth and seventeenth centuries it must be emphasized that Western education, or whatever there was of it in the early years, was confined to a few widely scattered trading posts on the Atlantic seaboard; with the possible exception of the kingdom of the Congo, the schools' influence hardly touched the tribal interior.

The modern impact of Western education on African society dates from the political conquest of West Africa by Western European powers in the last quarter of the last century. Once again the missionaries were the pioneers. In the last quarter of the eighteenth century a new enlightenment swept through Europe. This enlightenment originated, in part, with Christian and humanitarian groups, and in part with the American and French Revolutions. All of these forces preached the brotherhood of man and all worked toward the same end—namely, the abolition of the iniquitous traffic in men. One of the main results of the Abolitionist movement was that it altered the European attitude not only toward the slave trade but also toward the peoples of Asia and Africa. Already, with regard to British rule in India, Edmund Burke had put forward the theory that political relations involve moral obligations. The American and French Revolutions, which occurred around this time, insisted on the "rights of man" everywhere, and incidentally on those of the "noble savage." The Evangelical movement gave new life to the Church of the day and made the emancipation and regeneration of distant peoples the duty of Christendom. Its activities resulted in the formation of missionary societies. Thus the Baptist Mission was founded in 1792, the London Missionary Society in 1795 and the Church Missionary Society (C.M.S.) in 1799.

From the point of view of educational development the missionary movement coincided with the European attempt to penetrate the interior of Africa politically and economically, and hence the aims of the new educational pioneers went beyond the sphere of evangelization. In fact, missionary propagandists of the time insisted that commerce and Christianity, "the Bible and the Plough" were both essential for the regeneration and the redemption of the "Dark Continent." The missionaries still led the way in education, but where possible they collaborated with traders, explorers, and government agents. The schools which grew out of the nineteenth-century movement for African penetration were intended to supply clerks for the emerging European government offices and commercial houses, priests and schoolmasters for the schools and churches. This paper is concerned with this more recent impact of Western education upon the Federation of Nigeria.

The history of the introduction of European education in the Nigerian interior may be briefly stated. In the western region of Nigeria the Wesleyan Methodists first established primary schools in Badagry in 1842 and moved to Lagos in 1852. The Church Missionary Society landed in Badagry three years later and moved on to Abeokuta and Lagos in the 1860's. In the eastern region the Presbyterian Church of Scotland established their first church and school at Old Calabar in 1847. The C.M.S. followed them in 1857, establishing themselves not only at Onitsha but in many other towns on the banks of the River Niger. The first Catholic mission was established in Lagos in 1868, and during the 1880's the Catholics extended their activities to the southern Nigerian hinterland. From then until 1899 all education was under the control of missionaries. These missions depended on their home churches and gifts from friends for their sustenance. It was after nearly half a century of missionary educational activity that the government founded its first school in the country—a school for Moslem children in Lagos.

It was not until 1877 that the Lagos administration provided the first grant of £200 for each of the three missionary societies carrying on educational work in Lagos. Thus from the very beginning education in Nigeria was a virtual monopoly of the missionary societies, and in fact it has remained so. As late as 1942, the missions controlled 99 per cent of the schools in Nigeria, and more than 97 per cent of the students were enrolled in their schools. Even in 1960, the year of Nigerian independence, the Voluntary Agencies (as the missionary educational agencies came to be called) controlled in the western and eastern regions and in the federal territory of Lagos something between 70 per cent and 80 per cent of the existing schools. What has been the significance of this missionary predominance for Nigerian and indeed for African education?

As Professor Victor Murray pertinently remarked in his book, *The School in the Bush,* "To all intents and purposes the school is the Church. Right away in the bush or in the forest the two are one, and the village teacher is also the village evangelist. An appreciation of this fact is cardinal in all considerations of African education."

It is this close identification of education with evangelization and in turn with Western culture and civilization that led African nationalists to attack missionary-sponsored education as an arm of European imperialism. The mission schools taught young Nigerians to aspire to the virtues of white Christian civilization, and to emulate European culture; and consciously or unconsciously the schools implanted in most of the students a deep contempt for African culture and way of life.

Products of mission schools tended to view African culture as "pagan" and "heathen"; education was designed to emancipate them from the supposed evils of tribal thralldom. Briefly, then, some missionaries saw the African as a *tabula rasa* upon which could be written a completely new civilization. One direct consequence of this philosophy of education was that a new class of Africans arose who, although they may have understood tribal life, were not of it; who, having imbibed the learning of the white man, fought to share in the liberties and rights which it preached. Viewed in this light missionary education did help to prepare Africans for the new nationalism of the twentieth century.

Missionary education has also been under attack not only from the Africans whom it sought to benefit but from dyed-in-the-wool imperialists such as Lord Frederick Lugard and his school, who attribute to missionary education the African revolt against colonialism. Such critics insist that Western culture (as introduced by the missionaries) undermined and in some instances destroyed African customs, beliefs, family life, and the institution of chiefdom. They allege that the mission schools were a little too academic and the system of education they introduced was not adapted to the Nigerian background. This criticism is summed up by Miss Perham in her book, *Native Administration in Nigeria*: "The missionaries confused Christianity with Western civilization or even with English social habits; and there was little in the educational theories the teachers brought from home to show how education should be adapted to the environment and especially to the civic duties of the recipient."

There is much truth in this criticism; but it is by no means the whole truth. A nodding acquaintance with the missionary records of the last century will reveal that Miss Perham's criticisms were by no means new. Missionary bodies subjected their own educational policies to constant criticism along the lines suggested by the above quotation. They sought for the right educational policy and strenuously tried to practice it. Records of Nigerian missionary societies show that they consciously tried to devise a system of education suitable for the country, and particularly one geared to encourage industrial and commercial development. For this reason the teaching of English was encouraged at the primary school level, while at the secondary school level the emphasis was on industrial, technical, and agricultural training. For instance, from the nineteenth century to the early years of the twentieth there were missionary industrial schools and other institutions at Abeokuta, Lagos, Onitsha, and Calabar in Nigeria teaching how to clean and pack cotton and other agricultural produce for the European market, as well as brick and tile-making, carpentry, masonry, tailoring, printing and so on.

In other words, the ideal of most missions operating in Nigeria was to found self-supporting institutions combining education with industrial labor. It is what came to be known in mercantile and government circles as the "Basle method." This was the system by which the Basle missionaries in Ghana attempted to make their mission stations self-supporting by cultivating farms, training and employing carpenters and masons, and having a trade section to dispose of their surplus produce and, incidentally, to provide a considerable source of revenue. The governors of Lagos, the leaders of thought, and commercial agents throughout the country never tired of expressing their preference for industrial education, and at every opportunity admonished the missions to follow the Basle method. This was largely the position as it existed in the closing years of the nineteenth century.

On the whole, and in spite of the emphasis laid on technical and industrial education by the missions, it was the seminaries, the teacher-training colleges and the secondary grammar schools of the purely literary type that survived into the twentieth century. Why was this so? To begin with, industrial education was much more expensive than the missions could afford. Rarely did the budget of the C.M.S., the biggest mission in Nigeria, exceed

£5,000 a year. It was natural that the missions should channel their meager funds where the best results could be obtained.

On the other hand, schools of a purely literary type cost much less to run, and encouraged as they were by the commercial expansion in Nigeria at the time, they proved much more successful than the industrial institutions. This point is important. Today we rightly criticize the shortcomings of a wholly literary type of education, and we see its inadequacies for our present needs. But we tend to forget that the missionaries had such spectacular success in the early years because they came to a country largely anxious for contact with the outside world. The first demand was for education to establish this contact, largely through trade. The schools mostly provided the much-needed clerks. It is not without significance that the Lagos government, after criticizing the missionary emphasis on literary education for over thirty years, in the end bestirred themselves not as one would imagine, to start a technical school, but rather to start another literary grammar school—in 1899, called King's College. The fact was that the clerks were needed in even greater numbers than they were being produced. Indeed, the missionaries were wrong in their basic conception that the country could be industrialized before a greater commercial expansion had taken place. Thus all the theories about putting industrial and technical education first were, to put it briefly, against the grain of reality.

Finally, even in the earliest days, the Africans to whom this European education was offered knew what they wanted. The demand for literary education, the urge to acquire the ability to read and write, came from the Africans themselves. And many of the African leaders never confused education with religion and culture. In Bonny (a port in eastern Nigeria) in the 1860's, the chiefs who had to pay for their school told the missionary teachers that "they did not want religious teaching, of that the children have enough at home; they teach them that themselves; that they want them to be taught how to gauge palm oil and other such mercantile business as soon as possible." In other words, the African authorities of Bonny made it clear that they sent their children to the white man's school to learn the business methods of the West. The African had an educational system of his own inherent in the family life. There was moral and religious training with clear precepts reinforced by taboos. There was training in the etiquette and conventions of society. As Dr. Ade Ajayi put it, "There was intellectual training, too, as the child learned to count ears of corn or learned the answers to conundrums, or tried to tell the fables he had heard last, or listened to the old men tell their family (and tribal) history. In the moonlight he played games and learned alliterative verses. And as he grew older he might be apprenticed to a job or be initiated into further mysteries of life." The child was therefore sent to school to acquire additional arts—the art of reading and writing, the art of piloting steamboats, or of manufacturing gunpowder. The possession of these unaccustomed techniques conferred great powers on the white man. To Africans, knowledge was power. It was knowledge that had raised Ferguson, a black man, to be governor of Lagos. It was the excellent education which the ex-slave boy Samuel Adjayi Crowther had received which enabled him to be the first Nigerian Bishop of the Anglican Church, and in the nineteenth century. Men such as these wielded great powers in Church and State. The mission schools therefore supplied the African society of the time what it needed: clerks, schoolmasters, administrators, lawyers, and doctors. The emphasis on literary education was therefore not so much the result of the mistakes of the missionaries as of the demands of the society in which they worked. As Dr. Ajayi pertinently remarked, "The humble clerks . . . made a valuable contribution to our national economy. They did jobs which without the mission schools would either not have been done, or would have been deferred till a European could have been got to come . . . and do it. We often say that the main difference between East and West Africa at the turn of the century was the climate, the one favoring European settlement and the other not; I suggest that the existence of an economy based on African peasants, with a large and growing staff of African clerks and agents ready at hand before the coming of the British administration, was a very important difference. Towards that mission schools made a significant contribution."

I I

Why, then, was this system of education which met the needs of Nigerian society in the nineteenth century so bitterly attacked by Nigerian nationalists in the twentieth? Why did the missionaries, once the object of admiration, incur the wrath of many nationalists in this century? To begin with, the European penetration of the Nigerian hinterland from 1885-1914 had carried the trade frontier from the Atlantic seaboard to the tribal interior. The coming of the trading Europeans opened the eyes of the tribal Africans (as it did those of Africans on the coast) to the vistas of a new world in which the magic of the white man's power could be learned only through their schools.

The Nigerian discontent was concerned not so much with the contents of education. To a great extent the argument as to whether there should be more of industrial and technical than of literary education did not very much concern the majority of Nigerians. The overriding complaint was that there was not enough education—of any kind—for the masses of people. The key to the understanding of the whole problem of education in Africa is the appreciation of the fact that the whole region thirsts for knowledge. The wealthy and the poor, the aristocrats and the lowest peasants, Christians, Moslems, and the "pagans," cry out for it. This demand for education has not been artificially induced by the nationalist agitators or by the West African governments. It is the genuine and spontaneous response of a people who have come to realize that they cannot hold their own in the modern world without the rapid advancement of knowledge on a wide front. This statement requires qualification. In addition to the demand for *more* education there was increasing disquiet that the education, such as existed, was aimed at keeping the Colony and Protectorate of Nigeria economically backward; in fact, that education in the days of British rule was designed to enable the imperial power to tap cheaply and speedily the raw material of the Nigerian forests. To this end, it was alleged, literary education was perpetuated at the expense of the industrial and technical arts. Again, some leading Nigerians opposed colonial education because they believed it was designed to serve a small elite. The nationalist realized that no impression can be made on the colossal ignorance of the country until education, of all types, permeates every sector of the community, and until it is available to the majority of the people.

The Nigerian discontent with the status quo in education at the beginning of this century was therefore the result, first and foremost, of the British government's unwillingness to recognize that the demand for education was insatiable and that no government which ignores this force can continue to enjoy the people's confidence.

For reasons which cannot be fully entered into here, the British government throughout the period of their rule in Nigeria gave low priority to education. During the years 1877 to 1882, government spent only £200 on education. From the years 1898 to 1923, government expenditure on education was less than 2 per cent of the revenue. For instance, in 1923 while the total revenue of Nigeria was £6,509,244 the expenditure on education was £100,063, or 1.5 per cent of the revenue. From 1925 to 1939 educational expenditure was under 5 per cent. In 1936, whereas the total revenue was £6,585,458, £231,983 or 3.5 per cent of the total was spent on education. Despite the sustained African agitation for more schools, it is noteworthy that at the outbreak of World War II only 12 per cent of the Nigerian children of school age (350,000 out of 3,000,000) were receiving instruction. Again, the fact that elementary education was not free, as it was in French and Belgian colonies, was an additional source of grievance.

Another aspect of the question is the fact that Africans believed, rightly or wrongly, that the kind of education offered under the British Colonial regime prepared them only for subordinate positions in all walks of life. Little or no emphasis was laid on higher education, or for training in the higher grades of the professions or the civil service. In nationalist parlance, therefore, Nigerians were being educated by the British overlords to fill the role of "hewers of wood and drawers of water." Even when a university institution was founded in the years 1930-1934, in the form of the Yaba Higher College, its graduates were rated inferior, in terms of salary and status, to graduates of British universities. Admission to Yaba Higher College was restricted in two respects. In the first place the number admitted was largely conditioned by the existing vacancies in the technical departments of the government. For instance, only eighteen students were admitted in 1934, and in the following ten-year period the highest entry for one year was thirty-six, even though the number of qualified applicants for entry averaged 150 annually. Those who gained admission were drafted to courses according to the needs of the government and the training was almost entirely vocational. Of the first 181 graduates of the college, thirty-eight became either medical, agricultural, or forestry assistants; nineteen graduated as engineers, and six as surveyors. The rest ware absorbed into educational, administrative, and technical services as subordinate technicians and clerks. In short, the Yaba Higher College was attacked by Nigerian nationalists on many grounds and was never regarded by them as an adequate answer to their higher educational aspirations.

On account of this dissatisfaction, government gradually modified its long-standing opposition to education abroad, and inaugurated a program of awarding government scholarships for study in British universities. From 1937 to 1945, sixty-nine awards were made to Nigerians to study in the United Kingdom. These scholarships were, however, grossly inadequate, and did not cover fields of study in which Nigerians were interested and which they believed would enable them to occupy eventually responsible positions in the professions and in the political service—spheres which were at the time the preserve of British officials.

It has been indicated earlier that the Christian missions assumed the greater part of the burden of education in Nigeria. In the thirties and forties the government welcomed this state of affairs and not only encouraged missionary preponderance in education but later gave the missions financial subsidy for running their schools. This government's arguments in favor of mission schools were:

1. They were more cheaply run than government schools,

2. Missionary education placed great emphasis upon moral and character training,

3. Their curriculum, which concentrated heavily upon the four R's (religion, reading, writing, and arithmetic) produced the much-needed evangelists, clerks, and teachers for the colonial society of the time.

This marriage of convenience between the missionary societies and government in education emphasized the latter's indifference to education as a function of the state, and rendered the missions more and more suspect of colluding with the government and, in the eyes of Nigerian nationalists, with imperialism itself.

It must be stressed that during the period under review, the indigenous inhabitants of Nigeria were not merely content to attack government's indifference to education or to point out the inadequacies of the existing schools. They took the initiative in founding schools, in sending their sons and daughters for study overseas. During the thirties secondary schools owned and managed by Nigerian proprietors arose. The first of these, Aggrey Memorial College, Arochuku, was founded in 1933, to be followed by five others between 1935 and 1936. The growth of these schools gained momentum with the end of the war. Two factors largely stimulated that growth. First, the demand for education was so great that the existing government and mission schools could not cope with the situation. Enterprising businessmen and educators began to invest in what appeared to be a paying concern. The hope of reward was not, however, the only motive behind this movement. The growth of nationalism clamored for a philosophy of education that would emancipate the masses from the colonial-type mentality which, it was alleged, was propagated by the mission and government schools; and which, it was believed, retarded the rise of a strong Nigerian nationalist movement. Before the attainment of independence, schools of this type greatly increased and, as with missions schools, the best of them received financial subsidy from the state. Indeed, most of the schools now commonly known as mission schools in fact owe their origin to community effort, and in the late thirties and early forties when government contribution to higher education in Nigeria was negligible, improvement unions collected funds and awarded scholarships tenable in Europe and America. In 1945, of the 193 Nigerian students studying in the United Kingdom only forty-four were government scholars; the rest were private students sponsored either by their families or by town and tribal unions.

What has been written so far applies almost entirely to education in southern Nigeria; that is, in the eastern and western regions. The position in northern Nigeria, which has been under the dominance of Islamic culture for many centuries, is very different. In 1900, when the Protectorate of Northern Nigeria was proclaimed, Lord Lugard estimated that there were some 20,000 Koranic schools in which no less than 250,000 pupils were receiving instruction. These Islamic institutions helped to keep the torch of Moslem civilization burning for centuries before the advent of British rule. When Western-type education was introduced by the British early in this century, it was many decades after it had become established in the south. The disparity which exists in the educational facilities of the north and south has been the result of the differences in the timing and intensity of impact of modern education on the two sections of the country. This gap is noticeable at all levels of education, but particularly so in primary, secondary, and teacher-training education. Thus, although the North possesses nearly twenty million people—that is to say, more than twice the population of the eastern and western regions put together—it had, in 1958 only 230,000 pupils in primary schools as against 2,258,658 in the East and West.

These differentials in educational facilities can be explained in part by geography and in part by differences in historical developments. Proximity to the coast meant earlier contact with the influence of missionary societies. But the more important factor was the hostility of the natural rulers of the North to Christian teaching and the Western type of education, and the British policy of supporting them in this opposition. Lord Lugard agreed, at the inauguration of the Protectorate of Northern Nigeria on January 1, 1900, to maintain all the pledges which had been given the northern emirs by the Royal Niger Company, including that of not supporting the planting of Christian missions in the Moslem North. This continued for many years to be the main official excuse for excluding missionary activities from northern Nigeria. Actually, there were other reasons for this policy. It was feared that because of the opposition of the emirs, missionary evangelization would be dangerous to political tranquillity. Secondly, Lugard was convinced that Christian ideas and Western education would militate against the successful development of his system of indirect rule. In one of his first annual reports on northern Nigeria, he said: ". . . the premature teaching of English inevitably leads to utter disrespect for British and native ideas alike, and to a denationalized and disorganized population." There were, however, some exceptions to the policy of barring missionary enterprise from the North. Missionaries were at liberty to work in the pagan Middle Belt and were in fact encouraged to do so. Secondly, they were granted authority to open schools in the Moslem emirates on invitation by the chiefs. It was under this provision that C.M.S. opened a school in the Nupe country in 1903, and also, under Dr. Walter Miller, at Zaria in 1905.

Since the introduction of Western-type education in the North, its development has been very slow when compared to the position in the South. World War II and the sense of urgency which it generated in the educational advancement in the South made little impression on the pace of education in the North. In 1947 there were still only three secondary schools and just over 1,100 primary schools in the whole of northern Nigeria as against forty-three secondary schools and nearly 5,000 primary schools in the South. The official attitude of British authorities remained conservative. A policy statement prepared in 1928 by the education officer for Kano province epitomizes official attitude and policy during this period: "Students . . . should as a rule follow in the occupation for which they were destined. The standard should be low so that the boys will not be alienated from their friends and parents by too great a sense of superiority. After a generation or more, the standard might be raised."

In the years following the end of World War II, Nigerian nationalists felt and expressed strongly that Britain's program of education for Nigeria was designed to keep the African "in his place," that Britain's primary interest was economic exploitation rather than educational emancipation, and that this very fact dictated its own imperatives: territorial self-sufficiency, balanced budgets, and stringent economy. There was some substance in the above views. The underdeveloped and precarious nature of the Nigerian economy meant that there was insufficient revenue for costly programs of educational expansion. Again, since British rule as understood and applied in Nigeria was the maintenance of law and order, the government deliberately avoided any expensive schemes in education that might lead to the introduction of unpopular taxation or that might provoke riots and disturb the peace. Hence the government's conservative approach to educational questions can partly be explained by the character and policies of the Colonial period in Nigerian history.

III

It was to be expected that with the coming of independence or the imminence of it in the 1950's the African nationalists, now in power, should give great impetus to educational development.

Unlike the British administration, the nationalists had always recognized that education is a great political force in Nigeria. During the campaign for freedom they had promised the masses compulsory free primary education and they had also promised to alter the character of colonial education by relating it more closely to the needs of the country. Another factor which stimulated educational expansion after independence was that the exodus of foreign personnel created gaps which had to be filled if the machinery of government was not to be seriously impaired. Above all, the implementation of the ambitious economic, agricultural, and industrial programs demanded the expansion of training facilities at all levels. How far did the nationalists abide by their own propaganda when they assumed power? How high a priority have they given to education in their development plans?

The first nationalist government to take office in West Africa did so in Ghana in 1951. Effective power came into the hands of indigenous governments in southern Nigeria, i.e., in the eastern and western regions, in 1953. One of the first major acts of these governments was to launch accelerated plans for education. The educational programs formed part of the general development plans. In Ghana, 10 per cent of the plan funds was allocated to education; in Nigeria, 20 per cent. It is noteworthy that whereas the number of children in schools in Nigeria was about 350,000 in 1940, in 1958, when the expansionist programs of the indigenous governments had begun to take effect, the number had risen to over two-and-a-half million children at some 17,000 schools. Today in the western and eastern regions, over 40 per cent of the budget appropriation is for education. Clearly, then, education is regarded by the new Nigerian governments as the golden key to success. Everywhere education is looked upon as the most potent instrument for equipping the people at large for their new responsibilities. This emphasis on education is indicative of the growing concern of the governments of underdeveloped countries to reduce poverty and to narrow the gap between themselves and the more advanced countries. To that end many of them have launched development plans the implementation of which calls for the expansion of manpower training at all levels.

It is quite clear that in Nigeria the coming of independence has created new upsurgings of demand for education in the public mind. This desire for a better-educated people is a common expression of vitality and confidence in newly independent communities, and properly harnessed, it can lead to great things. But it carries its dangers too, and one of these is that enthusiasm may outstrip resources. In the eastern and western regions of Nigeria there is a danger that educational expenditure, which as already indicated is about 40 per cent of the total revenue, is already too high. Most authorities consider that, in an agricultural economy (Nigerian economy is over 80 per cent agricultural and primitive agriculture at that), the government should budget for no more than 50 per cent of the children of school age to receive primary education and for 4 per cent entries into secondary schools. The view is held that education "cannot realistically exceed 20 per cent of the budget, however great popular pressure for it may be."

Apart from the rather disproportionate amount spent on education in southern Nigeria, and to some extent, in Ghana, there is a lack of balance both in the structure of the educational system and in its geographical distribution. In an ideal educational system there is a balance between primary, secondary, and post-secondary education. In southern Nigeria over two-thirds of the educational budget is spent on primary education, leaving very little for the needs of secondary, technical, agricultural teacher-training, and higher education. The geographical distribution of these primary-school children is uneven. Attempts at introducing universal primary education have been made with varying degrees of success in the eastern and western regions and in the federal territory of Lagos. It is fairly certain that in these three areas the majority of children will complete primary education. In the northern region, on the other hand, only about one in eleven children of school age is at school, and in some areas the proportion is as low as one in fifty. To put it differently, whereas well over 50 per cent of the children go to school in the South, in the north of Nigeria only about 9 per cent of the children are at primary schools, and in many districts the percentage is as low as 2 per cent. In the Moslem parts of the North, therefore, the foundations of a European educational system are only beginning to be laid; and this uneven spread of education is one of the gulfs dividing the northern and southern peoples socially as well as politically.

Another important lesson which has emerged from the recent educational experiment in Nigeria, and indeed in West Africa, is that an underdeveloped territory, which seeks to provide universal primary education, or to expand other sectors of the educational pyramid, without an adequate supply of qualified teachers stands in danger of undermining standards. This is the position in which Nigeria finds herself today. The few trained teachers who were adequate for the narrow educational pyramid of the days of colonial rule have been swallowed up by the unexpected swell in primary school enrollment. The result is that the proportion of untrained teachers remains very high. Most of the 80,000 teachers in Nigerian primary schools are pitifully unprepared for their task. Nearly three-fourths of them are uncertificated, and among those who are certificated, two-thirds have had no more than a primary education themselves. In brief, nine-tenths of the teachers in primary schools are not properly trained for the job.

The situation is very similar in the secondary schools. Because of the sudden expansion of the educational pyramid at the base, there are now many more pupils wishing to enter secondary schools than there are places. Moreover, there is a gravely inadequate supply of trained and educated teachers in this sector of education. Of the 4,378 secondary school teachers on the rolls in 1958, 3,470 (about four out of every five) were not graduates, and 1,082 (about one in four) were neither graduates nor trained teachers. This emphasizes the urgent need for strengthening and expanding the teacher-training colleges. At present, primary and secondary education are insecure, so long as the majority of teachers have had enough of neither general education nor professional training. In fact, under existing conditions Nigerian teachers are among the worst-paid workers in the country, and as a result the profession is not attracting the best of the nation's manpower. No educational system can be stronger than its teachers, and until this fact is appreciated by those in a position to effect changes, not much headway can be made.

The weakness is not only in the number of trained teachers. The pupil population in the first year of secondary schools was 12,344, while that in the first year of primary school was 648,748. At the same time only about 553 pupils in the whole country were doing sixth form work—that is, were being prepared by the secondary schools for entry into universities. These facts illustrate graphically the weakness of the foundation on which higher education rests. It must be admitted, however, that many students— as many as about 500-800 a year—prepare themselves privately for the General Certificate of Education which is the recognized entrance examination for the universities. It is, of course, impracticable that everyone who completes a secondary school course should go to a university; but there are at present many able children who performed creditably in secondary schools and who find their further education blocked for lack of opportunity for more advanced study.

This brings us to one of the weakest links in the educational structure of Nigeria. As we have indicated earlier, the first Western schooling brought to the country was a literary one. This literary tradition and the university degree have become the indelible symbols of prestige in Nigeria; by contrast, technology, agriculture, and other practical subjects have not won esteem. The reason for this state of affairs is fairly obvious. Practically all West African countries entered upon independence with political and other institutions taken over more or less intact from their old overlords. These institutions, which were transplanted with

hardly any modifications from Europe to Africa, may have served
Europe well; experience is proving increasingly that they may
not be suited to the African environment to which they have
been imported. In no field is a reappraisal of such a legacy more
vitally necessary than in the field of education. Even now, in
most parts of West Africa, the man of the classics has traditionally
been thought a more respectable person than a farmer or a tech-
nologist. Whatever the reasons for the perseverance of this undesirable phenomenon, it is certainly not a good thing to perpetuate
it in countries where the most insistent need is for improved
farming and more advanced technology. Technical and vocational
education must be accorded a prestige and priority in keeping
with their importance in the country's economy. This neglect of
technical education is clearly reflected in the existing budgets on
education. In one region in 1959, while 66.7 per cent of the
amount allocated for education was spent on primary education
and 7.2 per cent on secondary schools, only 1.4 per cent was
reserved for technical schools and handicraft centers. What applies
to the technical sector applies with equal force to agriculture. In
spite of the fact that three out of every four Nigerians work on
the land and that seventeen shillings out of every pound earned
from Nigerian exports come from agricultural products, the traditionally literary schools continue to educate the youngsters
away from the needs of the farm and the village. There is obvious
need for a rapid development of technical and vocational schools
and of in-service training in the existing industries to meet the
serious manpower shortage in this vital sector of the Nigerian
economy. But over and above the needs of vocational education,
immediate steps should be taken to introduce technical and agricultural "streams" to the existing literary grammar schools. Only
thus can the academic tradition so firmly planted in the educational structure of Nigeria be modified to meet modern needs.

The provision of facilities for practical education in senior
primary and secondary grammar schools should be regarded as a
necessary part of the general education of every Nigerian school-

boy. It is absurd to suggest that no boy receive instruction in woodwork or metalwork except with the idea that his future occupation is likely to be that of a carpenter or worker in metal, and that the training which girls receive in domestic science be considered strictly vocational rather than as a natural preparation which any girl might expect to receive for domestic life. The instruction in practical subjects generally should be regarded as a normal part of any child's general education, and can be just as valuable to those who will later enter white collar occupations as to those who may become craft workers, engineers, cooks, or nurses, or work on the land.

IV

During the past ten years, 1951-1961, it will be evident from what has been written above that the new governments of Nigeria have been giving much thought to the future of education; above all they have been trying to alter the character of the existing system. In the enthusiasm for reform, many mistakes have been made. It is hardly an exaggeration to say that educational policies and practices in Nigeria during the past decade have been little more than a series of improvizations. To describe the situation thus is only to recognize the speed at which major changes in education were required by events. In the long run, the educational changes of the past ten years will be regarded as bold and progressive if the developments of the next ten years are soundly guided and resolutely undertaken. It is broadly true to say that the governments of the Federation of Nigeria recognize that the "crash" programs in education which characterized the years immediately following independence cannot go on indefinitely.

Since 1958, three out of the four governments of Nigeria have appointed commissions of inquiry to examine the existing structure of education and to make recommendations for a balanced and orderly advance. The first of these commissions investigated the educational system of the eastern region covering the primary, secondary, teacher-training, commercial and technical institutions; the commission examined the organization, administration, and management of education in the region, and commented critically on the operation of the Universal Primary Education Scheme and its effect on the finances and budget of the region. Its recommendations, which are about to be published, have been accepted by the government and will guide future development in all educational planning below the university level.

In April 1959, the federal minister of education appointed a commission "to conduct an investigation into Nigeria's needs in the field of post-school certificate and higher education over the next twenty years." This commission was initiated by the federal government in association with the regions, and its findings in the sphere of higher education were expected to influence developments in the Federation as a whole. One of the tasks which this commission undertook was to assess the manpower needs of the country as a whole and to relate the educational development to these needs. The report admitted that "it would be short-sighted policy to allow the educational system of a country to be controlled solely by 'consumer needs' for manpower." Nevertheless the commission members stressed that "it is part of the duty of an educational system to meet these needs, and in a young country particularly they must be given prominence." They went on to say that "modern dams, power stations, textile factories, or steel mills can be constructed within a few years. But it takes ten or fifteen years to develop the managers, the administrators and the engineers to operate them." The commission laid stress on the urgency of relating educational planning to much-needed developments within the country; its emphasis on this particular aspect of Nigerian education reflects the dissatisfaction felt by all observers with the existing academic and literary system to which we have often referred.

In round figures they estimated that Nigeria's minimum high-level manpower needs, i.e., people with post-secondary education, over the next ten years would be in the region of 80,000. About 30,000 of these are described as senior: managerial, professional, and administrative personnel. Ideally, all of these should be graduates or the equivalent, and in any case some 20,000 of them must be graduates. This involves an annual flow of at least 2,000 graduates from Nigerian universities. The present flow is of the order of 300 from Ibadan University College, which was, until less than a year ago, the only university institution in the country. About 600 graduates are produced annually from among Nigerian men and women studying in British, European, and American universities. In addition to the 30,000 men and women with "senior" qualifications, no fewer than 50,000 people with "intermediate" qualifications will be needed. By intermediate qualifications the commission means those which call for two or three years of full-time study after School Certificate, i.e., end of the secondary school course, in technical institutes or agricultural colleges, or a correspondingly longer period of part-time study associated with apprenticeship schemes or schemes of in-service training. If the proposals of the commission are accepted as the target for Nigerian educational advance in the next ten years, then the number of primary school pupils will be doubled, the number of students in secondary schools quadrupled, and those in university institutions increased five-fold. The commission recognizes that the Nigerian economy cannot bear this enormous expansion and urges that international aid in men and material be sought.

This comprehensive report, covering in great detail every aspect of Nigerian educational development, must be regarded as the first attempt to carry out a full-scale survey of the educational needs of a West African country. Since its appearance, other West African countries have made plans to undertake similar surveys. The third commission to investigate education in Nigeria was that appointed by the government of the western region to carry out a survey of all education in that region up to the School Certificate stage. It was designed to do for the western region work similar to that performed by the Eastern Region Commission.

It is significant that within a short period of three years, 1958-1960, three commissions have been appointed to examine the Nigerian educational system. These commissions were all international in character. The commission which investigated the system of education in the eastern region was made up of American, British, and Nigerian educators, and the project itself was largely financed by the Ford Foundation. The commission which investigated higher education in the Federation as a whole had altogether nine members, three each from Britain, America, and Nigeria, and was financed by the Carnegie Corporation of New York. The Western Region Commission also had outside members.

The international character of these commissions reflects the determination of the governments of the Federation not to imitate, slavishly, the educational system of any one country. In the past, and largely through historical accidents, Nigerian educational theory and practice had been decisively influenced by the British pattern. Emphasis on the grammar school and its elitish tendencies is not necessarily the recipe for Nigeria. One important fact that has emerged from the work of these commissions is that most Nigerians are now skeptical about leaning too heavily upon the educational system of any particular country. They are recognizing, increasingly, that the American or British systems were fashioned out of the needs and historical forces operating in those countries and that the patterns they have evolved may not necessarily apply to Nigeria. This elementary fact, it must be admitted, has not been grasped by some Nigerian educators; there are still fanatics who imagine that their mission is to impose on Nigeria a particular brand of education which has caught their fancy; and who have not bothered to study the particular needs of the country or tried to adapt their educational practices and precepts to the Nigerian situation. The truth, of course, is that education in Nigeria today is in a state of flux. It will take at least a decade, possibly a generation, before the many experiments now being tried out can take root. Until then one cannot yet speak of such a thing as a *Nigerian* educational system.

Mention must also be made of the great interest being shown in Nigerian education in this critical period by many countries and organizations. As noted, the commissions discussed above have been mainly financed by American foundations. Outside aid has been of great value in reassessing the existing system, and in relating education to the needs of the country. The psychological effect of this generous gesture from the outside is that Nigerians now feel that the outside world wants their great experiment in education to succeed; that with the coming of independence when the destiny of the continent is entirely in the hands of Africans themselves, the more advanced parts of the world are willing and ready to share their educational experience and technical knowhow. The task has only begun, but the willing and generous co-operation already manifested by the highly developed countries of Europe and America in African educational advance augurs well for the future.

CHAPTER 13

e§

LEISURE AND THE INDIVIDUAL
IN THE UNITED STATES

e§ AUGUST HECKSCHER

Leisure Today

In the past ten years a vast amount of attention has been
focused on leisure in the United States. The subject has been
researched from various points of view; institutes have been
built around it and compendious bibliographies compiled.

At this juncture we take up the subject again with less inno-
cence and wonder, with a little more knowledge and with awareness of some newly significant factors which are affecting present-
day leisure. Not long ago we tended to begin our thinking in
this area with the idea that contemporary America was recapturing a kind of leisure which existed in aristocratic societies or in
classic ages; but we have come gradually to a realization that
something different, and on the whole less profound and startling,
has been achieved. As a people we have gained little real leisure,
but we have gained a very considerable amount of free time.

This reformulation may seem a disappointment to some. It
was a charming thought that the leisure which had once belonged
to a small class had been spread across the whole population. It
was simple and striking to believe that we had begun to build

250

on the foundations of technology what the Greeks had so brilliantly achieved through a society of slaves. There was, however, a hitch. The more we tried to equate the leisure we saw about us with what we had read about in other ages, the less resemblance there seemed to be between the two. The result was widespread discouragement, and a tendency to disparage many aspects of American life.

The way out of this discouragement is to recognize that we had gained something more modest than leisure, but nevertheless of value. The free time which has been given to the citizens in growing abundance—time away from job—is by itself an immense boon, not to be minimized because it falls short of making us all into philosophers, sages, or artists. The human race has sought throughout its history for escape from backbreaking forms of labor and from unremitting toil. It has achieved these ends at rare moments and in isolated spots—usually where men had chosen to live in a simple, unambitious style, and had been permitted to do so by a kindly nature and peaceable neighbors. But for the most part the human race did indeed earn its bread in the sweat of its brow. Its fate was to toil ceaselessly; its pleasures were all too few.

The past half century has shown enormous gains for the average man—in this country and wherever industrialism has developed in a society harmonious with its needs. Not only has labor itself become less arduous, but the hours devoted to it have been greatly shortened. It should hardly be considered surprising, given the spectacular progress of modern technology, that these results have been attained. The machine was devised for precisely this purpose. There was, it is true, a period during which the ill effects of the machine were chiefly experienced. The nineteenth century in Great Britain, as to a lesser extent elsewhere, saw men, women, and children bound to the wheel of technology, yet deprived of its fruits. But as the underlying rationale of the machine has been fully developed, the benefits which theoretically belonged to it have been revealed in full measure.

Modern leisure, then, is really technological leisure; and that, more exactly, means time off from the job. We have seen over the past hundred years the hours of work in factories go down steadily, from about sixty-nine a hundred years ago to something under forty today. We have seen vacations and holidays increase, as well as certain interludes of relaxation (such as the coffee break) develop within the working day itself. The working force as a whole has been granted dividend in time in the form of earlier retirements and more extended periods of education in youth. The result for the average man is a really striking amount of time off the job in the course of his existence.

The day may come when we refer no longer to "time off the job." The sum total of work required in a lifetime will have so far diminished that it can be expected to occupy only a fraction of a man's years. He will then look forward to an expanse of leisure interrupted for brief periods by the requirements of formal jobholding. But for the immediate future work will undoubtedly remain at the center of a man's concerns. No longer his only interest, perhaps not providing him as heretofore with his major standards and his status in the community, it will still be for most the focal point around which all else revolves. The machine has given us "time off" from the job. It has not yet given us time that we can call entirely our own.

In playing down the more ambitious and abstract concepts of leisure and concentrating our attention on free time, we are in a position to think more sensibly and concretely about many contemporary problems. What do men actually do when they are not on the job? What do they do on the job which resembles or takes its character from free-time activities? What are they likely to do if they have more free time? What about those women who did not hold jobs before and now as jobholders find their free time lessened? What commitments do we undertake which cut down free time? What about second jobs—the so-called moonlighting? These and many related questions still leave scope for clarification. Meanwhile, by focusing on time off the job, which we do very definitely have, and worrying less about leisure, which is still a goal to be achieved, we can see American life in its own colors and judge it for more nearly what it is.

Talking in these terms we may be able to cast some light upon two areas which have recently become increasingly worrisome. The first of these is the capacity of the machine to give more time than people want—or to give it unevenly and haphazardly. "Technological leisure" can very easily turn into "technological unemployment." We have been witnessing, indeed, the effects of a second industrial revolution. Machines capable of calculation and control are multiplying the output per worker, as new machines are rapidly supplanting physical labor. The result is a malaise throughout the whole social order, which could make a mockery of talk of the new leisure.

To speak of measures dealing with unemployment or underemployment would be outside my present purposes; obviously many short-term palliatives must be undertaken. But in the long run unemployment will have to be dealt with in the light of our concern with leisure values. Just now the emphasis is upon men's right to a fair share of the work available. "Full employment" remains an ideal with practical and compelling applications. What constitutes "full employment," however, must be determined in the final analysis by the amount of man-hours which a society can expect to spend in satisfying its needs. The work will be "shared" according to the kind of free time we wish to give to various groups in society. Is free time an asset for youth, to a greater degree than for the middle-aged? Is it wise to give so much free time to men after sixty? The effectiveness and capacity for work among different groups will be one factor determining our standards of how the jobs are to be parceled out; the capacity to make use of free time should become almost equally important.

"Creeping unemployment" is upon us with far greater force than is commonly recognized. In industry after industry the effects of new machinery are only now beginning to be felt; elsewhere technological improvements will be introduced overnight as soon as a rise in the minimum wage, or a drop in the weekly hours, takes place. What seems too often like an isolated case of hardship, or the lingering result of a recession, is in fact part of a deep transformation of our society. Men will fight for jobs in the years ahead; and at the same time, without feeling there is any inconsistency in their attitude, they will fight for an enlarged share of free time. Without work, they will be saying in effect, there can be no leisure. Without "time on" there can be no meaningful "time off."

A second troubling question: Will this search for more free time run counter to the national drive for economic strength? In a way it seems strange even to be talking of leisure when hostile powers are challenging us and threatening to overtake us. It may seem that those of us who are concerned with leisure are forgetting what sort of age we live in. I confess that during the last several years when at the Twentieth Century Fund we have been engaged on a study of leisure I have sometimes asked myself whether we were not perhaps dealing in trifles while the world was on fire. But I am convinced now that a serious concern for free time—how it may be enlarged and how well used—is essential to any effective national achievements. Except in an ultimate test of survival an advanced industrial economy will find that it can give enlarged time and still continue to increase production. The history of the past hundred years in the West has been one of steadily mounting output while hours of work were being as steadily shortened. Today, moreover, the worth of the economy must be judged as much by the kind of life it provides its citizens as by the sheer volume of goods it turns out. The Soviet economy, notwithstanding the charge to "beat" the United States which Mr. Khrushchev constantly lays upon it, is committed to rapid attainment of a working week which even by our standards would seem short.

A point must occur at which free time does significantly curtail a nation's capacity to produce. In the foreseeable future the United States will be able, as has been the case for a hundred

years, to determine, by conscious or unconscious choices, what
share of increasing productivity it will take in the form of enlarged output and what share in increased time off. The way these
factors are balanced may indeed be influenced by the national
rivalry with the Soviets. Some day we may awake, moreover,
to find that the limit has been reached beyond which we cannot
hope to keep producing more (or even producing the same
amount), while working steadily less hard. That will come only
when technology has reached a point of diminishing returns
beyond anything now to be envisaged. In some of the services,
to be sure, fewer hours on the job can only mean less in the way
of results achieved, but even here large increases in productivity
are possible. In agriculture, and throughout the industrial complex, there remains a striking potential for technological advance.

For these various reasons, I suggest, we should begin to think
about leisure today in a moderately optimistic mood. Interpreting
it primarily as time off from the job, we can see that the modern
citizen is favored as few have been in the history of the long-
suffering human race—and certainly to a far higher degree than
any since the start of the industrial revolution. The young man
can count on ample time for his education. Entering the working
force, he surveys a life span where the restraints of the job are
combined with opportunities to indulge in a wide variety of
interests and pursuits; and with the hope, at the end, of years
free of obligatory toil. Looking more generally at the social order,
the observer can believe that under-employment will be turned
into a more widely shared and more adequately compensated
leisure. As for the fear that by working less we shall fall behind
in the world contest, it does not seem to be well grounded—at
least so long as American inventiveness and resourcefulness do
not fail.

How Free Is Free Time?

The point at which we can begin to feel concern is when we
examine the nature of this free time. How free does it actually

turn out to be? To what extent can it add to the true satisfactions and the deepest well-being of the citizen?

We would like to think that this time is not merely free *from* work, but that it also is free *for* the things we enjoy doing. Work, after all, has its own pleasures. Even under advanced industrialism the job brings rewards in terms of tasks accomplished and human associations realized. It would be quite possible—indeed in the case of many individuals it is all too possible—on leaving the job to enter into a state of existence far less meaningful and agreeable. The degree to which the job brings rewards has increased, moreover, as a result of the competition of free time. Many of the elements of leisure penetrate today's working hours. Factories and places of business take on in their architecture and surroundings the air of the country club or shopping center; and within the job itself the routines and pacing are subtly adjusted to habits gained in the off-hours. For these reasons it is the more important that free time be something more than freedom *from*.

Little advantage is gained for the individual or for society if people leave pleasant offices and factories to return to a squalid environment, through roaring streets to a quarrelsome and demanding family. The average worker is normally expected to perform tasks at home more menial and less intrinsically satisfying than anything he does during the working day. The contrast is particularly striking between the life of the executive at the office and at home. He comes from surroundings where his every wish is attended to, where his entertainment is often in the grand style and at company expense, to the limitations and frustrations of the suburban household. What must be the compensating factor is the freedom which time off brings. The office worker who would hesitate to wash the coffee cups after an office party will set willingly upon a mountain of dishes at home. Why? Because at home the work is her own; leisure is in some degree related to freedom.

It is curious that in the modern history of freedom, leisure has rarely figured as one of its elements. The philosophers have almost invariably been concerned with political freedom; even so, one would have thought that the time in which a citizen could theoretically do as he pleased, without constraint, would count as a determining factor. It has been argued that the citizen was free when he was pursuing his own interests—those interests usually being economic in nature. But the thought that to be free was to be at leisure—to be able, in Emerson's phrase, "to saunter and sit and be inferior and silly"—was really not entertained. For the freedom that springs from leisure one must go back to the Greeks; and they, characteristically, spoke not so much either of freedom or leisure, but of virtue and the good life.

In the end we shall all perhaps have to make ourselves students of the Greeks in these matters. With our more modest aim it is enough for the moment to pursue our inquiry into the degree to which free-time is free in itself—open to the various choices of the mind and heart. Time away from the job is obviously pre-empted in part by many factors. The need to eat and sleep cuts into free time. The chores of home are inevitable and can be time-consuming. There are other factors which are not written into man's lot, but seem to be part of the way our society is organized. The time expended in getting to and from work has tended to increase greatly, and except in the rarest cases these hours can hardly be considered "free." For some the chance to play cards with a regular group of friends riding homeward on the 5:32, or to read or doze, may be one of the pleasantest periods of the day. For most, the journey to and from work is a frustrating experience which they vow they will one day find the means to avoid.

Each individual could make his own list of obligations and commitments; in a general form we can get an idea of these through studies of how people spend their time or even spend their money. The results of such inquiries are apt to be discouraging. The impression seems inescapable that people alternate between periods of rather complete emptiness and passivity on the one hand, and periods when they are acting under various

forms of necessity or compulsion. From watching television aim-
lessly or enduring grudgingly the disarray and noisiness of family
life, the individual flees to various forms of semi-obligatory tasks.
Sometimes it will be a formal second job in which he finds escape.
Sometimes it will be so-called voluntary activities, which actually
impose their demands as insistently as any for which pay is being
received. The middle area, where men and women find themselves
agreeably engaged amid manageable things—neither under compulsion nor pressure, not confused or hurried—is what seems
missing in free time today.

Subtracting from hours off the job those that are obviously
not free, we may ask ourselves what are the characteristics of
free time at its best. It cannot mean time at which our momen-
tary whim is completely in control of our activities. It cannot
mean wholly unstructured time, when we wander without any
bounds or limits. In every lifetime, and particularly in youth and
old age, there is need for such idleness or contemplation; but
the times that in the main are most free are those in which we
find ourselves engaged in what we have chosen, with some attainable objective in view and some rough pattern to govern our
endings and beginnings. Hobbies can fulfill this function; so can
do-it-yourself activities, participation in civic activities, sports,
travel, even shopping and cooking. I can say they *can* fulfill the
function of freedom. Too often they do not; for they are undertaken with a sense of compulsiveness and without any clear conviction that what we are doing at one moment is any more profit-
able or enjoyable than what we are doing at another.

The quality of free time—the degree of freedom that is in
it—depends upon characteristics of the individual citizen and of
society at large. The conformist is never free—not because he
happens to be doing the same thing as others, but because he
is doing it for superficial reasons which have no relation to his
inner being.

There is a widespread feeling, moreover, that leisure creates
the very conformity which it should have the effect of abolishing.

How can this be? If leisure is freedom, and freedom is to follow an inner bent, how does it result in people copying one another and trying to be as similar as possible?

Our answer must be somewhat carefully framed. This worry about conformity is not new. When Americans were a people still wholly devoted to the gospel of work, it was regularly complained that we tended to wear the same clothes, hold similar opinions, and pursue convergent goals. Now that the gospel of work is largely replaced by the newer gospel of leisure, the complaint continues to be heard. There may well be in the American a strain of conformism, and this may find expression in one period as readily as the next. Leisure to a large extent is merely a way of expressing ourselves. "The soul," to quote Emerson once more, "is the color of its leisure thoughts." But the coming of leisure to a society does nevertheless in some measure change it, and it is worth inquiring with some precision as to whether in our society leisure has accentuated new traits in the citizenry.

If we grow more conformist under leisure—if our free time becomes steadily less free—it may be because the range of choice opened to us is so wide as to be dazzling and to drive us back toward reliance upon external standards. In a society of work the citizens all knew what their roles were supposed to be. They had a certain status and were expected to behave in certain ways, to live in certain types of house, and follow certain pleasures. Work kept people from coalescing, imposing its own discipline upon their lives, creating a variety of skills and routines. But with the relaxation of work standards, people found themselves at sea. They were supposed to know what they wanted to do. But they were not very sure they knew, and they found it safest to follow the course that others had set.

The difficulties of adjusting to a society of abundant free time cannot be overestimated. Growing up in it is to have before one no convincing image of what life is to be. While emphasis on success still exerts a powerful influence, the ways in which success can be achieved are obscure. The nature of work is changing. It looks less and less like work and more like a form of leisure; while leisure itself is chameleon-hued and without standards as to what is approved or what is meaningful. The younger generations protest by their own peculiar methods: Since there is nothing positive to revolt against, they adopt an evasive nihilism. The older generations, meanwhile, try to look as if they were busy, or at least as if they were amused. But what can profitably engage or delight them has been sanctioned neither by nature, religion, or tradition. Therefore they seek to identify themselves with some group. The group itself does not know where it is going, or why; and the individual is thus put in the position of wanting to adjust himself to something which is itself unsure and changing.

Conformity is the most obvious enemy of the freedom of free time. Other enemies are forces which have their origin in technology and in urbanism.

I have already spoken of the machine as the chief source of today's free time. We must recognize that the giver has put its own mark upon the gift. Without accepting all the arguments of those who see the machine as a corrupter and belittler of humanity, we must recognize that it has its clear effects upon man. It sets its own rhythms, exacts its own standards and style; to derive its full advantages is necessarily to yield in some measure to its subtle compulsions. The leisure which results from its efficiency will be a different leisure from that which emerged from a culture based on agriculture or handicrafts. The clock will dominate it; a certain mechanistic quality will color its enjoyments.

So will the consumption of material things. The machine says, in effect, to modern man: "I will give you an unprecedented degree of freedom from regular work; but you can have this only if you employ your new leisure in making use of my output." In accepting the gift of free time, modern man accepts also the challenge to occupy this time to consuming the machine's progeny. The result is a leisure necessarily active, involving men and women in the purchase and use of all kinds of equipment and gadgetry. It is a leisure in which passive contemplation or idle enjoyment of nature seems to have in it something of oddness and even of infidelity.

In the same way, modern leisure is the child of urbanism. Only the great city could provide the market for mass-produced goods. The instancy of communication within it, the rapid spread of each latest fashion or fad, creates a public ready to absorb and to discard in an accelerating rhythm. The individual may attempt to set his own pace, enjoying in some rural retreat the time which the city did so much to create. For better or worse, the city exacts its revenge. Its standards pursue the fugitive. The further reaches of the countryside—to say nothing of suburbia or exurbia—still echo the urban note.

In tradition-bound agricultural communities leisure had been given structure and form. Morning brought the inevitable and inescapable chores; evening its needed rest. The holidays of the year fell in with seedtime and harvest, each tending to have its own character, often overlaid with religious connotations. Even the longer spells of idleness, when the farmer was much indoors, were related to the turn of the seasons, to the changing moons, and the shortening and lengthening days. But the pace of the city is continuous. It keeps going at all hours of the day and night—as the machine, to attain maximum efficiency, runs without account of the human routine. People take their time off without the sanction of nature and contrive their amusements according to the latest dicta of the merchandisers.

The clock, the gadget, and the crowd—these three give to modern leisure much of its particular tone and quality. I am tempted to add a fourth: the child—or, more accurately, the children. Family life is no longer the creator of free time, as it was in simpler societies where a numerous offspring provided hands for the harvest and security in old age. But the family to a remarkable extent has become the object to which free time is devoted. The shorter working hours, the weekends, the vacations, have all become occasions for family rituals—from washing the baby to piling into the car for a cross-continental tour.

This return to a preoccupation with the family might have provided a healthy counterweight to the mechanistic and materialistic aspects of modern leisure. It could have restored to free time a natural organic quality—a sense of live textures and slow growth, a feeling for associations nurtured from within. Unfortunately these results have been blurred by the fact that the family was itself undergoing rapid change in its relationships and in the forms of its mutual dependencies. Parental authority was breaking down; the older doctrines of child-rearing, based largely on instinctive wisdom and folk remedies, were giving way to oversimplified and imperfectly understood dogmas of Freud. The children were withdrawing from parents who seemed to have surrendered their former role as authoritative guides; they were rebelling against a society which seemed to offer them no relevant goals. On the material side, meanwhile, the disappearance of the servant class had left the household in disarray. So it was that leisure spent in the family circle was not likely to be any less tense or nerve-ridden than time spent in the melee of the social order itself.

The Management of Time

The question "How free is free time?" must therefore be answered in a qualified way. Commitments, pressures, and conformities make the hours spent away from the job less than free; the subjection of the modern citizen is to something else than work. Within the job, as other participants at this conference will no doubt argue, a higher degree of freedom can be achieved than is now generally the case. Certainly this is true also in regard to contemporary leisure. Men and women can learn to use time. They can in the deepest sense "find themselves" in leisure, as many of them in their happiest moments have found themselves while occupied in some demanding task. It is important, however, that in despair or confusion they should not deliberately turn away from freedom, denying it, and seeking to escape its burden.

Much of what may be called "unfree time"—time away from the job but bartered to compulsion or necessity—is the result of a desire to escape leisure. The "second job" must be very often a flight from the chance to be master of one's own time. Many civic or charitable activities, like many exhausting rounds of social engagements, are less a way of spending leisure than a way of avoiding it. Within the work process, routines and habits seem to be carried forward with the subconscious urge to make work consume a larger part of life and thus to reduce the threat of having to decide for oneself what to do. Much of today's red tape and all-encompassing paperwork is a subtle evidence of the same drive that makes the worker indulge in feather-bedding and other delaying tactics. It is dangerous to generalize in this area, where motives are various and mixed; but surely the general compulsion to buy must come in part from a desire to put oneself in bondage to the installment plan and thence to over-time or a second job. At the very least it can be said that a people who really valued leisure would be less apt to encumber themselves with purchases which keep their nose so assiduously to the grindstone.

To accept time as a boon is the beginning of the power to organize and manage it. The wise individual can then decide how to give it content and form. Some of the hours which might otherwise be free he may deliberately choose to forfeit to some regular, obligatory tasks, in effect accepting the concept of two jobs, one paid and one unpaid. Other stretches of time he may keep wholly unplanned. The larger amount of disposable time will fall between the obligated and the wholly free; these will be hours when the individual accepts repetition, pattern, and routine, yet keeps the sense of being able to move at his own pace, to stop when he feels ready, and to set himself moderate and attainable goals.

Efforts by polls and other inquiries to distinguish leisure from non-leisure activities invariably come up against the dead end of subjectivity: What is pure pleasure for one man is work for his neighbor, or what is pleasure in some circumstances is not so in another. A man may play golf for the sake of the game or because it is a way of making a business deal; one will genuinely enjoy participation in civic affairs, another will look upon it as a bore undertaken only because the community or his corporation expects it of him. But the very fact that the line between leisure and non-leisure is drawn subjectively gives us a clue as to how time may be given meaning. The sociologist's despair may be the saving of the individual, for it becomes plain that we can ourselves determine within a wide range whether or not our time shall be genuinely free, whether it will be enjoyable or merely burdensome.

Take cooking, for example. It is the most inescapable of housewifely chores. It was once unquestionably accepted as woman's work, with the attitude that nothing could be done about it. But the new emphasis on leisure has affected the kitchen, making it less sanitized and cheerless, bringing into it recipes and ingredients from all parts of the world. For the housewife who wants to make it so, cooking can be both easier and more exotic than any other period; nor is the husband immune from being lured to try its art. Similarly, the new shopping centers can have the effect of making marketing once again, as it has been in the past, something akin to going to a fair. The tendency to bring the whole family, and to shop at hours ordinarily given for recreation, is obviously part of a new pattern. The whole do-it-yourself movement has been of ambiguous implication; for it is in part, surely, a necessity imposed by the decline of personal service. But it can also become, for the man who has some skill with tools and has pride in his own possessions, a leisurely and enjoyable way of passing the time.

Civic affairs seem in many ways to enter most bewilderingly into the leisure pattern. Work for the community should in one sense be the first end of leisure. The Greeks conceived of the citizen as essentially the man who was not bound by work; in eighteenth-century England the land was governed by the aristocratic leisure classes. Yet for those Americans who today carry on the voluntary associations in which the national life is so rich, the involvement is often a pure chore, either imposed by pressures from without or a sense of stern duty from within. Indeed, leisure in general has been accompanied by a marked return to private, as opposed to common, enjoyments. Why this should be so is a complicated matter to analyze; the cause must reside partially in the emphasis on consumption of which I have already spoken. Having taken on possessions and made the home a center of gadgetry, the citizen finds public activities drawing him away from the true center of his life.

Yet these activities can—and if democracy is to be vital they must—be a part of the substance of leisure. When they become professionalized and a matter of routine work, they lose a significant quality. When they are mere chores they lose something also. By observing certain rules in regard to civic undertakings it is possible, I suggest, to keep them truly voluntary and truly leisurely. No one citizen should be encouraged to take on more than he can easily carry. What he does undertake in this sphere should either be related to his work or else give him outlets and associations which his nature requires but which are *not* expressed through his job. It is a good idea also to keep some flexibility. Short terms of office encourage the amateur attitude. And a man who of necessity cannot change his job often may well profit from varying the portfolio of his extracurricular activity. In every case the means for an honorable exit should be provided if the individual finds himself growing harried or distraught.

Thus various activities can be infused with the quality of leisure. No less important, the expanse of time can be reapportioned and redivided. If all our vacations came in the form of one long sabbatical, or if all the hours devoted to cooking or shopping in a lifetime were imposed upon the housewife in one unbroken period, time would have a different substance from what it possesses when vacations or cooking or shopping come at decent intervals and in reasonable bulk. We accept certain patterns of time-allocation, without asking ourselves whether they lead to the most varied and fruitful use. The two-day weekend is undoubtedly preferable to two single days—say a Sunday and a Thursday—because of the distances at which most Americans live from their place of work. But in many of the smaller communities of this country the pattern is a one-and-a-half day weekend, with an extra half day Wednesday afternoon. There is much to be said for this arrangement. Not only does it make it possible for country folk to come in and do their shopping Saturday morning; it gives to those who labor a welcome change of pace at midweek. If more time is added to the weekend, as seems likely to be the case within the next several decades, a real choice will arise as to where this time is to be placed.

An extra day or half-day in the middle of the week will aid the merchants. A weekend starting Friday noon or even Friday morning will be to the benefit of those who have "vacation houses" or are in the habit of making brief trips away from home. The problem of the children must also be considered; for the processes of education, unlike those of manufacturing or even most services, do not lend themselves to a rapid increase of productivity. When the three-day weekend was tried a few years ago in a major plant in California, it was found that since it was at odds with the children's school pattern, it allowed no real expeditions or change of pace. The husband simply spent an extra day around the home. One such husband referred to his as his "honey-do" day. When asked what he meant, he explained that his whole day off was "honey, do this; honey, do that."

The whole question of vacations must be reviewed in the light of people's changing habits and preferences, as well as in the light of what we know about the effects of time. Does a month bring more rewards than two periods of a fortnight each, summer and winter? In what circumstances and for what groups in the population is the longer vacation, comparable to the academic "sabbatical," to be encouraged? Within limits these choices are left open to individuals and then a wide range of options and calculations come into play.

What is true of vacations is true to an even greater extent of the life cycle as a whole. Is our present way of grouping time off, with the large bulks of it at the beginning and the end of the life span, necessarily the best? An older friend of mine used to claim that he had been much and happily idle in youth, when it was a joy to him to wander in the woods and be at home with nature; while in his forties and fifties he was quite satisfied to turn to the daily routine of toil. My inclination, on the other hand, would be to say that in the United States today we delay too long the entrance of young people into the working force, and then retire them too precipitously in their sixties. A mixture of work and leisure at both the extremes would seem more healthful. To accomplish this we would need reforms in the educational system. A training in youth more bent to practical ends would be combined with a chance in mid-career to return to liberal and humane studies. Actually a tendency in this direction is discernible, and it may well be the genius of a leisure society to evolve in this way.

In all these calculations as to how time may be bulked and divided, the nature of the work process must, of course, also be considered. It is all very well to say that people should have more to do after sixty; but if we are told that after sixty their efficiency as laborers sharply declines, we might want to reconsider. Yet up until recently *only* the factors springing from efficiency and a maximum of productivity have been considered. In a social order where leisure values are considered important, questions would want to be looked at from at least two points of view. Merely to say this is to open new vistas of choice, and perhaps to lead to a whole series of insights that have hitherto been closed to us.

The Landscape of Leisure

The choices of individuals and the customs of society will cumulatively, over a span of time, bring about changes in the physical environment. We are already beginning to see such changes created under the influence of increasing free time. Some of them are for the good, others not. It is worth looking at some of these briefly, for the light they throw on the nature of our choices and the effects of free time.

Leisure needs space. Many forms of passing free time, such as reading or hobbies, can be performed in small areas, without moving about. Yet even here a transformation in the home is required. The library may be vanishing from modern housing, along with the separate dining room; but the television room, the recreation room, the dark room, and the home workshop, all call for added areas; and the demands on the backyard increase proportionately. Privacy and separateness are requisite to many of these leisure activities. Yet the openness of much modern planning cannot be merely a fad of the architects or a measure of economy. It conforms, I suggest, to the informality and free contact which leisure at its best has always involved. The family in the family room is much like the citizen in the forum of Greek civilization—or like the man in the street, when the streets were places of meeting and talk.

The household, however, is not the main focus of leisure. Certainly it should not become so. The authors of Utopias have generally urged that the house be comfortable, but not so luxurious as to beguile the citizen away from the forum, with its wider contacts and responsibilities. Today a retreat into the isolation of the home seems apparent; we are told by the consumer magazines that the public domain has become so crowded and unkempt as to make necessary this falling back upon a private haven. The beaches are polluted; the roads are traffic-laden; the parks are domesticated by the very hordes who crave some touch of wilderness. Therefore, the backyard barbecue and the private swimming pool. One is suspicious of a privacy so obviously induced by the high priests of consumerism.

Besides, certain kind of snobbishness must be overcome in our attitude toward the public scene. We tend all too easily to idealize a state of things which perhaps never existed, and which could certainly not exist under modern conditions. To have perfect quiet and unencumbered spaciousness is out of the question. Other civilizations have made a virtue of the jostling crowd. Roman baths or the taverns of Chaucer's day—to take two random examples—were institutions which would have lost much of their attraction without their busyness. The modern traveler, stopping at some replica of a colonial inn, may be taken aback by the coming and going, the waiting for a table, the general air of haste and confusion; yet in the great days of inn-keeping all this would have seemed an inevitable part of the picture. The only difference is, there would have been more noise, and undoubtedly more odors, than now greet us.

Much that strikes us as ugly in the environment is a part of new values, born of leisure and the spirit of recreation, striving to find the forms in which they can fittingly express themselves. Roadside architecture can be an affront to the sensibilities; looked at from a slightly different point of view, it may also be seen as the undirected efforts of modern citizens to find an idiom in architecture and communication which will make sense to people moving down the highway at sixty miles an hour. The new expressways lack the charms of the country lane; but at their best, when well-designed and passing through a landscape of large scale, they offer views and perspectives which no other generation has been able to enjoy. These new roads are a kind of ribbon sculpture, and the automobilist traversing them at high speed, with their turns and hills, has an experience in space that is unique to our age. They can make motoring strangely exhilarating. It is not to be discounted that the very fact of the automobile's being an adjunct of leisure has caused the roads to be what they are. In their leisure, men of all ages have instinctively sought beauty; and our particular kind of leisure is creating in this age a beauty of its own.

To look for the emergent form in the midst of today's confusion is part of what is required. In addition, of course, there is need of a general resolve to organize and control space in a way consonant with our society's basic needs. The relationship between space and time would be an interesting subject of theoretical analysis. We might begin with a simple, rough generalization: the more free time, the greater the space required. A rationally organized environment would, for example, provide small parks near the centers of living and work for people in the short interval of their lunch hour or an after-dinner stroll; larger and less immediately accessible areas for a Sunday expedition; and finally, large stretches of wilderness for the individual or family with two weeks to spend. It would provide access to fresh and salt water, to mountains and desert. It would recognize how large a role in leisure the return to nature plays in our society, cut off as it is from so many of the elements which first shaped its values and formed its instincts.

The difficulty is that space is bounded and finite, while population is expanding and while increasing free time brings people out in crowds to enjoy the limited resources which space offers. The dilemma posed by the over-running of the national parks by masses of humanity is illustrative of what is happening in all countries—on the beaches, the ski trails, the waterways. The national parks provide, however, a particularly ironical example; for their charm is their very wildness, and wildness enjoyed by the many becomes an absurdity. There is a solution, but it is a radical one and therefore not likely to achieve widespread acceptance. The solution is to keep the wilderness free and open, yet to make it somewhat difficult of access so that it is reached only by those with some degree of will and energy.

An automobile road up Pike's Peak or Whiteface Mountain may be touching evidence that we are concerned for the old and weak in our society; for now even these can have the advantages of the great views. But we are all young once, and there is no reason why these mountain-top experiences should not belong to the leisure of one's earlier years. The democracy that makes it possible for everyone—no matter how soft or decrepit—to reach a mountain peak is false; the true democracy provides the time and the means to health so that each *in season* has the chance to make the climb. It should be so, with the national parks. If the aunts and grandmothers could not go along on one of these expeditions the ideal of "togetherness" might suffer. But by keeping the parks for those who are fit to make a substantial physical effort, something would be preserved which is in danger of vanishing from our civilization.

The principle of "more leisure, more space" is subject to many qualifications once we turn back from the wilderness to take a good look at our cities. The cities have certainly been eating up at a rapid pace a disconcerting amount of hitherto unurbanized land. It is a little difficult to say what advantages have been gained thereby. The desire for a patch of country, in the form of a suburban plot, proves too often illusory; even the objective of securing a better environment for bringing up children is not invariably achieved. In any case, it can be said that the interests of leisure are served very imperfectly. The garden to tend, the front lawn to mow, the basement workshop and the local bridge club—these provide useful free-time activities. But leisure has its fulfillments in the city also—different, as we have seen, from the old rural pattern, yet not without traditions and ceremonies of its own. Socrates would have been at a loss without the forum, Ben Jonson without the Mermaid Tavern. It is hardly necessary to enlarge on the free-time attractions of the modern great city— or at least upon the attractions that would exist if the city lived up greatly to its possibilities.

The trouble is that the city has lost many of its functions as a result of the push outward to the suburbs and the gross mismanagement of space within its center. What should be a place for varied and easy human contacts, rich in diversions and entertainments, becomes in all too many cases a blighted core. It grows difficult to move about in the city, while to stay still is to run the risk of being mowed down. The automobiles and the roads which are designed to let everyone get from the suburbs to the downtown areas have made the downtown areas increasingly unattractive once one does get there. In the centers of many cities the crowds have now shown a reverse tendency to thin out. Without a healthy degree of concentration neither the market-place nor the theatre can find its public.

The management of space to serve leisure values requires, I am suggesting, a certain tightening and crowding at the center, with a decrease in density as one moves outward. What we are actually seeing is a tendency for population to even itself, as the central cities lose numbers and the suburbs and countryside gain. A few real estate developers are discovering that they can derive maximum usefulness from their tracts by building row houses, closely connected but with small individual courtyards or gardens. The remaining land, which would have been used up by separate houses each on its one- or two-acre plots, is then preserved as a sort of common—a place primarily for recreation. If such ideas can occur to the minds of real estate developers, and if they can actually find profit in carrying them out, it is perhaps not too much to hope that a similar principle might be set in motion with respect to our cities.

The Future of Leisure

We began by suggesting that leisure today had best be thought of in terms of free time—time away from the job. This definition helps us to think sensibly and clearly about some of today's social problems and lays out lines for fruitful research. It should be clear by now, however, that the matter is not as simple as it seems. There are many variables in the social complex—not just this one variable of free time. There are myriad tendencies acting and reacting upon one another; and all of them in a highly permeable atmosphere which allows the effects to be felt almost instantaneously and in turn to create new effects. So while we are looking at time off from the job, we find that the nature of the job is itself altering radically. Work is changing in form and substance, is becoming suffused with leisure values; and leisure, meanwhile, is taking on some of the characteristics of work. Exec-utives on an expense account hardly know whether they are at leisure or at work; they assume it must be the latter since they are getting paid for what they do. The same executives pushed into some time-consuming civic activity, have only the somewhat melancholy reassurance of receiving no compensation to testify to this being leisure. What is true for this comparatively small group in the population is becoming recognizably so for many others, as the companies for which they work provide an environment pleasing to the eye and the mind—often in melancholy contrast to the disorder of the world outside.

What is happening is that time-off is not merely increasing: the whole relationship between work and leisure is undergoing a radical transformation. What this will mean for the future is hard to determine.

Surely, however, the amount of work in the traditional sense is going to decline. It has been easy to argue that automation creates as many jobs as it displaces. This may well be true in the short run, but over a longer span it is hardly likely to hold. No matter how feverishly we devise innovations to tempt the consumer, men and women will at some point feel stuffed; and neither arms, nor public works, nor even space efforts, can be counted on to take up the slack provided by an advancing technology. Workers in the agricultural sector of the economy have already declined till they comprise less than 10 per cent of the population. Services have passed manufacturing in terms of the numbers employed. But the services, too, are becoming rapidly automated. It may be true that a barber can still give roughly the same number of haircuts per hour as barbers could before automation or the industrial revolution; but it is also to be noted that our elevators operate without elevator men and that on the telephone "the voice with the smile" has given way to the clicking silence of mechanical dialing.

This decline in work is bound to cause one of the great upheavals in the institutions and in the morale of the Western countries. We have thought of toil for so long as an indignity that we have tended to forget what a potent boon it was to society and how usefully it engaged the human being. Labor unions fought for a century and more for shorter hours, largely on the ground that work was something so far as possible to be avoided. It is no wonder if they are now confused, finding instead that they must fight to preserve "the right to work," or to "share" the work that is available. Discovering work to be so salutary, they try to create more of it by many absurd feather-bedding tactics. Already we see the unions agitating for *longer* hours in the form of "overtime."

In many areas besides the labor unions the battle against the decline of work will be fought. The moralists will certainly be heard, as they have always been when "idleness" seemed to be a threat. Successive older generations will look back upon a world in which they worked harder than the youth who are now disporting themselves so shamelessly. Conservationists will decry the shortening work week, which leaves the great mass free at virtually all times to roam the dwindling wilderness. Even the professional recreationists may feel that they have too much of a good thing, and plead for a revival of work to make their jobs manageable once more. But these will be voices out of the past. The newer voices will leave the old shibboleths behind and seek ways to organize the industrial and social system so that men and women can live meaningful lives in the wholly altered conditions which for them exist.

The concept of "time off"—so useful as an interim device—will have lost most of its relevance. If applied at all, it may be applied to time spent on such regular work as remains; for in these comparatively brief work periods, in the hushed halls of technology, men may find ultimate freedom from the distractions and compulsions of their endlessly leisurely existence. The mere escape from work will not be a reward in itself. The time one possesses when not working will hardly be called "time of one's own"—for it will be clearly seen to belong to society, to the family, to the higher needs of man's nature. The problem will be to take this new existence and without the prop and support of work as we now know it, to create something which makes one want to go on living.

I would guess that as work in the old sense begins to loosen its bonds, many other enterprises will rise in significance. The obeisance we give to the industrial system will seem but a part of our life, comparable to that which we now give to the military forces. Men were once all fighters, or all hunters—all the time. So the industrial era required the full time of virtually the whole population. But in the post-industrial phase of man's history, the citizen may be called for but a season to man the machines. Only the old captains—bemedaled and honored—will devote their lives to the service of industry.

Not in work but in *works* (how meaningfully the old plural use of the word comes back!) will men find their needs met. No longer subjected to one taskmaster, they will give to their crafts, to their family, to the community such skills of heart and hand as they have. The instinct for workmanship which went out to so large a degree under the influence of mechanization will find itself again in fields apart from the industrial process. We have seen industrialism blight much that was once original and creative in men's approach to work; we have seen its contagion spread into all areas. As a consequence we have done by the clock, mechanically and routinely, many of the things which in another environment could have been filled with the breath of life. To restore to the many tasks which lie outside the realm of necessity and compulsion a spirit of freedom and love will be the challenge of the post-industrial epoch.

Over this prospect, of course, lies the danger that the great mass, bored and aimless, will cause a general deterioration of standards and a corruption of virtue. We have seen enough in our time to recognize this danger, and to be able to imagine what the results might at their worst be if the iron hold of the job were suddenly released. Whether we shall in fact be a society of free men or a mass-dominated community depends upon ourselves. And the key question we face is whether we shall be able to take the free time which is now at our disposal and to begin converting it into a true leisure.

CHAPTER 14

❧

TWO MODELS OF HUMANIZATION
OF LABOR

❧ JULIAN HOCHFELD

W HAT IS THE NATURE of labor relations in the era of developed
industrial societies? What are the main patterns in the approach
to, and solution of, the problems stemming from alienation of
labor and its postulated humanization? How far is the approach
to these problems, and their solution, affected by ideological
positions? What are, nowadays, the conditions and limitations of
liberating labor from alienation? What are the prospects of humanization of labor, and the possibilities of affirmation through
work?

This is a range of problems involving a great many detailed
questions which ought to be taken up by a philosopher along
with a sociologist, an economist along with a psychologist, a historian along with a lawyer, an experienced manager along with
a scholar, a politician along with a businessman, and a labor
leader along with a man representing modern technology. It is not
my intention in this paper to cope with those detailed questions;
I shall try to tackle the issue in its most general form, I proceed
from the assumption that the existing ways of approaching and

276

solving the problems stemming from alienation of labor and its postulated humanization can now be reduced to two essential models. One of these models belongs to the legacy passed down to us by Karl Marx; it is the vision of labor totally freed from total alienation. The other model can be abstracted from various versions of the reformist concept of ameliorating the situation of the working people; in this case, the postulate of social changes in the interest of labor borders directly on the ideology and technique of manipulation in the interest of management.

I think that, though different, the two models are no longer in collision with each other. In a certain sense, they are even complementary. Against the background of the realities of a developed industrial society, the strength of the Marxian vision lies mostly in its critical contents; the program it contains is rational only insofar as it is considered to be a value giving general direction to reformatory efforts, a tool to measure all partial achievements, and an instrument to expose mystification. As to the program of gradual improvement of the situation of labor, its strength lies in its concreteness and adaptability to the existing possibilities and conditions, and in its links with the empirically-established shape of aspirations of certain human groups and with various social structures, empirically given. But Marx's concept in its entirety is the only one to supply the instruments of critique which can reveal whether the postulates or achievements within a reformist program actually constitute a degree of humanization of labor, or are merely a mystification of manipulators or an illusion of ideologists.

MARX: ALIENATED LABOR AND THE VISION OF EMANCIPATING LABOR FROM ALIENATION

For Marx, man as a creature of his species is, above all, *homo faber*. Although he draws his means of subsistence from nature, the character of his livelihood is completely different from that of animals. According to Marx, animals are directly identical with their livelihood. The essence of the human species consists of work in the productive activities within which man carries out, regulates and controls the exchange of substance with nature. His is a conscious and purposeful activity. Man is not identical with it; he does not merge into one with his action—on the contrary, he makes it subject to his own will and consciousness. This form of life, specific for humans, gives birth to what can be called the artificial environment of man-produced objects. In the objective world he has created, man sees his own reflection —as if reproducing himself in it, not only intellectually but really and actively. Thereupon, the objective world of man's own products becomes the sphere of man's activities; in fact, it is only through this artificial environment, created by himself, that man enters into a relationship with nature. Hence, work which enables man to create the objective world, external but his own, and to mold his own shape is the true affirmation of man as a creature of his species.

In terms of material progress rather than philosophical accomplishment, the millennia during which mankind was gradually emerging from the animal kingdom to form a separate species, potentially capable of such an understanding of affirmation through work, must have been rather unprepossessing. On his entrance on the historical stage man was, to quote Engels, helpless in face of the forces of nature and not quite aware of his own—poor as an animal and hardly more productive. Labor productivity was so small and production so little developed that there was practically no surplus above the necessities of simple and crude life. Since primitive societies were relatively static and their productive forces developed at a very slow rate, it took a long time to produce enough surplus to allow the evolution of the division of labor to take the form in which, amidst the mass of people employed in simple manual labor, there emerged a privileged handful occupied in management, trade, state administration, and later in fine arts and sciences. This marked the opening of the era of class societies—and of alienation of labor. The source of the alienation was in private ownership of means of production, or, to be more precise, in monopolization of qualified superior economic disposal in the hands of the possessing and ruling minority of the society.

Marx distinguishes three aspects of alienation of labor. *First,* alienation of the product of labor, lost by the laborer to the owner of the means of production, who (the owner) uses a portion of the product for the purpose of reproducing this very same relationship of superiority and subjection. The product of labor has thus not only been taken away from the laborer but has been turned into the force which subjugates him. *Second,* alienation of the performance of labor. When performing labor, the laborer does not belong to himself but to a representative of the class which has monopolized economic disposal; no wonder that he regards the performance of labor as something forcibly imposed from outside—an action in which he, the laborer, negates rather than affirms himself, and becomes his own self only after his work is over. Instead of satisfying man's need to work, labor is a means to satisfy other needs. And the result is, says Marx, that the workman feels free only in his "animal functions," such as eating, drinking, procreating, dwelling, dressing, etc; while in the performance of his specifically human functions, he feels like an animal. This leads us to the *third* aspect of alienation of labor, the alienation of what is the essence of the human species. Work is the way of life of the human species; this specifically human way of life becomes alien to man—is estranged from, and opposed to, the personality of man. In other words, to quote Marx, men have become alien to one another, and each of them to the essence of human society. Here Marx's characteristic of alienation of labor turns into a general characteristic of dehumanization, depersonalization, and atomization of social relations which make man unable to shape his own lot consciously and freely.

As Marx pointed out in his earlier works and emphasized in his later works on political economy, alienation, although unhuman, was an indispensable stage in the development of human societies. Similarly, Engels disclosed the important historical role played even by slavery, the most primitive and most barbarous form of class relations. But capitalism brought in its wake a tremendous upsurge of productive forces, owing to which total alienation of labor could be counterpoised by a program of its total liberation. Any class which monopolizes economic disposal, labor management, state administration, jurisdiction, fine arts, and sciences, and which, consequently, possesses the privileges inherent in domination—any such class has become redundant. It ought to be eliminated and it shall be eliminated. Marx realized from the very beginning that this implied a long and difficult process rather than a single act of revolutionary upheaval. But in effect, work will recover its ability to affirm man, to develop his talents, to give him satisfaction in life, to shape his personality in all aspects. The human essence of man will be restored to him; the conflicts between freedom and necessity, between individual and species, will be solved. Work will be freed from the fetters of alienation and from the bondage of economic necessities which in the past ages changed the essence of human existence from an autonomous end into a means to satisfy other needs; indeed, work, as the specific activity of man, will ensure total identification of species and individual.

Presented mostly in the earlier works of Marx, this revolutionary vision of labor's emancipation from alienation appears to have been somewhat altered in later years. The emphasis seems to have been shifted, slightly but perceptibly, to the minutiae dictated by a more concrete historical and economic analysis, or perhaps by the necessity to outline more immediate and realistic prospects.

According to the initial concept, productive activity, emancipated and released from the "kingdom of necessity," would cease being labor and would be completely identified with an activity fully affirming the personality of man, with free creative work of individuals associated, as a species, in the "kingdom of freedom."

Hence this vision can be called the revolutionary program of total identification of species and individual. Marx and Engels made an obvious distinction between *labor* and *work* (as confirmed, *inter alia*, in Engels' footnote on page 14 of the first English edition of the first volume of *Capital*) —between the labor of human body, physiological expenditure of manpower, and creative, differentiated work performed by human hands and brains to attain the objective set by the performer. When commodity production is abolished—when the society, released from all forms of alienation, reaches "the kingdom of freedom"— uniform, non-differentiated labor producing *exchange* values will have disappeared, and the production of *use* values will have become an entirely free action affirming the personality of man and reproducing him in the product of his work.

However, judging from some statements made by Marx and Engels later on, this concept was somewhat modified. For instance, in *Anti-Dühring* Engels gives a general description of the way mankind had passed since the birth of the class society to the capitalist system, which opened the prospects of eliminating the division of society into the laboring majority of performers and the privileged minority of disposers. Under the system which would replace capitalism and due to the gigantic growth of productive forces, it would be possible to distribute labor amongst all and to cut down labor performed by everyone, so as to give everybody sufficient time to take part in public matters, management, fine arts, and sciences. This was not a vision of creative work totally identifying species and individual, but a program of dividing social life into a sphere of economic necessities, i.e., a sphere of labor which, though susceptible to gradual reduction, must be shared by everybody, and a sphere of freedom, i.e., a sphere of affirming and creative work, to which everybody would be able to devote more and more of his time. Also, referring in the third volume of *Capital* to reduction of labor hours, Marx says that the "kingdom of freedom" begins beyond the sphere of strictly material production. Marx makes a distinction between freedom within the bounds of the "kingdom of necessity" and "the true kingdom of freedom." Within the "kingdom of necessity," freedom can mean no more than that the associated producers exert social control over production, rationally regulate it, expend their labor as economically as possible, and produce in conditions most befitting their human dignity. But it all remains within the bounds of the "kingdom of necessity." It is beyond these boundaries that full development of human forces begins in "the true kingdom of freedom." But Marx adds that even "the true kingdom of freedom" can only flourish on the ground of the "kingdom of necessity," on the ground of regular economic activities, with huge expansion of productive forces and reduced time of labor as its essential prerequisites.

It would call for a detailed analysis—which seems superfluous here, and which, besides, would take up too much space—to find out what is the relationship between the initial Marxian vision of total identification of species and individual and the subsequent program of freedom within the "kingdom of necessity" and the blossoming of "the true kingdom of freedom" beyond, but on the ground of, the "kingdom of necessity." In Marx's works there are many reflections based on keen observation of actual tendencies of economic development, and pertaining to such matters as the future society, future education, future universality of labor, future changes in the kinds of labor preconditioning the all-round development of the individual, and gradual disappearance of the differences between manual and intellectual labor as a result of technical progress. These reflections are invariably associated with a critical estimate of the forms of alienation carried to an absurdity by capitalism. To judge from them, it seems that the program which Marx deemed immediately feasible and, indeed, already initiated, was intended to be a bridge leading to the implementation of the original ideal. Such an interpretation is suggested by the well-known passage in the *Critique of the Gotha Program* where Marx mentions the conditions wherein a higher phase of communist society will emerge. These conditions are: disappearance of the enslaving subordination of the individual to the division of labor and of the antithesis between mental and physical labor; transformation of work into life's prime need (while maintaining its functions as a means of subsistence) ; and, finally, all-round development of the individual, thus multiplying productive forces and bringing about a more abundant flow of all the springs of associated wealth. The vision may seem hazy, and one may have one's doubts as to its being in line with some other statements of the founders of Marxism, but it is of a momentous importance. For it can always serve as a yardstick to measure partial achievements, a tool to expose illusion and mystification, a precision instrument to detect the distance between the ideal of culture of the Greek *polis,* corrected and passed down to us by the great humanistic tradition, and the "perverse fulfillment" of this ideal, the cultural developments in mass society.

TWENTIETH CENTURY: MARX'S CONCEPT AND THE DEVELOPED INDUSTRIAL SOCIETY

The realities of developed industrial societies of the second half of the twentieth century differ a great deal from the capitalist conditions which supplied material for the Marxian analysis of alienated labor and the Marxian vision of emancipation of labor from the bondage of alienation. In the light of the new system of social relations, new facts of social life, new tendencies of social development, and the shift in the previous ones, what does Marx's concept look like?

To begin with, it is indubitable that, in spite of all changes, the critical aspect of Marx's concept has retained its value. Production in the developed industrial society is machine production which, already raised to the second power, is being raised to an even higher power. And, although the living and working conditions in the area of the second industrial revolution differ totally—at least in the countries economically well-developed—from the horrible situation of workmen in the years of the first industrial revolution, the basic features and tendencies of the organization of the process of labor in the era of machine production, as depicted by Marx, continue to manifest themselves the more prominently the less they are tinged by primitive forms of exploitation.

According to Marx, the necessity of social regulation of the process of labor arises on introduction of large-scale cooperation and collective means of production, especially machines. But when labor is alienated, such regulation turns into its own caricature. The machine, which is supposed to release man from hard manual labor, also relieves him of the contents and sense of his work. Instead of setting the means of labor in motion, he has to follow their motion. Instead of handling the conditions of labor, he is being handled by them; it is machine production which gives a tangible technical shape to this inversion. A big modern factory is a powerful and autonomous mechanism, independent of the working individual—a mechanism which incorporates workmen as its living accessories, technically subordinated to the movement of the means of labor and to impersonal organization. The workman becomes increasingly dependent on industrial relations in their entirety; his helplessness, growing continuously, surpasses factory limits and can only be comprehended on the scale of the whole society. Transformed long ago into a fraction of a fractional machine, the workman has become in turn an unwitting, impotent, helpless, and bewildered fraction of the organization of social relations; and this organization, regular but impersonal, has its own rhythm but escapes the control of the individual.

Such a paraphrase of Marx's writings is prompted by the results, frequently described, of the organization of the process of labor in the era of the second Industrial Revolution. Some of these results are:

1. Fissure of the process of labor into elementary actions, and its reintegration in the impersonal form of technological and organizational assembly lines.

2. Contraction of strictly production work and expansion of the designing, planning, organizing, and controlling functions, which are also subjected to parceling, reshuffling, bureaucratic uniformization, and, consequently, routinization.

3. Organization, along the same lines, of trade, services, and clerical work, which swell to absurd proportions in developed industrial societies.

4. Concentration of fundamental economic decisions in centers as far away from the factory shop as from the office of the manager of a single factory.

5. Ever-closer links between concentrated economic disposal and the powerful and equally concentrated organizations of political administration, military, propaganda, and information disposal on a national and international scale.

6. Growing complexity and diversification of the problems of management in a factory and of leadership in the society, in conjunction with growing specialization and complexity of the division of labor.

7. Ever-greater distance between the average working man and the place where decisions are made affecting the fate of the individuals, or of the mass of individuals—which distance has grown so large that, in the eyes of both the disposing and the disposed-of ones, the place of decision-making seems to be non-existent and is identified with the impersonal functioning of the entire social machinery.

Exaggerated as it is as regarding its actual prevalence, but only too true regarding the tendencies and typical features of the most highly developed industrial societies, does not the image just presented prove how profound is the de-personalization of labor relations against the background of de-personalization of social relations in their entirety? To be sure, the notion of alienated labor seems to be too narrow; the Leviathan of modern political relations, completely interlocked with economy and culture, makes it imperative to detect in the tendencies of development of present-day societies the forecast of total alienation, which has been given by sociologists the euphemistic label of mass society.

As yet, the image does not reflect the situation in the countries technically and economically underdeveloped. Their labor relations represent various mixtures of the forms described by Marx with some others, either more primitive or imported from highly-industrialized organizations. But this does not diminish the degree of alienation; it only alters its outward appearance. The Marxian critique spoke of a society where division of labor is the unfolding and development of the motif of division into a mass of powerless performers and a handful of disposers, privileged but obedient to the logic of their own function in the impersonal mechanism of social relations—and this critique has remained terrifyingly and overwhelmingly true.

It is however a fact that we are also witnessing the continuity and, indeed, intensification of the processes traditionally regarded as the basic prerequisites of humanization of labor.

I have in mind, above all, the increase in productivity of labor. This is the potential source of abundance of goods and reduction of labor hours, owing to which one can contribute the time free of labor to public matters, cultural interests, political participation. But when outlining such prospects, Marx never underestimated the circumscribing factors. One of them lies in the type of society where the performance of managerial, political, and cultural functions by the privileged minority is balanced by the routine monotony of labor carried out by the majority which has no access to those functions. But even in case such division is overcome, it does not mean that the increase of time free from labor can keep in step with growing productivity of labor. For indispensable labor, as Marx calls it, is of dynamic character; it augments in pace with the rise in the necessities of life and the level of civilization. Moreover, indispensable labor must supply funds for different collective needs and social services and for the general costs of administration not belonging to production. No great effort of imagination is needed to realize what that means today; the volume of indispensable labor is being influenced not only by the cost of growing public services in the ordinary sense, intelligible to anybody, but also by the cost of the peculiar reproduction on a large scale of the bureaucratic administration and military machinery, the cost of technical emulation between nations which feel endangered if lagging behind, the cost of non-coordinated but competitive aid to underdeveloped countries, and the cost of conspicuous consumption, collective and individual. As a result, the potentialities inherent in growing productivity of labor—shorter hours, labor less hard, fewer people looking for a job to earn a living—come short of the rate of growth.

Nonetheless, increased labor productivity continues to be the prerequisite of humanization of labor. Deep and all-affecting as alienation of labor may be in the conditions of a developed industrial society, such a society opens the prospects of increasing the abundance and variety of goods, of reducing the time of labor, of eliminating hard manual labor, of seeking a job not so much for the sake of salary as for the satisfaction that it may give. And this tendency gathers impetus in ratio with automation and the scope and dimensions of the new technical revolution.

But technical equipment, organization of production, and the structure of political power in a mass society make us face new problems, so far unsolved. Those problems arise, to a certain degree, irrespective of the form of direct property relations, although the contents of the latter—division into the disposing and privileged minority and the laboring majority dispossessed of influence and the power of control—is by no means unimportant.

As I have mentioned, Marx and Engels strove for an improved and expanded cultural ideal of the Greek *polis*. Freedom within the "kingdom of necessity," as well as "the true kingdom of freedom" which is supposed to be the sphere of full development of man's spiritual and physical forces, was correlated by Marx and Engels with creative and conscious participation in public life, in the management of common affairs of the society, in super-

vision of the issuance and performance of tasks, and in fine arts
and sciences. Productive labor, reduced in time, coupled with
public functions, performed consciously and freely, enriched by
universal consumption and even universal production of cultural values—this was to be the meaning of work affirming the
personality of man and totally identifying human individuals with
the human species. What in the Greek *polis* fell to the selected
few was to be multiplied and shared by everybody. But for the
time being, mass society culture is as far from this ideal as man's
"animal functions" are from the essence of his species. Food,
drink, propagation, home, clothes, if understood as a goal in
themselves, were regarded by Marx as elements of man's "animal
existence." And this cannot be altered by adding to the list a
radio and television set, a motorcar and refrigerator, luxurious
trips and sumptuous feasts. In the meantime, where does the
mass society man look for affirmation of his personality and satisfaction in life? Deprived of the chance of affirmation in work, lost
in the perplexing jungle of political events which he cannot
understand, pestered by the nauseating media of mass misinfor-
formation and stupid mass distraction, he uses the shorter hours
of labor and the abundance of goods for self-affirmation or self-
frustration as a private person, lonely in the crowd and governed
by what the crowd likes in his spiritual loneliness. And what is
the difference if the man seeks success in life, career, prestige,
fame—since they, too, become a goal in themselves?

As we see it, mass society culture is the "perverse fulfillment"
of dreams associated with technical progress. It is a side line on
the great road to humanization of labor. Perhaps this is the
cause of the malady of our age which preys on the hearts of
the learned social reformers. When compared with the realities
of a developed industrial society, the Marxian vision dispels illusions, exposes mystifications, and lays the problem bare.

What is the way out of the entanglement? How to come back
from the side line to the main road? How can the increase in labor
productivity, with its immense possibilities of abundance of goods
and constant reduction of the routine of labor, be relieved of the

drawbacks of bureaucracy, competition, and prestige-seeking? How to remove the contradiction between intellectual work and organizational management on the one hand, and labor on the other? How to curb the process of professionalization and specialization of intellectual work and organization management without detracting from their positive aspects? How to cut down and finally erase the distance between the performer and the center of disposal, and how to give universal access to the disposal, while making it human and personal? How to transform the media of mass propaganda and misinformation into the means of informing the intelligent public, and how to make entertainment nobler, non-commercial, and more individual? The list of questions could be prolonged. The very fact that they are so differentiated proves that we must not delude ourselves with panacea; no one can believe in a universal means to solve all the problems involved in these questions.

PREREQUISITES AND LIMITATIONS OF THE REFORMIST MODEL OF IMPROVING THE SITUATION OF LABOR

In his essay on George Orwell, Lionel Trilling says that, like Cobbett, Orwell did not dream of a new kind of man; he was content with the actually existing kind, with all its vices and shortcomings. Trilling adds that what moved Orwell in his social, literary, and political activities was the desire that the imperfect kind of man should have more "freedom, bacon, and proper work." This seems to be an accurate characteristic of the reformist approach and a correct definition of the psychological motives of the reformist model of improving the situation of working men. When reformulating the fundamental ideas of reformist socialism, C. A. R. Crosland recalled the traditional philosophy of the British labor movement, where the slogan "more welfare and greater equality" continues to play a dominant role. And this is another striking definition of the gist of the reformist program, not at variance with the preceding one.

The problem of "bacon"—or material welfare and material

security—is the comparatively simple component of this program, although it gives rise to controversial interpretations whenever actual solutions are concerned. At any rate, unless it includes a means of ensuring adequate amount, quality, and accessibility of the means of man's "animal subsistence," any program of overcoming this "animal existence," of delivering man from its exclusive domination and crossing the boundaries of the "kingdom of necessity," is so much blabber. The "kingdom of freedom," unless it is presumed to exist only in some other world, is not for the undernourished slum-dwellers, harassed by sickness, want, and insecurity. Indeed, the gates of the "kingdom of freedom" are locked to all those who—while regarding primitive exploitation, utmost poverty, and unemployment as things of the past, exotic events or distant memories—are still wearily and worryingly racing against time, overcrowding the insufficient means of public transportation, queuing up to do their shopping before or after working hours, who are deprived of the devices to cook a speedy meal and to keep the house clean, confined to shortage of space and ugly surroundings at the places where they work, live, and relax, condemned to unrefined pleasures and refined displeasures of life.

I have dealt so far with things so "elevated" that it might appear that, following the example of some apostles of "matters of the spirit" who are apt to pooh-pooh the annual world harvest of bodies dead of disease and starvation, I fail to see the fundamental human task of developing productive forces, increasing labor productivity, and struggling for a social and economic system which will ensure ample quantities and more proper distribution of consumer goods. But these are still issues of first-rate importance for the majority of inhabitants of this world; and steadily increasing material welfare, its improvement and security, cannot be a matter of indifference even to the members of those societies which are the most industrialized and relatively most affluent.

The ideological tenets and political forms of "the struggle for bacon" may vary; so may its conditions, immediate results, and prospects. But in a certain sense it is clear that whatever the historical conditions, ideological foundations, and political forms of this struggle, whatever level it has reached in a given moment— its program can always be reduced to a certain model of reforms intended to raise the material welfare of the working people. Some time ago, on another occasion and in another place, I put forth the idea that, whether statesmen and politicians are aware of it or not, what is involved are the various and often intricate ways of the world-wide transition from the capitalist to the social- ist phase of the industrial era; and that, if this were brought to man's consciousness, it might facilitate and accelerate the process and lead to mutual acceptance of the best facets of each specific way. It might lead to a realization that it is quite possible for the different ways to be complementary instead of contradictory, and thus greatly enhance the chances of peace which, being the indispensable condition of saving our civilization, must be the object of first interest for representatives of even extremely dif- ferent political concepts. Despite the divergence between the sys- tems in the Soviet Union and the United States, the rivalry of reforms which would strive, in both cases, for more welfare should constitute a common feature of civilization in the two worlds and, consequently, a prerequisite of the formation of one world.

But as to the postulate of proper occupation and the program of freedom and equality formulated in the model of gradual improvement of the situation of millions of ordinary people, it is very far from the comparative simplicity of the idea of material welfare. Which occupation can be considered to be proper? What kind of freedom and equality? Within the vision of total libera- tion of labor from the bondage of alienation, the issue acquires a certain meaning, which disappears outside that vision. Examin- ing the tendencies of development in contemporary societies from the angle of prospects of technical revolution today, the programmed increase of productive forces and labor productivity and the resulting growth of material welfare can be regarded as completely realistic and capable of acquiring different but concrete shapes. However, the same tendencies are the origin of the conditions which, taken in their entirety, augment the alienation of man in mass society. For millions of people, an occupation may seem proper because it gives them decent wages, a certain degree of security, and the right to regular rest; but the same occupation may be considered completely improper because the men have no way of controlling its conditions, cannot understand them and are bewildered by them, seeking affirmation in private life, in more or less sophisticated forms of man's "animal existence." For millions of people, freedom may mean the right to choose from a menu which, be it scanty or abundant, has been prepared beyond their range of influence and control, and which, if abundant, supplies an abundance not so much of dishes as of appetizing flavors and impressive names. For millions of people, their freedom may seem so all-embracing that, the brain-shaping media being out of their control, it never occurs to them that their freedom is not absolute and that the menu has not been generated by nature itself.

As to equality, myths have always had an astounding power. When the myth of equal political rights can be sold for the cheap price of a chance to acquire refrigerators, television sets, and cars—what is equality then? Some ideologists maintain that small political participation of the population helps stabilize democratic relations; some others think that universal and enthusiastic participation of the population in political acts is an evidence of democratic relations. In one case—there is equal access to refrigerators, but no realized equality of rights; in the other case—equality of political participation may have the potential power creating equality in refrigerators. In the final analysis, what is equality?

These problems are not dealt with by the "more welfare" program. But—though it is only against the background of increased material welfare that they acquire proper dimensions—

they cannot and must not be slighted. For, to begin with, no-where has the mass society been evolved so totally as to eliminate frustration, dissatisfaction—and consequently *anomie*. Secondly, *anomie* directly affects the process of production, reducing its efficiency and effects. Awareness of the complex personality of the working man and his social and political aspirations which have not yet been eradicated and the eradication of which might spell failure to the efficacious course of the very act of labor—such awareness may enlarge the scope of the reformist model of humanization. And this is the source of the concept of *human relations*.

It has been repeatedly emphasized in the literature of the subject that the concept of *human relations* is tainted by the interests of the milieu that has molded its pattern. The idea is to obtain, not affirmation through work, but a well-functioning and skillfully arranged illusion of affirmation; not actual partici-pation of labor in the decisions made, but an impression of such participation by means of establishing ingenious links between the working man and the team, and the team and the institution; not to send down information and send up guidance for essential executive disposal, but, vice versa, to send down orders adequately prepared so as not to be objectionable and to send up information. In this version, the concept of *human relations* amounts not so much to a component of the program of humanization of labor as to the ideology and technology of manipulation in the rela-tions between management and subordinates, on factory scale and nationwide scale alike.

No one can deny that such a conservative version of the con-cept of *human relations* actually exists, is alluring, and influential. But it is not the only version, potentially or actually. There does exist a true striving for affirmation through work, and, hence there exists the problem of seeking real reforms in the interest of the working people, to bring them closer to affirmation. There does exist a true striving of the working people for honest infor-mation on matters important for them, and for real power over their own destinies; hence there exists the problem of reforms which, despite the complexity of modern industrial societies, would lead to actual participation of the working people in the management of production and all public life. And in different forms, with different impact and different success, the struggle for real power of the working people over the conditions of their own life is being waged the world over.

Perhaps the character of the industrial society of the second half of the twentieth century is not conducive to the objectives which this struggle strives to attain. Perhaps the idea of struggle for the creation of the initial conditions of humanization of labor, to be followed by reforms intended to carry humanization into practice step by step—perhaps this idea borders on Utopia. Perhaps those people are more realistic and sober-judging who say that only material welfare is obtainable and are skeptical as to the rest, finding justification—at least superficial—of such skepticism in the character of social relations of our era. Perhaps immediate success is in store only for those who have mastered the technique of adapting themselves and the others to the growing demands of rationality of action, and have excluded from their own life-program the shaping of the conditions to which people are supposed to get adapted, leaving that either to the impersonal course of technical progress or to the groups that dominate society today. Perhaps the only effective model of improving the situation of the working people is the restricted one which envisages increased productivity and material welfare; perhaps everything that exceeds the limits of improving man's "animal existence," that goes beyond the "kingdom of necessity," is an illusion.

Perhaps. But on the other hand, the little we know about social relations prevents our denying the sense of fighting for achievements the lack of which causes frustration and suffering, and weighs heavily on human life. This is the case of the program of humanization of labor. What it means in practice is that the search for reforms—necessarily partial ones—can go on and shall go on, regardless of skeptics and pessimists. But it also means that

Marx's great vision is going to last as an instrument to expose the mystification of manipulators, a measure of the reasonability of reforms carried out, and a directive and guidance.

That is how I understand the thesis of complementariness of the two models of humanization of labor. In actual fact, only a restricted model of reforms is ever put into practice. The program that the model contains is always based on the conditions, possibilities, and relations of social forces; it depends on the level of our knowledge, on the illusions of the performers, and even on conscious mystification of the disposers. But the model can be constantly controlled and verified; it can be altered and improved; it can be broadened to embrace ever more fully the sphere of affirmation of the personality of the working man; it can be continuously cleansed of the influence of mystification and illusion which are engendered, not only by lack of our knowledge and by zeal on the part of manipulators, but also by the class and ideological interests of the privileged few. Here is where Marx's total revolutionary vision comes in. Implementation of reforms without revolutionary critique invariably turns into "perverse fulfillment." Revolutionary critique alone, without concrete and actual reforms, restricted as they may be, is either barren or simply covers up its own negation.

APPENDIX

BRIEF BIOGRAPHIES CONFERENCE PARTICIPANTS

عچ

FRANZ ALEXANDER: Director, Psychiatric Department of Mount Sinai Hospital, Los Angeles, California. Born in Budapest, Dr. Alexander studied psychoanalysis at the Psychoanalytic Institute in Berlin, came to the United States in 1930, and in 1932 was appointed first director of the Chicago Institute for Psychoanalysis; later he served on the faculty of medicine, University of Illinois. He has published works on psychoanalytical aspects of criminology, on psychiatry, and on psychosomatic medicine. His main current interest is improving the methodology of psychosomatic research.

M. A. ALLAM: Secretary-General, Afro-Asian Youth Bureau, Cairo, Egypt. Also visiting professor at Ein-Shams University, the Higher Institute of Physical Education, and the School of Social Work; and technical director, the Supreme Council for Youth Welfare, United Arab Republic. He was secretary-general of the first Afro-Asian Youth Conference held in Cairo in February 1959, and assisted in the preparation of the third All-African Peoples' Conference, Cairo, March 1961.

LAWRENCE A. APPLEY: President, American Management Association. Former vice-president and director of Montgomery Ward & Co. and of Vick Chemical Co. Was executive director and later deputy chairman of the War Manpower Commission during World War II, and later a member of the personnel policy committee of the Hoover Commission; has also served on various other government positions; is a director of numerous corporations and a trustee of Ohio Wesleyan and Colgate Universities.

RAYMOND ARON: French journalist and university professor. Has taught at the University of Cologne, the French Institute, Berlin, the Lycée du Havre, and the University of Toulouse; is now professor at the Institute of Political Studies and The Sorbonne. Editor of *La France Libre,* London, 1940-1944; now a staff writer for *Figaro.* Chevalier of the Légion d'Honneur. Among his books are *The Century of Total War, On War,* and *The Opium of the Intellectuals.*

HARRY S. ASHMORE: Editor-in-chief and vice-president, Encyclopaedia Brittanica, Inc. Until recently, he was a newspaperman, starting as a reporter in Greenville, South Carolina, becoming executive editor of the *Arkansas Gazette* of Little Rock (1948-1959), and winning a Pulitzer Prize for editorial writing in 1958. Author of *The Negro and the Schools* (1954), *Epitaph for Dixie* (1957), and *The Other Side of Jordan* (1960).

ROGER M. BLOUGH: Chairman of the board of directors, United States Steel Corp. After graduation in 1931 from Yale Law School, he practiced law in New York City. Became associated with United States Steel in 1942 as general solicitor; in 1952 he was elected vice-chairman of the board and in 1955 became chairman and chief executive officer. He is chairman of the Business Council (formerly Business Advisory Council); a trustee of the Committee for Economic Development, and of the National Fund for Medical Education; a director of the Commonwealth Fund; a member of Yale University Council and chairman of its Committee on Law School.

HAROLD BOESCHENSTEIN: President, Owens-Corning Fiberglas Corp., Toledo, Ohio. He has been in his present post since the company was founded in 1938. Prior to that he was a vice-president and general manager of Owens-Illinois Glass Co. He is a former chairman of the Business Advisory Council (now Business Council); a trustee of many educational and philanthropic institutions; and a director of Dow Jones & Co., Inc., Ford Motor Co., International Paper Co., National Distillers & Chemical Corp., and the Bell Telephone Co.

AMORY BRADFORD: General manager, *The New York Times.* A lawyer, he practiced privately in New York City up to 1947, except for a wartime stint in State Department research and intelligence work. Joined the *Times* in 1947 as assistant to the publisher; general manager since 1957, a director since 1955. He is a trustee of the Carnegie Institution, Washington, D.C.; chairman of the New York City Publishers' Association; president of the Regional Planning Association; a member of the Council on Foreign Relations and the Yale University Council.

PAUL J. BRAISTED: President and trustee, The Edward W. Hazen Foundation, New Haven, Connecticut. The Hazen Foundation is a philanthropic endowment primarily concerned with international and intercultural cooperation. Before joining it as program and executive director in 1940, he served as professor of religion and chaplain, Judson College, Rangoon, Burma; master, Mount Hermon School; and executive director, Student Volunteer Movement. Trustee of the International Film Foundation, the National Council on Foreign Relations, the U. S. National Commission on UNESCO, and the Religious Society of Friends.

MARY I. BUNTING: President, Radcliffe College, Cambridge, Massachusetts. She has taught biology and related subjects at Bennington, Goucher, Yale, and Wellesley. Dean of Douglass College, Rutgers University, 1955-1959; lecturer on biology at Harvard since 1960; president of Radcliffe since 1960. At Radcliffe she has initiated a fellowship program to enable adult women to return to college for research work. Member of the National Science Foundation, the American Council on Education, and the Society of American Bacteriologists; vice-chairman, National Advisory Commission for the Peace Corps.

RANDOLPH BURGESS: Banker and diplomat. He is chairman of the board of the City Bank Farmers Trust Co., New York City, and was formerly U. S. Permanent Representative on NATO. Prior to that, he served as vice-president of the Federal Reserve Bank of New York; vice-chairman and chairman of the Executive Committee, First National City Bank of New York; and as Deputy Secretary and Under-Secretary of the Treasury under Eisenhower. He is a director of the International Banking Corp. and the Union Pacific Railroad.

RITCHIE CALDER: Professor of international relations, University of Edinburgh. Former science editor of the London *News Chronicle*. Member of the Council of the British Association for the Advancement of Science, 1946-1960; awarded Kalinga Prize, 1960, for promoting common understanding of science. Has carried out fact-finding missions for United Nations agencies regarding the deserts of North Africa and the Middle East; technical assistance needs of Southeast Asia; development possibilities in the Arctic; and the Congo crisis of 1960. Author of *After the Seventh Day*.

GILBERT W. CHAPMAN: President, the New York Public Library. Formerly president of the American Water Works and Electric Co., and later of Yale and Towne Manufacturing Co. Chairman of the Council on Library Resources, and of the Awards Committee, National Book Awards; director of the Institute for International Education, the Foundation for Youth and Student Affairs, *Saturday Review*, and Harper & Row, Publishers.

WILLIAM L. CHAPMAN: Vice-rector, University of Buenos Aires. Trained as an accountant, he was an employee of the international accounting firm of Price, Waterhouse & Co., 1943-1960; admitted to partnership, 1960. Since 1957, professor of auditing and financial analysis, University of Buenos Aires; vice-rector since 1960. He has published articles on financial reporting, corporation control, and legal aspects of auditing responsibility.

HAROLD E. CLURMAN: Stage director. His early theatre experience was as an actor, stage manager, and play reader; founder and director, Group Theatre, 1931-1941; motion picture producer and director, 1941-1945; wrote a monthly column on the arts for *Tomorrow* magazine, 1946-1951; drama critic of *The Nation,* 1953. Among the many plays he has directed were "Golden Boy," "Desire Under the Elms," "The Member of the Wedding," "Bus Stop," and "The Time of the Cuckoo." Author of *The Fervent Years,* and *Lies Like Truth*: *Theatre Reviews and Essays.*

JOHN B. COBURN: Dean, Episcopal Theological School, Cambridge, Massachusetts. Before his ordination, he taught English and biology at Robert College, Istanbul. Later rector of Grace Church, Amherst, Massachusetts and coach of the Amherst lacrosse team; still later, dean of Trinity Cathedral, Newark, New Jersey. He is a member of the Joint Commissions on Theological Education and Ecumenical Relations of the Episcopal Church, and author of *Prayer and Personal Religion, One Family in Christ, Professors are People,* and *Priests in a Pagan Community.*

MERLE CURTI: Historian and Frederick Jackson Turner professor of history, University of Wisconsin. Former president of the American Historical Association, and a member of the board of advisors of the American Council of Learned Societies; received the Council's award for distinguished scholarship in 1960. Among his works are *The Growth of American Thought,* which won a Pulitzer Prize in 1943; *Roots of American Loyalty* (1946), *Probing our Past* (1955), and *The Making of an American Community* (1959).

CORNELIS W. de KIEWIET: President, University of Rochester. An authority on modern European history and British Colonial history. Born in Rotterdam, Holland, and a United States citizen since 1939, he has been a college teacher in Southern Rhodesia, at Iowa State University, and at Cornell University, and was dean of the College of Arts and Sciences at Cornell from 1945 to 1948. Active on numerous committees concerned with sub-Sahara Africa. His books are *British Colonial Policy and the South African Republic* (1929), *The Imperial Factor in South Africa* (1937), and *A History of South Africa* (1941). (Since the conference he has become president emeritus of Rochester, and historian and consultant on Africa to the American Council on Education, Washington, D. C.)

WILLIAM C. DE VANE: Sanford Professor of English literature and dean of the college, Yale University. He originally joined the Yale faculty in 1922 and has remained there since except for four years as head of the English department at Cornell, 1934-1938. Director of Yale's Division of Humanities and Social Sciences, 1946-1958; a member of the Modern Language Association and of the American Council of Learned Societies; a former director of the American Institute of Management. He has written extensively about English literature of the nineteenth century.

KENNETH O. DIKÉ: Principal, University College, Ibadan, Nigeria. Member of the faculty at University College 1950-1952 and since 1954; principal since 1960. Senior research fellow, West African Institute of Social and Economic Research, 1952-1954. Currently active in his nation's student exchange program with the United States. He is founder and a director of the National Archives of Nigeria, and president of the Historical Society of Nigeria. Among his publications are *Trade and Politics in the Niger Delta, 1830-1885, A Hundred Years of British Rule in Nigeria,* and *The Origins of the Niger Mission.*

JOHN DOS PASSOS: Novelist. He has also written verse, plays, essays, and history. Among the best-known of his books are *Three Soldiers* (1921), *Manhattan Transfer* (1925), the trilogy entitled *U. S. A.,* consisting of *The Forty-Second Parallel* (1930), *Nineteen Nineteen* (1931), and *The Big Money* (1936); *Adventures of a Young Man* (1939), *The Ground We Stand On* (1941), *The Grand Design* (1949), *Chosen Country* (1951), *District of Columbia* (1952), *Most Likely to Succeed* (1954), and *Midcentury* (1961).

HALBERT L. DUNN: Special assistant on the aging, U. S. Public Health Service. Formerly chief, National Office of Vital Statistics. Trained as a medical doctor and in statistics, he has long been active in the fields of public health, medical statistics, human relations, and social affairs. Fellow: American Association for the Advancement of Science, American Statistical Association. Member of Advisory Panel of Experts on Health Statistics, World Health Organization. Author of *Your World and Mine* (1956), *High-Level Wellness* (1961), and many articles.

TENGKU DZULKARNAIN: Dean of the law faculty, University Islam Sumatra Utara, Indonesia. Also professor of political science, constitutional law and international law, and dean of the law faculty in the State University of Sumatra Utara, Medan; a participant in the Leader Exchange Program of the U. S. Department of State. He has been president of several land-courts in Indonesia, president of the High Court in Padang and Medan, and minister of justice of the United States of Indonesia.

SIBYLLE ESCALONA: Professor of psychology in the department of psychiatry, Albert Einstein College of Medicine, New York City. Formerly in various positions with the Menninger Foundation, and assistant professor of psychology at the Yale Child Study Center. Author of many publications for professional and lay readers, the most recent of which is *Prediction and Outcome: A Study of Child Development,* written with Grace Heider. Dr. Escalona's major fields of interest are the psychology of infancy and childhood and the methodology of clinical research.

WILLIAM P. FAY: Ambassador of Ireland to Canada. Called to the Irish Bar in 1931, practiced private law until 1937, when he entered the Department of the Attorney General; later served in various posts in the Department of External Affairs. Chargé d'affaires, Irish Legation, Brussels, 1947-1950; envoy and minister of Ireland to Sweden and Norway, 1950-1951; ambassador of Ireland to France, 1954-1960.

HERBERT W. K. FITZROY: Administrator, University Center in Richmond, Virginia. He has taught history and anthropology at the University of Pennsylvania and at Princeton, and served as assistant dean at Princeton. U. S. Air Force, 1942-1946: directed various pilot-training schools; dean of liberal arts, Shrivenham (England) Army University, 1945-1946; directed Army Lecture Bureau, European Theatre of Operations, 1946; colonel, Air Force Reserve. He is president of the Richmond Forum Club, the Richmond branch of the English-Speaking Union, and the Virginia Museum of Fine Arts.

FRANKLIN L. FORD: Professor of history, Harvard University. Has taught the history of modern Germany and of seventeenth-century France at Harvard since 1953. Author of *Robe and Sword* and *Strasbourg in Transition, 1648-1789.* Formerly taught at Bennington College. Member of the Committee on Educational Policy at Harvard; trustee of Radcliffe College.

WILLIAM K. FRANKENA: Professor and chairman of the department of philosophy, University of Michigan. A member of the Michigan faculty since 1937. He has been a visiting professor at Columbia, Harvard, and the University of Tokyo, and is a member of the American Philosophical Association. He has written articles and reviews in philosophical journals.

SIR OLIVER S. FRANKS: Chairman, Lloyds Bank, London. British ambassador to the United States from 1948 to 1952. He has been a teacher of philosophy at Queen's College, Oxford and at the University of Glasgow; provost of Queen's College, 1946-1948. Entered British Ministry of Supply in 1939; permanent secretary, Ministry of Supply, 1945-1946. He is chairman of the Friends' Provident and Century Life Office and of the Committee on London Clearing Bankers. (Since the Conference he has become provost, Worcester College, Oxford.)

GILBERTO FREYRE: Writer and social anthropologist, Recife, Brazil. Professor of sociology and Founding professor of social anthropology at Rio de Janeiro University, 1935-1938, and since then visiting professor or lecturer at many universities in South America, the United States, and Europe. He founded the Recife Institute for Research in Social Sciences and is supervisor of the North East Brazil Social and Educational Research Center; was a delegate to the United Nations General Assembly in 1949. Among his books are *The Masters and the Slaves, New World in the Tropics,* and *Order and Progress.*

JOHN A. FULLER: Chairman of the board, Shawinigan Chemicals, Ltd., with headquarters in Montreal, Canada. Also president and a director of St. Maurice Power Co., and Quebec Power Co. He is a director of various United States and Canadian corporations, including United States Steel Corp., Bell Telephone Co. of Canada, Rolls-Royce of Canada, Ltd., and Sun Life Assurance Co. of Canada. Member of the board of governors of McGill University.

CARL GERSTACKER: Chairman of the board of directors, the Dow Chemical Co., Midland, Michigan. He joined Dow in the accounting department in 1938, and became treasurer in 1949, vice-president in 1955, chairman of the Finance Committee in 1959, and chairman of the board in 1960. He is president of the Synthetic Organic Chemical Manufacturers' Association, and a director of the National Association for Mental Health, the Dow Corning Corp., and the Federal Reserve Bank of Detroit.

WILLIAM GLASSER: Psychiatrist, Los Angeles, California. He holds degrees in chemical engineering, psychology, and medicine, and the diploma of the American Board of Psychiatry and Neurology. At present, he combines private psychiatric practice with teaching, consulting in juvenile delinquency in the California Youth Authority, psychosomatic medicine at the Los Angeles Orthopaedic Hospital, and group therapy at the UCLA Neuropsychiatric Institute. He is the author of *Mental Health or Mental Illness?*

VICTOR GRUEN: Founder and president, Victor Gruen Associates, planning, architecture, and engineering. Born and educated in Vienna, he opened his own architecture office in 1933 and came to the United States in 1938. Among the outstanding projects of Victor Gruen Associates are the Northland and Eastland Shopping Centers, Detroit, Michigan; Southdale Shopping Center, Minneapolis, Minnesota; rehabilitation plan for Fort Worth, Texas; Wilshire Terrace apartment building, Los Angeles, California; Charles River Park, urban redevelopment project in Boston, Massachusetts; and redevelopment projects in Stamford, Connecticut, Fresno, California, and Paterson, New Jersey.

HENRY E. GUERLAC: Professor of the history of science, Cornell University. President of the International Academy of the History of Science. He has taught at Harvard, was chairman of the department of history of science at the University of Wisconsin (1941-1943), and has been a member of the Institute for Advanced Study at Princeton. Historian of the MIT Radiation Laboratory, 1943-1946, and author of the official history of radar development in the United States.

OSCAR HANDLIN: Professor of history, Harvard University. At Harvard he is director of the Center for the Study of the History of Liberty in America. Editor of the Library of American Biography; awarded a Pulitzer Prize for history in 1952. Among his books are *Boston's Immigrants, The Uprooted, The American People in the Twentieth Century,* and *Race and Nationality in American Life.*

PHILIP M. HAUSER: Professor of sociology, University of Chicago. Also chairman of the department of sociology and director of the Population Research and Training Center at Chicago University. Earlier he served in United States government posts as acting director of the Bureau of the Census, assistant to the secretary, Department of Commerce, and as United States representative in the United Nations Population Commission. Among his publications are *Population Perspectives, Urbanization in Latin America,* and *The Study of Population: An Inventory and Appraisal.*

ALEXANDER HEARD: Dean of the graduate school, University of North Carolina. As a youth he served with the U. S. Department of the Interior and later in the U. S. Indian Service and the War Department. He joined the staff of the University of North Carolina in 1950 as a political scientist. Consultant to the Senate subcommittee on privilege and elections in 1956-1957; now chairman of the President's commission on the financing of political campaigns. Among his books are *A Two-Party South?* and *The Costs of Democracy.*

AUGUST HECKSCHER: Director, Twentieth Century Fund, New York City. Formerly an instructor in government at Yale, and a journalist: editor of the Auburn (New York) *Citizen-Advertiser,* 1946-1948, editorial writer, and chief editorial writer for the *New York Herald Tribune,* 1948-1956. Trustee of St. Paul's School, New School for Social Research, Mount Holyoke College, and the American Civil Liberties Union; a member of the Art Commission of New York City. Author of *Patterns of Politics* (1947), and *Diversity of Worlds* (1957), in collaboration with Raymond Aron. Recently appointed special consultant to the President for cultural affairs.

DOROTHY HEIGHT: Associate director for training, Bureau of Personnel and Training staff of the National Board of the Young Women's Christian

Association of the United States of America. A member of the National Board staff since 1944, with a special interest in leadership training. Member, the Women's African Committee; president, National Council of Negro Women. Former member of the Defense Advisory Committee on Women in the Services. She has traveled extensively in West Africa. Visiting professor at the Delhi School of Social Work, New Delhi, India, 1952.

PENDLETON HERRING: President, Social Science Research Council, New York City. Formerly a member of the Harvard University faculty; currently a member of the visiting committee in Harvard's department of government; also a member of the visiting committee in the social sciences, Johns Hopkins University. Director, Woodrow Wilson Foundation, and former president of the American Political Science Association. Among his books: *Public Administration and Public Interest, The Politics of Democracy, Presidential Leadership,* and *The Impact of War.*

JOHN HERSEY: Novelist and journalist. Among his books are *A Bell for Adano* (1944), which won a Pulitzer Prize; *Hiroshima* (1946), *The Wall* (1950), *The Marmot Drive* (1953), *A Single Pebble* (1956), *The War Lover* (1959), and *The Child Buyer* (1960). Quondam member of the Westport, Connecticut Board of Education; member of the Fairfield, Connecticut Citizens School Study Council; trustee of the National Citizens' Council for Better Schools; and chairman of the Connecticut Committee for the Gifted.

MELVILLE J. HERSKOVITS: Professor of anthropology, Northwestern University. Also professor of African affairs there. Having previously taught at Columbia and Howard Universities, he has been on the Northwestern faculty since 1927; professor since 1935, director of the Program of African Studies since 1951. Former chairman, Commission on Negro Studies, American Council of Learned Societies; editor, *The American Anthropologist,* 1949-1952. Among his books are *Life in a Haitian Valley* (1937), *Dahomey* (1938). *The Myth of the Negro Past* (1941), and *Cultural Anthropology* (1955).

DAVID G. HILL: President and member of the executive committee, Pittsburgh Plate Glass Co. Joined the company in 1942 as an industrial engineer. He is chairman and a director of Pittsburgh Corning Corp.; president and a director of Ste. Ame des Glaces de Courcelles; and a director of various corporations, including Mellon National Bank & Trust Co. and National Union Fire Insurance Co. Trustee, the Committee on Economic Development; member the National Industrial Conference Board.

KENNETH HOLLAND: President, the Institute of International Education, New York City. Active in international education since 1935. Initially associate director, American Youth Commission of the American Council on Education, later served in the State Department and the Office of Inter-American Affairs. He helped set up the Fulbright Scholarship program and was first director of the Office of Educational Exchange. Author of *Youth in European Labor Camps* and *Youth in the CCC.*

JAMES A. HOUSTON: Administrator for Department of Northern Affairs, Canadian Government, West Baffin Island. Born in Toronto and trained as an artist at the Ontario College of Art and the Art Students' League, New York City, as well as in France and Italy, he has studied Indian Art in the southwestern United States and Mexico. He originally went to the Canadian Arctic in 1948 as representative of the Canadian Handicrafts Guild, and has lived there most of the time since then, at first in an igloo, more recently in a wooden house. In 1958, he studied block printing in Tokyo, and did research on the Ainu people in Hokkaido, Japan. (Early in 1962 he lectured on Eskimo art and culture in Scandinavia and Soviet Russia.)

HAROLD HOWE II: Superintendent of schools, Scarsdale, New York. Formerly principal of high schools in Newton, Massachusetts, Cincinnati, Ohio, and Andover, Massachusetts. Trustee of Vassar College, Yale University, and Taft School. Member of the College Entrance Examination Board Committee on Examinations; former chairman of the Mayor's Committee on Juvenile Delinquency, Cincinnati, Ohio.

JOHN A. HRONES: Vice-president, Case Institute of Technology, Cleveland, Ohio. Former teacher and dean at Massachusetts Institute of Technology. Since 1957, he has been academic dean at Case Institute. Contributor of numerous articles to engineering publications.

PATRICK HURLEY: Professor of geology and chairman of the faculty, Massachusetts Institute of Technology. His research activity is in the fields of nuclear geophysics and geochronology. Consultant to domestic and foreign companies in mineral exploration and evaluation. Fellow, American Academy of Arts and Sciences, and Geological Association of America; member of the American Institute of Mining Engineers. He first came to Massachusetts Institute of Technology in 1940 as a research associate.

SIR JULIAN HUXLEY: Biologist and writer. Between 1912 and 1935 he taught at Oxford, in Houston, Texas, and in London. Formerly secretary of the Zoological Society of England, and a member of a commission on higher education in West Africa. He was the first director-general of UNESCO, 1946-1948. Among his publications are *Essays of a Biologist, The Science of Life* (with H. G. and G. P. Wells), *Evolution, the Modern Synthesis, Africa View, From an Antique Land, New Bottles for New Wine,* and *The Captive Shrew,* a collection of poems.

ALFRED KAZIN: Literary critic, New York City. Author of *On Native Grounds, A Walker in the City, The Inmost Leaf, Contemporaries,* and many book reviews and critical articles. He has also edited books on Dreiser and Fitzgerald, and texts by Melville, Blake, and Emerson. Born in Brooklyn, and educated at City College of New York and at Columbia University, he has taught at many American universities, including Harvard, Smith, Amherst, and Black Mountain, and abroad at Cambridge and the University of Cologne.

J. WARD KEENER: President and chief executive officer, The B. F. Goodrich Co.; also the presiding officer and a member of the executive committee of its board of directors. With B. F. Goodrich since 1937. He has been advisor to the State Department at meetings of the International Rubber Study Group and as a director of the Rubber Manufacturers Association, and a member of the National Industrial Conference Board. Chairman of the board and a director of Goodrich-Gulf Chemicals, Inc., and a director of company subsidiaries in Africa, Canada, Malaya, and Australia.

BERNARD KILGORE: President, *The Wall Street Journal.* He has spent his entire working life with the *Journal,* starting as a copy editor in 1929. President of Barron's Publishing Co., and of Canadian Dow Jones, Ltd.; publisher of *The Packet,* Princeton, New Jersey. He is a director of Dow Jones & Co. and of Princeton Municipal Improvement, Inc., and a trustee of DePauw University.

JOHN R. KIMBERLY: Chairman of the board, Kimberly-Clark Corp., Neenah, Wisconsin, pulp and paper manufacturer. Also chairman of the board, Spruce Falls Power & Paper Co., Ltd. Director: Wisconsin Telephone Co., First National City Bank of New York. Trustee: Lawrence College, Episcopal Church Foundation, The Rockefeller Foundation, Institute of Paper Chemistry. Member of the Business Council (formerly Business Advisory Council); formerly served with the Office of Production Management and War Production Board.

DOUGLAS M. KNIGHT: President, Lawrence College, Appleton, Wisconsin. Formerly taught English at Yale, 1946-1953; in his present post since 1954. Member: Commission, on Liberal Education, Association of American Colleges, American Council on Education. Trustee: Edward W. Hazen Foundation, Woodrow Wilson National Fellowship Foundation. Director: Rockefeller Brothers Theological Fellowship Program. He is on the editorial board of *The Christian Scholar,* and is author of *Pope and the Heroic Tradition.*

ERIC LARRABEE: Managing editor, *American Heritage.* Associate editor of *Harper's Magazine* from 1946 to 1958. He was a member of the Carnegie Corporation reconnaissance team to West and Central Africa in 1952. Author of *The Self-Conscious Society* (1960); co-editor (with Rolf Meyersohn) of

Mass Leisure (1958); co-editor (with Robert Spiller) of *American Perspectives* (1961). (Since the Second Corning Conference, Mr. Larrabee has left *American Heritage* to become managing editor of *Horizon.*)

BARRY T. LEITHEAD: President, Cluett, Peabody & Co., Inc., shirt manufacturers, New York City. With Cluett, Peabody since 1929, president since 1948. He is a director of numerous corporations, of the American Arbitration Association, and of the Brand Names Foundation, a member of the Advertising Council and of the Business Council (formerly Business Advisory Council), and chairman of the executive committee of the Father's Day Council.

DAVID E. LILIENTHAL: Chairman and chief executive officer, Development & Resources Corp., New York City. He practiced law in Chicago, 1923-1931; became a director of the Tennessee Valley Authority in 1933 and was its chairman, 1941-1946. First chairman of the U. S. Atomic Energy Commission, 1946-1950. In his present capacity he is concerned with providing technical and managerial services toward the development of natural resources abroad. Trustee of the Twentieth Century Fund and of Radcliffe College; vice-chairman of the Advisory Council, Peace Corps. Author of *TVA: Democracy on the March, This I Do Believe,* and *Big Business: A New Era.*

JAY LOVESTONE: Director, international publications, Department of International Affairs, AFL-CIO, New York City. Also editor of *Free Trade Union News,* AFL-CIO monthly publication in English, French, German, and Italian. Born in Russia and raised in New York City, he has since 1918 been continuously active in the American and international labor movements, and a participant in many international labor congresses. He was the founder in 1929 of the Independent Labor League of America (Lovestonites).

SALVADOR DE MADARIAGA: Author and diplomat. Originally from Galicia, in northwestern Spain, he now lives in England. Head of the disarmament section of the League of Nations, 1922-1927; a professor of Spanish literature at Oxford, 1927-1931; Spanish ambassador to Washington, 1931, and to Paris, 1932. Took up residence in England in 1936; made weekly BBC broadcasts to Spanish America during World War II. Former president of the Liberal International; worked closely with UNESCO until he resigned owing to the admission of Franco Spain. His many books include novels, plays, poems, radio dramas, essays, and writings in biography, politics, and history.

CHARLES HABIB MALIK: University professor, The American University, Washington, D. C.; professor of philosophy, The American University,

Beirut, Lebanon. Former president of the United Nations Security Council. His academic training was in mathematics, physics, and philosophy. Ambassador of Lebanon to the United States, 1953-1955; envoy and minister of Lebanon to Cuba, 1946-1955; chairman of the delegation of Lebanon to many sessions of the United Nations General Assembly. Among his publications are *Problem in Asia* and *The Problem of Coexistence.*

LAURENCE J. McGINLEY: President, Fordham University. Former president of the Middle States Association of Colleges and Secondary Schools and of the Association of Urban Universities, Father McGinley has been president of Fordham since 1949. Director, Lincoln Center for the Performing Arts, and the New York World's Fair 1964-1965 Corp. Admitted to the Jesuit Order in 1922, he formerly taught at Woodstock College, Maryland and at St. Joseph's High School, Philadelphia, and was director of the Vatican radio station in 1939.

FRANK R. MORAES: Indian journalist and author. He is editor-in-chief of the *Express* group of newspapers, published in Bombay, Delhi, Madras, and Madurai. He was assistant editor, *The Times* of India, 1938-1942; war correspondent in Burma and China, 1942-1945; daily editor, 1949-1950; editor, 1950-1957. His books include *Introduction to India* (with Robert Stimson), *Report on Mao's China, Jawaharlal Nehru, Yonder One World, The Revolt in Tibet,* and *India Today.*

GABRIELE MORELLO: Director, Istituto Superiore Per Inprenditore Dirgente Azienda, Palermo, Sicily. Educated in law in Sicily and in economics at Stanford University; he has also studied law at Oxford. Formerly a professor of marketing, he became director of the Istituto Superiore for advanced training of business executives in 1957. He has lectured in Europe on economics and marketing.

ARTHUR E. MURPHY: Professor and chairman, department of philosophy, University of Texas. He taught at the University of California, the University of Chicago, Cornell, Brown, the University of Illinois, and the University of Washington before assuming his present post in 1957. A specialist in American thought, he has published, among other books, *The Uses of Reason* and *Philosophy in American Education* and has done studies of the work of John Dewey and Alfred North Whitehead.

WHITNEY J. OATES: Andrew Fleming West professor of classics and chairman of the council of the humanities, Princeton University. A member of the Princeton faculty since 1927. He is a director of the American Council of Learned Societies and a trustee of the Woodrow Wilson National Fellowship Foundation, the Wenner-Gren Foundation, and the Princeton University Press. Among the works he has edited are *The Complete Greek Drama* (with the late Eugene O'Neill, Jr.), *Greek Literature in Translation* (with C. T. Murphy), and *Basic Writings of St. Augustine.*

CHARLES E. ODEGAARD: President, University of Washington. He has taught history at the Universities of Illinois and Michigan; at the latter institution he was dean of the College of Literature, Science, and Arts, 1952-1958. Member of the U. S. National Commission to UNESCO, 1949-1955; chairman of the Commission on Human Resources and Advanced Training, 1949-1953. As executive director of the American Council of Learned Societies (1948-1952) he was a leading organizer of the First Corning Conference in 1951.

RICHARD M. PAGET: Partner, Cresap, McCormick & Paget, management consultants, New York, Chicago, and San Francisco. Formerly a staff member and later partner of Booz, Allen & Hamilton, management consultants. Former president, Association of Consulting Management Engineers. Trustee of the United States Trust Co. and of the Parsons School of Design, New York City.

JAMES A. PERKINS: Vice-president, Carnegie Corporation. He came to the Carnegie Corporation in 1950 as an executive associate and has held his present position since 1951. Previously he had been an instructor in political science at Princeton; assistant director of Princeton's School of Public and International Affairs; a member of various federal agencies during World War II; and vice-president of Swarthmore College.

RALPH REISER: President, United Glass and Ceramic Workers of North American, AFL-CIO-CLC. Associated with the Glass and Ceramic Workers since 1943 as district president, vice-president in charge of organizing and most recently as international president. He is serving his third term in that office.

DAVID ROCKEFELLER: President and chairman of the executive committee of the board of directors, the Chase Manhattan Bank, New York City. Chairman of the Downtown Lower Manhattan Association, which aims for the comprehensive rehabilitation of downtown New York City; director of the Equitable Life Assurance Society, The B. F. Goodrich Co., and Rockefeller Brothers, Inc.; trustee and vice-president, Rockefeller Brothers Fund, Inc.; trustee, the Museum of Modern Art.

J. STILLMAN ROCKEFELLER: Chairman, First National City Bank of New York. He joined the National City Bank in 1930 in the domestic inspection section of the comptrollers department, after a number of years with Brown Brothers & Co., investment bankers. Chairman and director of the International Banking Corp. and the National City Foundation; director of numerous banking and industrial firms; member of the board of managers of the Memorial Center for Cancer and Allied Diseases, New York City, and a trustee of the American Museum of Natural History.

JAMES J. RORIMER: Director, The Metropolitan Museum of Art, New York City. He joined the Museum in 1929 as an assistant in the department of decorative arts, and served successively as curator of the department of medieval art, curator of the Cloisters, and director of the Cloisters, before becoming director of the Museum in 1955. Chairman of the Museums Council of New York, and a member of the American Museum Association and the Medieval Academy of America. He is an authority on tapestries and medieval monuments, and on methods of verifying works of art.

MURIEL RUKEYSER: Poet, and biographer of Willard Gibbs. She is a member of the faculty of Sarah Lawrence College, and has lectured and taught in other schools and universities. In addition to her numerous collections of poems (among them *One Life, Body of Making,* and *Poems 1935-1961*), and her biography of the American mathematician and physicist Gibbs, she has published two children's books, *Come Back Paul* and *I Go Out.*

SAMUEL SANDMEL: Provost, Hebrew Union College-Jewish Institute of Religion, Cincinnati, Ohio. A specialist in the New Testament and its relationship to Judaism, he was appointed to the Hebrew Union faculty in 1952. Hillel professor of Jewish literature and thought, Vanderbilt University, 1942-1952. Author of *A Jewish Understanding of the New Testament, Philo's Place in Judaism, The Genius of Paul,* and a forthcoming book, *The Hebrew Scripture.* He is president of the Society of Biblical Literature and Exegesis.

CHARLES M. SCHEFF: President, the American Flint Glass Workers' Union of North America. Admitted to membership in the union in 1922, he was elected second vice-president in 1940 and secretary-treasurer in 1943. He became president in 1957.

LEO SCHULGIN: Eastern European news editor, *Helsingin Sanomat,* Helsinki, Finland. One of Finland's leading Russian experts, he has translated several Russian works into Finnish, and traveled extensively in Russia during 1957, 1958, and 1960. Member, Journalists Association of Helsinki.

GRAHAM SPRY: Agent general for the government of Saskatchewan in the United Kingdom and Europe. A former director of Standard Oil (California) and Ceylon Petroleum Co., based in London; personal assistant to Sir Stafford Cripps, 1942-1945; war correspondent in Italy and Germany, 1944-1945; member of an economic survey in Turkey for the Twentieth Century Fund, 1947; in his present post since then. He is co-author of

Social Planning for Canada and *Turkey, An Economic Appraisal*; author of *Canada*.

JANEZ STANOVNIK: Member of the Yugoslav Parliament, and director, the Institute for International Policy and Economics, Belgrade. He was in the Yugoslav Partisan armed forces from 1941 until 1945. He was chief, Cabinet of the Deputy Prime Minister of the People's Republic of Yugoslavia, 1945-1952; since then he has served in various posts with the Yugoslav delegation to the United Nations. He has published numerous studies on international economics in periodicals in Yugoslavia and elsewhere.

MARK STARR: Educational director, International Ladies' Garment Workers' Union, 1935-1960. As a miner in his native South Wales, he wrote three labor textbooks before coming to the United States in 1928. He has lectured on labor education and related topics at Harvard, Yale, Columbia and the Universities of Chicago, Illinois, Michigan, Minnesota and Florida; has served on the executive boards of the American Labor Education Service, National Educational Television and Radio Center, and the Institute of International Education. Labor consultant to various countries of Europe and Asia; workers' education expert for the International Labor Organization in Singapore, 1961. Author of *A Worker Looks at History, Trade Unionism: Past and Future, Labor and the American Way,* and many other books, pamphlets, and articles.

JULIUS STONE: Challis professor of jurisprudence and international law, the University of Sydney (Australia). He has been visiting professor at Columbia and Harvard Universities, and a Ford Foundation visiting professor in India. Author of articles on sociology and the philosophy of law. Among his books are *The Province and Function of Law, Law and Society* (with S. P. Simpson), *Legal Controls of International Conflict, Aggression and World Order,* and *Legal Education and Public Responsibility.*

EBERHARD STROHAL: Deputy editor-in-chief, *Kurier,* Vienna. A graduate of the University of Vienna with major studies in psychology and sociology. He has been with *Kurier* since that paper was founded in 1954 when the Russians left Austria. He accompanied the Austrian Foreign Minister on a trip to Russia and has traveled in Germany, Yugoslavia, the United Arab Republic, and Israel.

BYRON K. TRIPPET: President, Wabash College. Chairman of the Commission on Liberal Education, Association of American Colleges; a member of the National Lecture Panel of Phi Beta Kappa. A former Rhodes Scholar, he has since 1946 been a member of the Indiana Rhodes Scholarship Selection Committee. Before assuming his present position he was professor of history and assistant dean at Wabash, 1936-1942. He has written articles on teaching, college administration, and corporate support of higher education.

ARNAUD DE VOGÜÉ: Chairman of the board, Compagnie de Saint-Gobain, chemicals, Paris. He has been a director of Saint-Gobain since 1947, a member of the Executive Committee since 1950, and chairman since 1952. President of Centre d'Etudes et de Recherches des Chefs d'Enterprises; president of Comité France-Amérique.

WALTER H. WHEELER, JR.: Chairman of the board, Pitney-Bowes, Inc., office equipment. Associated with Pitney-Bowes and its predecessor firm since 1919, and was president of the firm from 1938 until he assumed the chairmanship in 1960. Chairman of the board and a director of Pitney-Bowes of Canada, Ltd. and Pitney-Bowes, Ltd., London. Director of numerous companies, and a member of the Business Council (formerly Business Advisory Council), as well as the Committee for Economic Development and the Council on Foreign Relations.

JOHN F. WHITE: President, National Educational Television and Radio Center, New York City. Former dean and later vice-president of Western Reserve University; former general manager of Station WQED, Pittsburgh, Pennsylvania. Member of the board of the Joint Council on Educational Television and the Learning Resources Institute; member of the Television Committee of the American Council on Education and of the Broadcast Advisory Committee of the United States Information Agency. Secretary-treasurer of the citizen's group that recently bought television station WNTA, New York City, for noncommercial educational operation.

FRAZAR B. WILDE: Chairman of the board and president, Connecticut General Life Insurance Co., Hartford, Connecticut. Director of the Connecticut Bank & Trust Co.; on the research committee and a trustee of the Committee on Economic Development. He has been in the insurance field since 1914 and has been president of Connecticut General since 1936.

JAMES C. WORTHY: Business consultant, Chicago, Illinois. From 1956 until recently, he was vice-president and director of public relations of Sears Roebuck & Co. and president of the Sears Roebuck Foundation. He is vice-president, Chicago Association of Commerce and Industry; trustee, Chicago Theological Seminary, Chicago Urban League, and the Library of International Relations; and author of *Big Business and Free Men*.

CHARLES E. WYZANSKI, JR.: United States District Judge for Massachusetts. He served as law secretary to U. S. Circuit Court Judges Augustus N. Hand and Learned Hand, with the Department of Labor, with the Department of Justice, and with a private law firm before becoming U. S. District Judge for Massachusetts in 1941. Trustee of the Ford Foundation and of the Institute for Advanced Study, Princeton; former president of the Harvard Board of Overseers; a Fellow of the American Academy of Arts and Sciences and of the American Law Institute.

SIR MUHAMMAD ZAFRULLA KHAN: Vice-president, International Court of Justice, The Hague. Described in British *Who's Who* as "Pakistani politician," he practiced law in India and later was judge of the federal court of India and held various Indian government posts. Leader of the Pakistan delegation to the United Nations General Assembly, 1947-1954; he also led the Pakistan delegation at the San Francisco Conference on the Japanese Peace Treaty, 1951, and at the SEATO Conference in Manila, 1954. (Since the Second Corning Conference he has been appointed Pakistan's ambassador to the United Nations.)

REPRESENTING THE AMERICAN COUNCIL
OF LEARNED SOCIETIES

THOMAS P. BROCKWAY: Executive associate, ACLS; on leave from Bennington College. He taught history at St. John's College, Dartmouth, and Yale before joining the Bennington faculty in 1933. During World War II he was administrative officer with the Board of Economic Warfare and Foreign Economic Administration, and in 1949-1950 was a research associate at Harvard. Author of *Basic Documents in United States Foreign Policy,* and articles. (Since the Conference Mr. Brockway has returned to Bennington College where he is professor of history.)

FREDERICK H. BURKHARDT: President, ACLS. President of Bennington College from 1947 to 1957. Earlier he taught philosophy at the University of Wisconsin, and served during World War II as a research analyst in Central European Affairs for the Office of Strategic Services; acting chief of the State Department's Division of Research for Europe, 1945-1946. In 1950-1951 he was deputy director, Office of Public Affairs, Office of the U. S. High Commissioner for Germany. He edited *The Cleavage in our Culture* and has contributed articles on philosophical subjects to periodicals.

GORDON B. TURNER: Executive associate, ACLS. A member of the Princeton history staff for ten years before he joined the ACLS staff in 1959; that year, he also occupied the Ernest J. King Chair of maritime history at the Naval War College. Among his publications are *A History of Military Affairs since the Eighteenth Century* and *National Security in the Nuclear Age.*

REPRESENTING CORNING GLASS WORKS

RICHARD H. ANDREWS: Manager, public relations, New York office, Corning Glass Works. Also vice-president and executive director, Corning Glass Works Foundation. During World War II he served in various capacities in the Lend-Lease Program and finally as its chief of mission to Norway. Executive director of the American-Scandinavian Foundation, 1948-1953; appointed director of Corning Glass Works Foundation in 1953, and to his present position in 1961. Trustee of the Jamestown Glass House Foundation, the College of Advanced Science, and the Committee to Salvage Talent.

JAMES M. BROWN: Director of corporate services, Corning Glass Works. Before joining Corning he was director of the William A. Farnsworth Art Museum, Rockland, Maine. Became first director of the Corning Glass Center in 1951. Director, division of public affairs, 1956-1958; director, Division of Management Development, 1958-1961. He is president, Corning Glass Works Foundation and has served as vice-president, Corning Museum of Glass; vice-president, Council for the American Association of Museums; president, International Councils of Museums-United States; and trustee, Arnot Art Gallery.

WILLIAM C. DECKER: Chairman of the board of directors and chief executive officer, Corning Glass Works. He joined Corning in 1930 as manager of the industrial sales department and was president from 1946 until April 1961. He is chairman of the board and a director of Corning Glass Works of Canada, Ltd., Corning Fibre Box Corp., and Corhart Refractories, Co., Inc.; and a director of Dow Corning Corp., and Pittsburgh Corning Corp.

AMORY HOUGHTON: Chairman of the executive committee, Corning Glass Works. He joined Corning in 1921 on the company's manufacturing staff. President, 1930-1941; chairman of the board, 1941-1961. United States ambassador to France, 1957-1961. Director, Metropolitan Life Insurance Co.; councilor, National Industrial Conference Board; trustee, Corning Glass Works Foundation. Member of the Harvard Board of Overseers, 1947-1953; member of the Business Council (formerly Business Advisory Council), Department of Commerce.

AMORY HOUGHTON, JR.: President, Corning Glass Works. He joined Corning in 1951 as accountant's assistant, and became president in April 1961. He is a director of Dow Corning Corp., Pittsburgh Corning Corp., New York Telephone Company, B. F. Goodrich Co., Corhart Refractories Co., Corning Fibre Box Corp., and Corning Glass Works of Canada, Ltd.; and a trustee of Episcopal Theological School, Corning Glass Works Foundation, and the Corning Museum of Glass.

ARTHUR A. HOUGHTON, JR.: President, Steuben Glass, New York City. He joined Corning Glass Works in 1929 in the manufacturing department, and has been president of Steuben Glass since 1940. He is a director of Corning Glass Works, Erie-Lackawanna Railroad Co., U. S. Steel Corp., and New York Life Insurance Co.; and a trustee of the U. S. Trust Co. of New York, Cooper Union, Metropolitan Museum of Art, New York Public Library, and The Rockefeller Foundation. In addition, he is chairman of the Parsons School of Design, and vice-chairman of Lincoln Center for the Performing Arts. From 1940 to 1942, he was curator of rare books for the Library of Congress.

CHARLES D. LaFOLLETTE: Financial vice-president, Corning Glass Works. He joined Corning in 1929 as sales manager of the Pyrex housewares division and has been in his present position since 1957. He is a director of Corning Fibre Box Corp., of Corning Glass Works of Canada, Ltd., and Corhart Refractories, and director and treasurer of Dow Corning Corp. President of the Corning Museum of Glass and vice-president of Corning Glass Works Foundation.

GEORGE DUFF MACBETH: Honorary vice-president, Corning Glass Works. He began in the glass manufacturing business with Macbeth-Evans Glass Co. in 1913 and was president and general manager from 1926 to 1936. His company merged with Corning in 1936, and he became a vice-president and director of Corning Glass Works. He is a director of Corning Fibre Box Corp. and Pittsburgh Corning Corp., and a trustee of the Corning Glass Works Foundation.

ROBERT D. MURPHY: President, Corning Glass International. He was a career diplomat from 1917, when he was a member of the American Legation at Bern, Switzerland, until 1960, when he was Under Secretary of State for Political Affairs. Among other things, he made preparations for the Allied landings in North Africa in November 1942, and subsequently conducted negotiations for the entry of French West Africa into the war; he has been ambassador to Belgium and to Japan, and was Deputy Under Secretary of State for United Nations Affairs from 1953 to 1959.

BENJAMIN S. PEIRSON: Director, division of public affairs, Corning Glass Works; president, Corning Glass Works Foundation. He was associated with several automotive firms before joining Corning in 1934 in the general sales department. He held sales positions in Fibre Products Division and Pyrex Housewares Division and served as general manager, Consumer Products Division. Assistant director of sales, 1948-1957; manager of sales staff, 1957-1958; appointed to his present position in 1958.

EUGENE C. SULLIVAN: Honorary chairman of the board, Corning Glass Works. He organized the early research and development work for Corning and set up its first laboratory in 1908, having worked previously with the United States Geological Survey. He is vice-president and a director of Cor-hart Refractories Co. and a director of Corning Glass Works, Dow-Corning Ltd., Owens-Corning Fiberglas Corp., and Pittsburgh Corning Corp. He has written articles on inorganic and physical chemistry, mineral and geological chemistry, and glass.

AUTHORS OF BACKGROUND PAPERS
WHO COULD NOT ATTEND

McGEORGE BUNDY: Special assistant to the President of the United States for National Security Affairs. He was political analyst for the Council on Foreign Relations, 1948-1949; associate professor of government at Harvard, 1951-1954; dean of the faculty of arts and sciences at Harvard from 1953 until he assumed his present duties in 1961. Author of *On Active Service* (with Henry L. Stimson), editor of *The Pattern of Responsibility*.

JULIAN HOCHFELD: University professor and sociologist, Warsaw, Poland. He was active in the socialist youth movement and the Polish Socialist Party before World War II, and in exile during it. Member of the executive committee of the Polish Socialist Party, 1945-1948; he is now professor of political sociology at the University of Warsaw, vice-president of the Polish Sociological Association.

INDEX

INDEX

و ۶

Format by Sidney Feinberg
Set in Linotype Baskerville
HARPER & ROW, PUBLISHERS, INCORPORATED